C000148316

First Published in 1995

ISBN 0 9510942 1 1

Printed in Great Britain by
G & A Printers & Stationers,
Stone Cross, Penkridge, Stafford.

1

THE GOOD OLD GRIT

**A History of
the
People of Penkridge**

1270 - 1939

By

Robert Maddocks

ACKNOWLEDGEMENTS

This book had its genesis in work done by pupils of Wolgarston School in 1987 to celebrate the 150th anniversary of the opening of the railway. The author would like to thank the generations of Wolgarston pupils who, from 1975, tolerated his history lessons and who, even now, may recognise some of his favourite quotations and opinions within the text.

Students of history in Staffordshire are very fortunate to have the services of the County Record Office and the William Salt Library. Their dedicated staff made the long searches through the Hatherton collection and the Staffordshire Advertiser possible.

Especial thanks must go to those people of Penkridge whose interest and expert knowledge sustained the author in his work. Mrs. A. Plant allowed the use of part of her unique collection of photographs of old Penkridge. The heritage of Penkridge would be much poorer without the care and attention of the Plant family. Mrs. E. Harris kindly contributed her memories of the village in the early twentieth century. Mr. Jack Tweed volunteered a stream of vivid anecdotes and information which confirmed the author's opinion that Penkridge truly had a story worth telling. It was a great privilege to interview the late Mr. Cyril Felthouse. His clear and affectionate memories of pre-war Penkridge were a joy to record.

Robert Maddocks
Penkridge
September, 1994

CONTENTS

List of Photographs

1.   The Marsh Common
2.   Map of Market Street
3.   Some Soldiers of the "Great War", 1914 - 1918
4. a) Mr. Joseph Brown
   b) Bellbrook Cottage
5.   Littleton Arms - Invoice
6. a) Co-op
   b) Plants Grocery Shop, before 1923
7.   National School at Penkridge, Account Sheet
8. a) School Children Singing, 1921
   b) The Stocks, 1920's
9. a) Stafford - Wolverhampton Road, Penkridge, 1921
   b) Albrighton Hunt, 1922
10. a) Cast of Sleeping Beauty, 1922
    b) Mr. J.R. Burd
11. a) Laying the Foundation Stone of the Peace Memorial Hall, 1926
    b) Members of the Peace Memorial Hall Committee
12.   Stone Cross, 1926
13. a) The Plough Team of Deanery Farm, 1927
    b) Funeral of Col. H.M. Whitehead, 1935
14. a) Col. H.M. Whitehead
    b) Reverend James Kempson
15. a) Early photograph of Penkridge from Church Tower
    b) Bert Plant's Grocery Shop
16.   *(Members of Penkridge Cricket Club with C. Felthouse, S. Barnes. c. 1950)*

Introduction

February 2nd 1936

On Sunday February 2nd, 1936, George Orwell came through Penkridge. The author was walking to Wigan to do the research for his book, "The Road to Wigan Pier". He stopped for a cup of tea. The generosity shown him by an unnamed Penkridge family did not prevent a painfully direct entry in his diary. To this great author Penkridge amounted to,

> "A tiny frowzy parlour with a nice fire, a little wizened oldish man and an enormous woman about 45, with tow coloured bobbed hair and no front teeth. Both of them thought me a hero to be walking on such a day. Had tea with them en famille."

Thus published in 1945 and reprinted many times since in "The Collected Essays of George Orwell", we have the most widespread and prominent reference to the village.

Orwell went on to become famous. But what about the men and women whose paths he crossed that day? The people of Penkridge clearly deserved better than the damp jottings of an old Etonian on a wet winter afternoon.

What, for instance, of the Reverend James Henry Kempson? He might have been seen hurrying to church to prepare for Evensong and his fifth service and third sermon of the day. A priest with a keen interest in the past, he must have had a profound sense of personal and public history as he recollected the previous week's memorial service for the late King George V, when he had draped the church in royal purple. He was approaching his twenty fifth anniversary as vicar of Penkridge, twenty five years of service in a church founded in the ninth century, seeing every day the alabaster effigies of Sir Edward Littleton and his wife dating from 1629, the wrought iron gates made in 1778 and remembrances of his predecessors like the plaque commemorating the Reverend Richard Slaney. A month later he wrote,

> "On this day I completed twenty five years as Vicar of Penkridge. I offer humble thanks to Almighty God for many mercies. Conscious as I am of many shortcomings and failures I yet in deep humility take up the words of the Psalmist, 'Oh give thanks to the Lord for He is gracious; and His mercy endureth for ever'."

History is made up of individuals like James Kempson. His personal faith and private life were bound up with great public events, producing a figure of great dignity. All people are similarly part of history and worthy of respect, whether they are important church leaders or labourers struggling against poverty.

Who else might have met the glance of the famous author as he made his way along the Wolverhampton and Stafford Roads? Perhaps Ernest Davies, landlord of the Railway Inn, might have spared him some time, unaware that on the following day his application for an extension of hours on cattle auction days would be turned down by the magistrates because the market adjoining the inn had been closed. "The Railway" was now as far away from the auction yards as many other pubs in Penkridge which were not allowed extensions.

Walking on a little further the stranger might have seen Thomas Robson, landlord of the Littleton Arms, a man destined to be happier on Monday as his extension was allowed. This man, continuing in a tradition almost as distinguished in the history of Penkridge as that of the church or the Littletons, was the proud landlord of an inn which had been the centre for the village's official and social life since the late eighteenth century and which had been in his family since his grandfather had moved from Wheaton Aston to take it over in the late 1840s.

In 1936 one dialled 11 to telephone the Littleton Arms. The number 45 would find Frederick Rostance, carpenter, whose premises Orwell would have passed next. At Crown Bridge he would have seen the shop of Mrs. Bridgewater, butcher. Both were following in the footsteps of countless generations of artisans who nevertheless can be identified and named as far back as 1379, like Johannes Barbere, "carpentarius" and Willelmus Cook, "carnifex".

It being a Sunday and raining, the streets of Penkridge would have been quiet, except for the builders who were working a seven day week erecting houses for the council. The Cannock Rural District Council was dealing with complaints about this breach of the Sabbath. Mothers would be keeping their children in as a "mild" epidemic of scarlet fever swept the village, putting pressure on local hospitals. Traffic would have been light although the Penkridge Police Court had lately found itself dealing almost entirely with motoring offences.

So, as George Orwell made his way to Stafford, to stay at a temperance hotel with grey, smelly sheets, the people of Penkridge faced another Monday. Work would begin, shops would do business and the banks would be open, as on every Monday and Friday. Many ladies would be looking forward to the monthly meeting of the W.I., at the Peace Memorial Hall with its short whist drive and lecture on Herbaceous Borders. They would be putting the finishing touches to their entries for the "something new made out of something old" competition. The History of Penkridge, which was made of the lives of ordinary men and women, was rolling on.

Chapter 1

The Middle Ages

During the second half of the thirteenth century William de la More was one of the most important men in Penkridge. He owned at least forty acres of the moor which stretched from the village to Moorhall, ten acres at Stretton in Shropshire and a croft at Pillaton. He had claims to be the Lord of the Manor of Great Wyrley and owned the mill and other land in Penkridge. He ran a large household with many servants on the moor and owned chattels worth nearly £70. In more recent times he would have been a magistrate or a member of the vestry and respected as a symbol of decent behaviour and law and order.

In the Middle Ages, however, things were different. During his lifetime the rich and powerful William de la More was charged with at least four murders, poaching and theft. William was brought before the courts many times, but the intermittent nature of royal justice left plenty of scope for a life of crime. His name first appears on the court rolls in 1274 when he was sued for ten marks for theft at Longnor. Three years later he was sued for a £10 debt. Showing a contempt for the law, William did not bother to answer the charge.

In that violent age the law was just one option when asserting your rights. William was willing to use the law when brute force failed to get him his way. William's right to the lordship of the Manor of Great Wyrley was often questioned. When someone as rich and powerful as himself, Richard de Loges of Rodbaston, challenged him in 1278, William settled the matter in court. When lesser men like Ralph the Miller and William Trumwynne claimed their feudal rights to firewood and chopped down some of his trees, William responded by rounding up Trumwynne's cattle in lieu of payment. Only when Trumwynne retaliated by gathering together a gang of men to take the cattle back did the matter come to court.

Living on the moor at Penkridge and claiming the Manor of Great Wyrley, William de la More often fell foul of the laws of the Forest of Cannock. Freeholders and farmers, like William, who lived within the boundaries of the Royal Forest were restricted by laws designed to preserve the game. They were allowed to keep a mastiff as a guard dog but had to have them expeditated, or mutilated by the removal of claws from one foot, so that they could not hunt. Despite this, in 1286, the forest was being ruined by dogs chasing and disturbing the deer. It was quite clear that the damage was being done by dogs belonging to William de la More. Mastiffs from Wyrley, in contrast to Penkridge, did not have to be mutilated because of an old privilege granted to the Bishop of Chester.

The forest officials were annoyed that such a right was being exploited by someone as lawless as William. He was brought before the Forest Court and challenged to explain how he came to be Lord of the Manor of Wyrley. Royal officials at the court contradicted his claim that he held the village from the King. Despite this set back William continued to enjoy the benefits of the manor for seven more years before finally being dislodged by Richard de Loges in 1293. Powerful men could commit great crimes when the law was so slow-moving and weak.

Unlike mastiffs, greyhounds had no use except for hunting. None, therefore, could be kept in the forest except with royal permission. This did not deter William de la More who kept a pack on the moor. In 1276 he took them hunting with his servant, Thomas, and two members of his household, Robert Byseche and Richard Spark from Wolgarston. They poached a buck and took it to William's house for a feast of venison. Although the crime was well documented it took nine years to bring William to court and fine him forty shillings.

William had probably been hunting illegally for all of those nine years since a second charge of poaching was proved for the year 1285. The court heard that two of his mastiffs had put up a doe and that they had "chased it in the forest as far as the ditch of Dunston." William, his groom William Heryng, his shepherd Alan de Eton, Adam le Whelp and some other servants skinned the doe in secret and only then brought it to la More for eating. If William was taking precautions against being discovered with stolen venison in his house it appears that the law was at last beginning to hem him in.

By 1293 William de la More's star was clearly in the descendant. At the Stafford Assizes the King's Attorney claimed that William was holding land in Penkridge illegally. William was deprived of his property, including the mill, which was returned to the King. Taking advantage of his old enemy's weakness, Richard de Loges of Rodbaston restaked his claim for the Manor of Great Wyrley. By this time William was under great pressure from the forces of law and order and failed to appear in court on three occasions. As a result Richard de Loges won his case and William lost the manor.

William de la More finally came to grief when the Court of Gaol Delivery arrived in Stafford. He was accused, before the royal judges, of murdering four local men. He had killed Robert of Gailey by trampling him to death under his horse. When Henry de la Hull of Levedale approached his horse he had kicked him so hard in the chest with his armoured shoe that he died the next day. William tried to avoid detection by taking the body of Robert back to the moor to hide but to no avail. He was also accused of the murders of Reginald Aleyn of Wyrley and William le Ro. Despite the mountain of evidence against him and the presence of the King's Judges William obviously felt that he could brazen it out with the help of a local, county jury. He failed to take the elementary precaution of someone facing a felony charge of transferring his possessions to his wife. When he was unexpectedly found guilty and hanged he lost not only his life but also his possessions of £68..6s..11d which were confiscated by the Crown.

In theory the feudal system was capable of preventing this sort of mayhem. As a tenant William paid homage to his Lord in a pyramid of allegiance leading up to the King. After the hanging, Hugh le Blund, Lord of the Manor of Penkridge, and the Canons of Penkridge Church, acting as Lords of the Deanery Manor were fined 5 marks (3 marks = £1) and 20 shillings respectively for failing to keep their tenant in order. Criminal or "over mighty" subjects can arise in any era but in the Middle Ages Penkridge suffered from power struggles and family feuds which made the maintenance of law and order very difficult.

During the reign of King John the two manors of Penkridge were united. The Archbishop of Dublin, who held the Deanery, bought the rest of Penkridge for his nephew, Andrew le Blund. Thereafter disputes arose over whether Penkridge Manor should be inherited by the office of archbishop or by a member of the Blount family. The arguments between the Archbishop's Deanery Manor and the Blount's Penkridge Manor produced legal battles for at least sixty years between 1250 and 1310. In 1293, for example, the Archbishop accused Hugh le Blund of stealing two carucates of land that belonged to "his Church of Dublin". The case collapsed in court because the lawyers carelessly missed out the name of the church (St. Patrick) from the writ. It was bad enough that the dispute produced this wasteful and costly exercise in law. Worse, for the people of Penkridge, was the fact that it created crime and violence in the fields and on the streets of the village itself.

When in 1250 John the Chaplain claimed the Deanery's feudal right to fish in the "free fishery" at Penkridge the Blounts took him to court, accusing him of violent conduct. Whilst this was probably a case of a civil action being couched in the forceful language of common crime, by 1309 the dispute had taken on the attributes of gang warfare. A band of twelve men led by William of Gailey, John Dod, Richard Jonesmandel and the chaplain, Henry of Otherton, forced their way on to Blount land, cut down oak, ash, poplar and willow trees and carried the wood away. When they were arrested by the sheriff they said they were working for the Dean of the Chapel and that Blount had no right to put up fences or plant trees on common land.

Although the church had great economic power in the Middle Ages it was fragmented into the many hundreds of holdings of the bishops, abbots and other clergy. The wealth of the church was jealously guarded and endlessly fought over in a process which drained the clergy of much respect in the eyes of the people. In Penkridge the church soared magnificently over the village and the countryside but the clergy themselves rubbed shoulders with the rest of the population in a tough and often brutal struggle for survival.

John Dod, who had led the raid on the Blount plantation in 1309, was a Canon of Penkridge Church. Living the life of a rough and ready bailiff, he could not expect to benefit from feelings of religious deference when he came face to face with his enemies. In 1313 Dod was caught alone on the streets of Penkridge by seven disgruntled villagers, the three de Wethales brothers, Thomas Bynde, John the Fox, Robert the Knight and John of Charns. He was surrounded and given a thorough beating. The same gang was still together two years later when they rode into the village and intimidated the coroner, preventing him from investigating the death of Henry the Parson, who had been murdered. Such was the weakness of the law that the County Sheriff was not ordered to arrest them until 1324.

In the Middle Ages the two most important questions about a church and its parish were, "in whose gift is it?" and "what is it worth? " Penkridge was an important parish because it was worth a great deal. The church owned about a third of the land of the parish and the tithes and fees from the parishioners amounted to 70 marks a year. Nine extra parcels of land or prebends, stretching as far as Cannock were attached to the church. The church had been in the gift of the Archbishop of Dublin since 1215 when King John had rewarded Henry of London for his support in the struggle against the barons. The gift was to be inherited by his successors "provided they be not Irishmen" and its wealth was taken from the area to support those great princes of the Church. Questions of religion hardly arose when church offices and sinecures were allocated. If a post fell vacant between the reigns of Archbishops the King stepped in and took economic advantage of the windfall. In 1316 the Penkridge prebend at Cannock became available and Edward II used it to pay the wages of one of his government clerks, William of Burston. William had no connection with the parish and spent his time abroad as a diplomat. Such practice may have been common in the Middle Ages but it remained objectionable. Local men, taking advantage of William's absence, moved onto his land and took his goods. The King had to order the County Sheriff to Penkridge to restore order and make sure that the absentee clerk's property remained safe.

The great power of the church during the Middle Ages did not ensure its respect. In troubled times or during the reign of a weak King the Crown itself could be treated with contempt in and around Penkridge. This was despite the fact that the feudal system was intended to maintain the authority and power of the Crown by granting land tenure in return for the payment of homage and the recruitment of soldiers in time of war. The tenant who held the Manor of Penkridge did so on the understanding that the village would provide one knight plus equipment and followers for military campaigns, especially in Wales. In 1277 Hugh and Henry le Blund performed their family's knight service by going as two sergeants. They both had to be fully armed but took fewer followers.

Penkridge supplied soldiers for a campaign in Gascony in 1253 and for battles against the Scots in 1301, 1310 and 1317. In 1346 Penkridge men served at the battle of Crecy. When reinforcements were needed for the French campaign writs were issued which reveal the relative importance of Penkridge in military terms. The King demanded four armed men from the village, the same number as Wolverhampton and Birmingham. Stafford was required to produce eight men.

The feudal military structure did not ensure obedience to nor respect for the King. Penkridge tenants, like most of the rest of Staffordshire sided with Simon de Montfort against the King in the Barons War of 1264 - 66. During the reign of a weak King like Edward II royal officials could be treated with contempt. In 1317 William Trumwynne and William of Pilatenhale were caught hunting in the royal forest at Cannock. Instead of being cowed they insulted, beat up and wounded the King's Officer who was collecting venison for the court.

The King's representative in the county was the sheriff. Even during the reign of a vigorous and respected monarch like Edward III his attempts to carry out the royal will could degenerate into personal feuds and banditry. In 1352 Sir Hugh de Wrottesley owed the King money and wouldn't repay it despite being a member of the royal household. The Sheriff of Staffordshire, therefore, raided Sir Hugh's land at Tettenhall during the night and took some of his cattle. Sir Hugh gathered together a band of outlaws, overtook the sheriff and ambushed him on the Penkridge to Dunston road. The sheriff was killed, run through by a German sword, and the hue and cry was set up. Sir Hugh and the rest of the gang were rounded up and put in the Marshalsea prison. Because of his royal connections Sir Hugh was allowed to escape within six weeks. Two other people, apparently unconnected with the murder, were pursued through the courts for another twenty years because of a family feud with the widow's family.

The biggest problem for a village like Penkridge during turbulent times seems to have been one of taxation. Changes in political fortune and downright corruption and extortion hurt the villagers. In 1323 at an Assize at Tutbury all the main tax gatherers of the region pleaded guilty to taking huge sums from the towns and villages and using the money for their own ends. A large number of tax agents were fined including Robert of Lynhille, William Engleton, Walter del Park and William of Longridge, all from Penkridge.

The main tax collectors were also accused of extortion. Robert of Congreve pocketed large sums of money from Penkridge people by threatening to tax them to the full amount unless they offered him bribes. Royal officials had endless opportunities for corruption. In 1323 Ralph of Grendon was raising an army for a Scottish campaign. He forced the people of Penkridge to pay him two marks so that the recruitment took place in the village, not at some remote place that would have entailed a long journey.

Medieval taxation could be an unpleasant experience for those concerned but it provides the historian with the most comprehensive evidence of who lived in Penkridge during the Middle Ages. In 1327 a tax of 1/20th of the value of all moveable goods was imposed to pay for a war against Scotland. Four of the "most loyal and best" men of the village were appointed to search everyone's property on Michaelmas Day and record the value of their goods. Everyone was included, even the unfree serfs, though those whose property amounted to less than ten shillings were exempt. Armour, jewels, the robes of the gentry and agricultural and trade tools were not taxed. Owing to the relentless nature of taxation we can say with some certainty that the better off inhabitants of Penkridge in 1327 are listed below. The value of their property can be estimated by multiplying their tax payment by twenty. The total contribution from the Penkridge area (including Wolgarston, Longridge and Congreve) was 109 shillings and ten pence. This was much more than Rugeley (62s.) and Wolverhampton (66s.) but less than Brewood and its surrounds (188s.) Five years later in 1332, another tax was imposed, this time a tenth, for the same reason. The two lists give a good idea of the family names and individuals of fourteenth century Penkridge.

1327			1332		
Walter Bygot	4s.		Blount	6s	8d
William de Modeshale	3s.	6d	William de Modersall		12d
Robert Curteys	4s.		Robert Curteys	2s.	6d
Richard Dun	2s.	6d	Richard Doon	2s.	
Richard Urry	2s.		Nicholas Attebroc	2s.	
John le Wayte	2s.		Adam Norman	2s.	6d
John Marchaund		7d	John le Merchent	2s.	
Simon de Wyston		18d	Simon de Wyston	2s.	
William Tope	2s.		William Tope	2s.	
John de Gauelye		18d	John de Gauelye		18d
William le O		18d	Richard Scute		18d
Alan Berde		21d	William Thurston		18d
William le Hunte		12d	William le Hunte		12d
John Skent		12d	William Attemere		12d
John Dunkan		12d	Thomas de Bradely		12d
John de Eyton		18d	Edith Huchens		12d
William Sweteman		12d	William Bache	2s.	
Nicholas ad Duttum		12d	John de Kersewell	2s.	
Nicholas le Merser		18d	Nicholas le Mercer		12d
Adam Muryman		18d	Richard de Betlehem	2s.	
Robert de la Bolde		18d	Robert Attebolde		12d
Cecilia de la Lowe		18d	John de Bethem	2s.	
			William de Engelton		13d
			John de Mora		13d
			Margaret le Barker		12d

Probably the most interesting character on the two lists was Richard Dun. He appears in the records as "de Onne", "Doon" and "Dun", an interesting example of a family name springing from a location. When the tax clerk wrote in Latin he was described as "carnifax". When the language was English he was recorded, more vividly, as "fleshehewere" or butcher. Richard either lived to a great age or had a son of the same name and occupation. Whichever was the case, the Penkridge butcher did not lead a placid shopkeeper's life. In 1339 he appeared to be working as a bodyguard for the bailiff of the Lord of the Manor when they broke into several houses belonging to Thomas de Mounpelers. In 1379 he was accused of raiding Acton Trussell and taking the goods of William Trussell. He did not appear in court and was outlawed. In 1390 he was sued by John Gifford for breaking into his field at Chillington and taking and treading down his corn. In 1396 Richard Dun was arrested for cutting down trees belonging to William Walters at Pillaton.

Apart from Richard Dun a high proportion of the family names on the tax rolls also appear in court records. In 1346 a gang of fifteen youths including Nicholas Muryman, John Bache, John Attemore and Laurence de Whiston beat up and robbed Thomas de Swynnerton in Penkridge. John le Hunte was an accomplice of Richard Dun on one of his escapades. In 1397 William Engelton had twelve people arrested for the rape and abduction of his daughter, Joan.

The most infamous imposition of the Middle Ages was the Poll Tax of Richard II which led to the Watt Tyler Rebellion in 1381. Whereas previous taxes had been based on the wealth of the people, the poll tax was hardly graduated at all. The richest man in England, the Duke of Lancaster, was taxed at ten marks. Bishops and the Lord Mayor of London paid £4. Most other people over the age of 15 were taxed a notional 3 groats (1 shilling or 5 pence). This meant that Penkridge, with a total of 105 such inhabitants was rated at 105 shillings. The collectors for Penkridge could charge a maximum of 60 groats (£1) and a minimum of 1 groat to raise that amount. In practice the richest villagers paid 2s..6d per married couple while the poorest labourers and servants paid 1s..4d per couple.

The largest group of people in Penkridge were described as "cultor", or husbandmen. This band of 24 farming families was headed by John Balle, the constable of the village and collector for the tax. He put himself in a low tax band, charging himself 2 shillings whilst many others paid 2s..6d. The other farmers were William of Engelton, Henry in the Moor, Alice of the Park, Richard of Lynhille, Roger Taillour, Robert of Alderstone, William Stut, Thomas Trone, Richard Bailey, Thomas Marchaunt, William Gybous, Adam of Bradely, Robert Congreve, Walter Kemp, John Geffrey, Thomas Monforde, John Hunt, Lucy of Longridge, Richard of Preston, William Walter, Richard Arthur, Petronilla Athetowne and Stephen Sparkes.

It is striking that whereas twenty four men are described as farmers, only three men are called labourers. Clearly most of the land in Penkridge was farmed in small holdings associated with the strips of the open field system which provided enough food to support a family but not enough land to require paid labour. The three Penkridge labourers were Richard Wayte, Walter Kilkorn and Hugo Symsone who paid 16 pence each in tax.

Four people in Penkridge were described as cottagers. As three of them were widowed women and one a single man it seems that they were older people who could no longer work large areas of land and were presumably "getting by" on a few acres. The widows were Petronilla Alkus, Joanna Stalbrok and the perhaps aptly named Agnes Spendelowe. The male cottager was Richard Att Ook.

The Poll Tax list reveals a high proportion of tradesmen and craftsmen to farmworkers. It is very unlikely that twenty four farming families could have supported twenty two tradesmen so Penkridge must have been the centre of trade for a large surrounding area. There were three "fabers" or blacksmiths, Richard Muriman, Henry of Bradely and a man named after his trade, John Smith. Penkridge had four butchers, Hugo Wayte, William Cook, Richard Attebrook and Richard de Onne. There were two bakers or "pistors", John Gyn and John Salte, and one miller who was named, in Latin, after his trade, Nicholas Molendinarius.

John Barber was the village carpenter and Thomas of Barre was the brewer. The largest group of tradesmen were the group linked to the cloth and clothing trade. Walter Elyngthorp was a skinner and William Glover was a "cirotecarius" or glove maker. Four men were in the cloth trade, William Brabancon, Adam Webbster, Thomas Horsebrook and William Brown. There were three "cissors" or tailors, Thomas of Standeford, John Hornt and William Taillor. There was one shoemaker, Roger Wele.

Chapter 2

Prosecuting Felons
1270 - 1842

Respect for law and order usually depends on respect for a clearly defined source of authority. In the Middle Ages this was often lacking, both at national and village level. During the reign of Edward I it was not at all clear who had what powers in Penkridge in a three way tussle between the Lord of Penkridge Manor, the Church and the Crown. In 1271 the Dean and Chapter of Penkridge Church claimed to hold "the View of Frankpledge, fines for infractions of the assize of bread and beer, and infangenthef with the mainour." The View of Frankpledge was the name of the manorial court whilst infangenthef was the right to arrest and judge thieves.

At the same time Hugh le Blund, the Lord of the Manor, claimed "a market by charter of King Henry, a fair, gallows and infangenthef as annexed to the manor from time out of memory." The King disputed these claims and all three parties had to argue their cases in court. While the greater part of the dispute was over the right to make money out of the fair it must have been inimical to good order to have the power to arrest thieves and hang offenders disputed in this way. Nevertheless, it seems it was a long established tradition that order was kept by the Lord of the Manor having his own set of gallows. Field names survive a long time and on the 1754 estate map of Penkridge a small patch of land at the crossroads by the Cuttlestone Bridge is named "Gallows Pit".

It is well known that raising the Hue and Cry was a medieval way of capturing criminals. Common sense suggests that this was not a very effective method of law enforcement. Penkridge in the Middle Ages was prone to what can only be called gang fights and the hue and cry system served only, it seems, to muddy legal waters. In 1311 John de Hyntes said that Robert de Wyston, four of his sons and John le Taillor "had beaten, wounded and ill treated him at Penkridge on the day of St. Michael the Archangel" and claimed £100 damages.

The defendants turned the accusation on its head. They said that John de Hyntes and his friends had beaten them "so that their lives were despaired of, and that they raised the hue and cry." They claimed that the bailiff of Penkridge had joined the chase and tried to arrest John de Hyntes. If John had received any injuries it was his own fault and "not against the King's peace". The incident shows that the authority of the Lord of the Manor, as represented by the bailiff, could be resisted violently in the streets and legally in the courts.

Judging from the number of court cases involving Penkridge, justice in the Middle Ages could be a time consuming and uncertain matter. Even in simple cases of common crime the manorial court, the county sheriff and royal judges could be involved. Sentences were harsh. In 1335 at the court of Gaol Delivery at Stafford,

> "William, son of John Gyn of Penkridge, (who had been) indicted before the sheriff at his great tourn of Cuttleston for feloniously stealing a horse which was worth 5 shillings (was found to be) a common and notorious robber and was found guilty and hanged."

By the sixteenth century the Justices of the Peace were at the centre of the campaign for law and order. Bringing wrongdoers before them regularly and locally at the Quarter Sessions was an improvement in justice and should have worked well. When crimes concerning the people of Penkridge came before them, however, a picture of inefficiency and incompetence emerges. Rather than being an organised system using the resources of the county or the state, law enforcement in the sixteenth century seemed to pit individual against individual. In 1589 the J.P.s at Stafford heard that,

> "whereas John Bowes Kt. sheriff, issued a warrant to John Berwicke his bailiff, by virtue of a writ from the Queen, to arrest William Preston, late of Preston, and the said John Berwicke arrested the said William at Penkridge 28 September 1589 to take him to the gaol of the Castle of Stafford .... the said William assaulted the said bailiff in the execution of his office and rescued himself."

This episode happened when a paid employee of the sheriff was involved. When the unpaid constables of the manor courts were ordered to enforce the law examples of inefficiency multiplied greatly. The records of the Quarter Sessions are full of examples of constables failing to do their duty. In 1593 the constable of Penkridge, Thomas Allen, elected as all constables were, for one year only, was brought before the justices by the Chief Constable of the "Seasdon Hundred",

> "for not receiving one Geffrey Yevans, a notoryous Roge, but sufferinge him to escape, being brought and delivered to him by the constable of Brewood or his servant together with a mittimus to the gayoler and a precept whereby the sayd Roge might be brought from Constable to Constable towardes the gayole."

A system of law enforcement that hoped to transport criminals across the country by passing them from one reluctant amateur constable to another was optimistic in the extreme. As more and more tasks were piled upon local government the task of the constable became more onerous and troublesome. In 1602 the constable of Penkridge, George Horne, was accused of dereliction of duty for, "not appearing at Huntington to make presentment for punishing of Roges and Alehouses and for not joining with churchwardens to levy and pay in the money assessed for maimed soldiers and the prisons of the Bench and Marshalsea according to the order made at the last sessions."

For local crimes the medieval manorial court continued to contribute its most valuable asset - local knowledge. The manorial court of Penkridge, known as the View of Frankpledge, co-operated with the Justices of the Peace in bringing criminals to book. In 1598 they sent a certificate to Stafford stating that,

"at the View of Frankpledge of Penkridge it was presented by the oaths of Richard Tonke, John Fletcher, Richard Collins, Thomas Woolley, James Southall, Thomas Burne, Thomas Thurstance . . . that Charles Harryson, late of Penkridge, labourer, broke into the dwelling house of Alice Preston, widow, at Penkridge and stole . . ."

It is obvious that the powers and abilities of manorial constables were best suited to local misdemeanours and local people. Their authority came from being elected at the court of the Lord of the Manor by a jury of the leading local tenants. The office of constable, first mentioned in 1252, was a survival from the Middle Ages and perhaps not suited to the growing problems of the sixteenth and seventeenth centuries.

By the late eighteenth century society was perceived to be in a state of permanent crisis. A rapidly growing population, the expansion of industrial towns and increased poverty produced the conditions for a crime wave. In London efficient parish constables were organised by Henry Fielding into the Bow Street Runners in 1748. In 1792 the Bow Street method became the model for the rest of the city, thus introducing the era of the organised police force. In places like Penkridge, with fewer and different problems, an alternative solution was adopted. The constable was by-passed and leading individuals of the village attempted to take the detection and arrest of criminals into their own hands. In 1795 the Staffordshire Advertiser carried the following notice.

SUBSCRIPTION FOR PROSECUTING FELONS

We whose names are hereunder written being inhabitants of the Townships and Villages of Penkridge have formed ourselves into a Society to pursue and prosecute at our joint expense any person who shall commit . . . any Felony, Grand or Petty Larceny, and more especially House breakers, horse stealers, sheep stealers and fowl stealers.

The subscribers are likewise determined to prosecute all persons found unlawfully fishing, stealers of plough irons, hooks and thimbles, Hedge tearers and springle getters, to the utmost rigour of the law.

The crimes listed by the Association for the Prosecution of Felons show unmistakeably the main concerns of an agricultural community. Poaching, obviously, was an important problem. Most of the surrounding arable land was enclosed, so the tearing down of hedges for firewood had to be stamped on.

The Association offered rewards of up to £10 for information leading to the successful prosecution of a felon but was much more than an organisation for the paying of informants. Members had to print and distribute leaflets containing detailed descriptions of their horses if they were stolen. When another member received the handbill they were honour bound to set out on long journeys within four hours to publicise the theft. The rules of the Association demanded that they

> shall use all possible diligence and make every necessary enquiry and shall also cause notice to be given by the public crier in such towns as are appointed for that purpose and in every respect use their utmost endeavour not only to recover what is stolen, but also to discover, apprehend and convict the offenders.

The geographical reach of the Association was impressive. The vicar had to send his servants as far as Rugeley, Burton and Derby. John Hodson promised to cover Uttoxeter and Ashbourne. John Haddersich was responsible for Lichfield, Tamworth and Loughborough. The forty five members of the Association tracked thieves as far as Birmingham, Kidderminster, Cleobury Mortimore and Nuneaton.

Sometimes the Penkridge Association considered it necessary to advertise in newspapers. In July 1801, with a fine disregard for fairness, they announced,

FIVE GUINEAS REWARD

> Whereas James Rochell of Bradely was lately detected breaking open a barn belonging to Mr. Picktock of the Taft, in the Parish of Penkridge, the said Rochell effected his escape, and a reward of 5 guineas is offered for his apprehension. James Rochell is a labouring man, about 46 years of age, 5 feet 7 or 8 inches high, stout made, fresh complexion, light hair, speaks short, has a down look, and rather squints.

The Penkridge Association was still going strong in 1839, 44 years after its foundation. By that time new crimes had been added to the list, giving the distinct impression of being an accumulation of personal grievances and fears of the changing membership. Among the crimes at the forefront of Penkridge minds in 1801 were,

> Breaking and entering at night into a dwelling house, counting house, office, shop or warehouse, stealing, maliciously killing or maiming any horse, or wilfully setting fire to any house, outbuildings etc.
> Robbing gardens, orchards, damaging walls.

Any domestic servant stealing or giving away property of master.
Any waggoner selling or disposing of any coal, lime, hay, straw etc.
Stealing turnips, peas, potatoes or any other vegetables.

The Penkridge Association was prepared to offer rewards of up to £21 for information leading to the capital conviction of offenders but most local crimes were of a less dramatic nature involving poaching and theft by servants. Nevertheless the punishments, even for minor crimes, could be severe. In 1818 it was reported from Quarter Sessions that,

> "Matilda Corser, for stealing two £5 notes, the property of Mr. Charles Worsey of Pileton with whom she lived as a menial servant, and which notes he missed on the third instant, and upon being searched on the sixth, they were found to be concealed in her hair she was sentenced to be transported for seven years; the learned chairman observing, that when servants betrayed the trust reposed in them, and purloined property it was their duty to protect, no master could be safe, and it was necessary to pass a severe sentence to prevent the repetition of such offences."

During the third week in March Matilda Corser was removed from the county gaol, taken to Deptford and put on a ship bound for New South Wales. Her fate was a clear example of society's main solution to the problem of inefficient law enforcement, namely deterrence through harsh punishment. Nine years later another servant, Mary Brindley, was found guilty of stealing some beads from her mistress, Mrs. Devie. In court Mr. Devie "humanely recommended his unfaithful servant to the mercy of the court and the Bench commiserating on her situation sentenced her to be imprisoned for the space of *six weeks only.*"

There was not a great deal of very serious crime reported from the Penkridge area. It was a small, peaceful village. Everyone knew each other and the leaders of society, including Lord Hatherton himself, were able to exert a restraining influence. Once a Penkridge person escaped the improving atmosphere of the village, however, it was possible that he would go off the rails. Joseph Wilkes was born at Pillaton in about 1825. His father was a waggoner and then became assistant gamekeeper on the Teddesley estate. All might have been well but Joseph's father was sacked by Lord Hatherton and the family had to move on. Joseph got work as a farm labourer at Acton and Butterhill but eventually moved to Walsall with his brother. They fell into bad company and in 1842 became involved in a burglary during which Joseph hit and killed an old man.

Joseph was arrested and convicted of murder at Stafford. He was sentenced to death but many supposed that his sentence would be commuted since he was only 17 years old and had not taken a weapon to the scene of the crime. He was described as a "blunt" and uneducated lad who did not seem to appreciate the seriousness of his dreadful situation. Appeals to the Home Secretary for clemency failed despite being supported by the Governor of Stafford Gaol. Joseph Wilkes therefore suffered the ultimate sanction of England's system of law and order.

On the day before his execution he attended a service at the gaol which included the "condemned sermon". The chaplain addressed him directly, telling him that,

> "Your life has not yet reached its meridian, you have not attained the vigour and strength of manhood and yet ere the light of another Sabbath dawns your body will be restored to the dust and your soul will wing its way to the presence of a Holy God. How awful and tremendous the thought - that in a few hours your soul will be in a place of happiness or misery - in heaven or hell."

Joseph slept for several hours the night before his execution. He was woken up early in the morning "to attend to his spiritual exercises". While he was thus occupied great crowds were gathering in front of the gaol. The train from Walsall was late and many people could be seen running from the station in a vain attempt to be in time for the hanging. A few minutes before 8 o'clock on Saturday April 1st the hangman, "the last functionary of the law" entered Joseph's cell. After his arms were pinioned they walked out to the gallows. Joseph walked steadily and did not show any emotion while the Chaplain read the burial service.

> "On the arrival of the procession at the lodge, the unhappy youth shook hands with the Chaplain, the Governor and other Officers and ascended the drop without assistance. He gave a hasty glance at the crowd whilst the rope and cap were adjusted and at a few minutes past eight the drop fell and closed the world upon him forever. He struggled for some time and appeared to die with difficulty."

James Wilkes was luckier than his brother. He had been sentenced to transportation for life and was at that moment in a prison hulk before being sent to Australia. Joseph Wilkes was beyond help but the long slow process towards a policy which emphasised more efficient policing rather than harsh penalties had begun and Staffordshire was appointing parish constables as a first stage in establishing a rural police force.

Chapter 3

Reformation to Restoration

During the Middle Ages the people of Penkridge were familiar with many of the abuses which were to lead to demands for the reform of the church. Most would probably have been ignorant of church politics and the ology but they would have noticed that their spiritual welfare was being endangered. This happened in the 1330's when the Archbishop of Dublin and the Bishop of Lichfield fought over the bodies and souls of the parishioners of Penkridge's Prebendary at Cannock. Charges made for the burying of the dead formed an important income for the church. In 1330 the clergy of Lichfield secretly dedicated a new churchyard and took over the Chapel at Cannock. When Penkridge clergy arrived to conduct funerals they had to fight off their Lichfield colleagues who attempted to grab the bodies. As Dorothy Styles, an historian of Penkridge Church, has commented, "If this were true there must have been some gruesome incidents at Cannock."

One of the most serious allegations of those who protested at the state of the church was that it encouraged superstitions, partly in order to raise revenue. In 1517 Martin Luther complained of the sale of Indulgences to pay for the building of St. Peter's in Rome. Agents for the Church were promising remission of time to be spent in purgatory in return for "gifts from the faithful". On a much smaller scale a similar scheme had been adopted in Penkridge. The Archbishop of Dublin, in his role as Dean of Penkridge, granted an Indulgence of one hundred days "to all such as are contrite to confess their sins and shall bestow any charity upon the Chapel of St. Leonard of Dunstan and shall come hither for that purpose."

Simony, the sin of buying and selling of church offices, was blatant in Penkridge. One John Pudde complained in Chancery that he had been promised a Prebend in the Collegiate Church of Penkridge worth £20 a year. He had been charged £18 and he had already put down a deposit. Despite this he had only been offered a Chantry worth £5 a year. Penkridge was a wealthy church, its income in the early sixteenth century being £74 a year. When the college was dissolved, like the monasteries, during the Reformation, its property was sold off. When it came into the hands of the Littleton family, fifty years later it cost £604 and was described as consisting of (albeit in suspiciously round figures) the site of the college, 7 ancient prebends, 100 messuages, 100 cottages, 40 tofts, 4 mills, 10 dovecotes, 100 gardens, 100 orchards, 400 acres of land, 40 acres of meadow, 10 acres of moor and 10 acres of marsh and land covered with water. The revenue of this property had previously to support the College consisting of the Dean, seven prebendaries, two residential canons, who lived in a "mansion house" and acted as the rectors of the parish, and a sexton. Most of the spiritual work was done by six curates who were paid about £4 a year.

Nevertheless, the hold of the church on the people of Penkridge was strong. On the eve of the Reformation the Archdeacon of Stafford conducted a survey of those attending church. It showed that on Palm Sunday 1532 fifty three families attended the church. The five priests wrote down the names of the communicants. The list, which predates the parish register by forty years, is the first in which modern surnames are used. Not surprisingly, there is very little correlation with the names on the medieval tax lists but many of the names were to be familiar in the village for at least the following three hundred years. Where a man appears to have more than one wife it has been assumed that the priest included the names of deceased spouses.

William Swenerton, Catherine, Joan
Robert Teylors, Joyce
Richard Henney, Catherine, Margery
Robert Mower, Joan
Hugh Becham, Joyce
Hugh Lyott, Thomasin
Robert Barton, Agnes
William Finchely, Margaret, Joan, Ellen
John Flecher, Elizabeth
John Finchely, Margaret
John Douncalf, Elizabeth
Roger Morton, Elizabeth
William Warde, Margaret
William Ryder, Joan
Robert Ryder, Margaret
William Lyott, Joan
William Garlett, Thomasin
Randal Bassett, Isabel, Thomasin
Thomas Bere, Ellen
John Venabull, Joan, Joan
John Clarke, Catherine
John Birne, Margaret
Roger Mason, Catherine
William Benet, Elizabeth

Ralph Tonks, Gillian
Miles Cowley, single, mother Margery
John Torne, single, mother Joan
Robert Corbett, Gillian
Edmund Dekynson, Agnes
William Wolley, Margaret
Alexander Kinge, Joan
Edward Avery, Agnes, Agnes
Thomas Wytfeld, Joan
Richard Meke, Joan
Thomas Smyth, Joan
William Pool, Catherine, Elenor
Roger Styles, Margaret
Roger Alen, Margaret
John Corner, Agnes
John Cox, Alice
Roger Hoppas, Engott
John Douncalf, Elizabeth
John Talbott, Elizabeth
Henry Hounde, Margaret
Hugh Preston, Alice, Joan
Robert Emson, Alice
Thomas Colens, Joan

During the reign of Edward VI (1547 - 53) the Protestant Reformation was pushed to its fullest extent. The Latin Mass was abolished and services much simplified. Greater emphasis was placed upon instructing the laity in the Scriptures and churches were stripped of images and side altars. High altars became, merely, holy tables. An inventory of the possessions of Penkridge Church, taken two years before the end of Edward's reign shows that puritan zeal did not go too far, in Penkridge at least. The church retained a plentiful supply of colourful ornaments and vestments including two silver chalices, one silver censor, three dark tawny copes and three suits of vestments, one blue, one black and one crimson "bought by Mr. Littleton at the suppression of Stone monastery."

Changes, however, were inevitable. One of the church bells was sold to finance a Protestant Reformation of the church. The money was used "in plucking down the altars and defacing the church, in painting the table at high altar with scriptures, in glazing the church windows and in having a young man to teach in writing school."

It might be supposed that the problem of badly paid and poorly qualified priests was solved after the Reformation. The great wealth of the church was now, however, diverted into lay hands and during the sixteenth century the quality of the Vicars of Penkridge was variable. George Hordern, Vicar in the 1590's continued the medieval tradition of battling clerics. He appeared in at least four court cases because of his involvement in brawls. His first fight was on the significant day of 29th September in 1590 and against a Robert Mole. In the next couple of years he fought John Clarke, a shoemaker, Katherine Bennett, the wife of a shoemaker and Thomas Hanly, a tailor. Hordern is described in the records as "scholaris ruralis, male conversationis ut penitus illiteratis" which marks him down as a badly behaved and troublesome illiterate. Such was his lack of moral authority that large brawls involving up to eight villagers broke out in the churchyard despite the threat of severe punishments.

After the Reformation the next great crisis for the church came with the struggle between King and Parliament in the 1640's. One of the first indications of troublesome times ahead for the ordinary people of Penkridge came in 1640 when Charles I attempted to raise an army to suppress the Scottish Covenanters. The plan in Staffordshire was to muster the trained bands of men who had served in the army before and could therefore be expected to have some enthusiasm for the project and then make up the required numbers from about three hundred pressed men who were rather less reliable. The trained men chosen from Penkridge, Pillaton and Dunston were William and Richard Tonks, Thomas Worsey, John Wright, Thomas Steedman, Thomas Broome and Humphrey Hawkins. Their more grudging, pressed colleagues were Thomas Ap Hugh, William Hockinn and Thomas Ansley.

The constable of the Cuttlestone Hundred had the thankless duty of conducting the unhappy pressed men to Uttoxeter where they would be handed over to the officers who would train them and then march them north. The task of the constable was fraught with difficulties. Although the soldiers' pay of 8d a day was quite generous for the time it did not become available until the actual muster and the county had to provide for the men until then and control their impulse to forage for food in the surrounding countryside. The constable had all the problems of an army officer without any of his powers. These ill-trained, undisciplined and reluctant men were not under army law and the constables only had the hopelessly inadequate common law to deal with outbreaks of dissent and crime.

The men from Penkridge were called to Uttoxeter with the rest of the Cuttlestone and Seisdon Hundreds on the 1st June 1640. Nervous preparations were made to receive the men, numbering about a hundred. The camp was guarded by the anxious constable of Uttoxeter and fifty of his townsmen. The travelling constables were given strict instructions to " take care of their soldiers and to provide them with convenient lodging and **not to leave them**." They were ordered to "prevent all uproars and other myschiefs that might happen upon such an assembly."

If the authorities had thought that they had done enough they were soon disillusioned. The pressed men "made haste to do mischief" and made two bonfires out of uprooted park fencing. The men of Uttoxeter were utterly outnumbered. They made "all faire pswations to pacifie them" but the riot increased in size. The constable complained that "we were disinabled to record the said riot or to inflict condign punishment on the said rioters being men unknown to us." After three days of "disorder and tumulte" and " gross insolence" reinforcements were brought in to restore order. It is not surprising that the army put up such a poor show and managed to lose Newcastle to the Scots. Charles I had to pay the invaders £850 a day and was forced to recall Parliament.

The effect of the Civil War upon the lives of ordinary people often depended upon the relationship of their local magnate with Parliament. At the outbreak of the war Sir Edward Littleton was a member of the Long Parliament. At first he sat on the Parliamentary Committee at Stafford but eventually he was "disabled", in 1644. He was designated a "delinquent" and had his estate sequestered. Most of the Littleton tenants were ordered to pay their rents to Colonel Simon Rugeley and sometimes the Committee sent troops into the village to collect corn from Pillaton and other farms.

While the people of Penkridge seem to have been under the thumb of Parliamentary forces for most of the war the Committee at Stafford could not prevent Royalist incursions into the area. Tildesley quotes State papers for March 1645 which reported that,

"This day came letters that Prince Rupert marched on Wednesday last from Newport to Penkridge Heath, within four miles of Stafford and quartered his army there."

A couple of months later "The True Informer" reported that,

> "On Monday May 19th Captain Church went out of Stafford with seven horses to discover the enemy's motions. He fell upon their quarters at Penkridge, killed three, took four prisoners and seven horses, by which means the enemy are so awed by our forces that they march close together and dare not struggle abroad to plunder as they were wont." (Tildesley)

Nevertheless Penkridge did not suffer a violent upheaval during the war. The Littletons managed to maintain their position and Sir Edward's wife was allowed to "quietly enjoy and receive" one fifth of the income from the estate, the rents of Preston Walker, John Webb, John Haddersich, Edward Smith, Constance Ingram, Edward Hand and Mr. Tytley. At the end of the war Sir Edward was allowed to buy back his land.

Perhaps the worst aspect of Parliamentary rule for the people of Penkridge was the presence of soldiers and the imposition of new taxation to pay for them. In 1652 forty two inhabitants of the Cuttlestone Hundred complained to the Justices that "our Hundred hath beene much prejudiced by soldiers being sent into the county to quarter upon us." From 1643 all individuals were assessed" for the value of every pound" for a new tax called "Weekly Pay". The money was collected by the constables and headboroughs and allocated locally to particular garrisons and army commands. Penkridge, as part of the Cuttlestone Hundred paid the wages of the regiment of foot soldiers that garrisoned Stafford town. The duty of being village constable had always been irksome. Now that he was the main link between the Parliamentary Committee and the village and the main tax gatherer the problems were overwhelming. With Sir Edward absent supporting the Royalist cause the manorial court had broken down and new constables could not be elected. There was also a shortage of Parliamentary magistrates to appoint replacements. In 1645 the constable of Penkridge complained to the Quarter Sessions that he had not been discharged, "by reason that there was no court kept there last Michaelmas in regard of the present distractions" and that "he was no scholar but all together unfit for that service". He handed over a list of names of other villagers "far more able and fitter" who had not served for up to twenty years.

The Vicar of Penkridge when the Civil War broke out was Joseph Creeke. He died in 1643 just before the victorious Puritans attempted their reform of the Church of England. The Book of Common Prayer was forbidden in 1645 and eventually about three thousand incumbents were ejected from their parishes by Parliamentary Committees. Creeke's unnamed successor lasted until 1646 when he was ejected. Luckily for the traditionalists of Penkridge the Parliamentary Committee for Plundered Ministers appointed in his stead Nathanial Hinde who appeared, by the standards of the day, to be a religious moderate. One undeniable benefit of the changes was that the Committee increased the stipend of the Vicar by diverting £50 a year from the income of the Rectory, part of Sir Edward Littleton's sequestered estate.

The upheavals caused by the war and subsequent changes at the church do seem to have affected the lives of some villagers. According to the Parish Register no marriages were solemnised in 1644, only two in 1645, four in 1646, one in 1647 and 1648 and two in 1649. This could have been the result of a break down in social order due to the troubled times. It is also possible that local couples were going to churches more to their taste after the changes of 1646. An alternative explanation is that the Vicars of Penkridge recorded the marriages in a half hearted and haphazard way during the troubled years. A major change occurred in 1653 when Parliament decided to take the solemnisation of marriage away from church ministers and give the task to the magistrates. In the 1650's, therefore, Penkridge saw its first civil marriages. The banns were called "three severall market days in the Market Place at Penkridge" and the couples were married by the magistrate, Mathew Moreton.

Whilst the people of Penkridge seem to have had a moderate Vicar during the years of the Commonwealth they were not to escape the attention of extreme puritans entirely. John Jackson, the Puritan Vicar of Lapley, cast a jaundiced eye on his neighbouring parishes and found them wanting. In 1655 he complained bitterly that wakes were being observed by feasting on Sabbath days and that "a great part of the weeke after are the wakes continued and upheld by loose people, especially by Ale houses without restraint." He observed that the "great part of the wakes weekes is spent in promiscuous dancing, maurice dancing, tippling, gameing, quarrelling and wantonesse." He felt that God was being dishonoured and superstition being encouraged by particular days still being dedicated to saints. He was particularly angry when he discovered two bands of dancers in Lapley, one from Stretton in the Parish of Penkridge. Although superstition and loose living continued in the countryside Penkridge posed no real threat to zealous Protestants. When a list of Roman Catholics, or Recusants, was compiled in 1657 only three lived in Penkridge. In contrast Roman Catholics under the protection of the Giffards at Brewood numbered seventy three.

When Charles II was restored to the throne in 1660 the first task of local government was to administer a poll tax in order to pay off the Commonwealth soldiers. County Committees were appointed, bringing together the old loyal royalist families like the Littletons and former members of the Parliamentary Committee at Stafford. This re-uniting of the natural leaders of society was seen also at Penkridge. Nathanial Hinde, the Vicar, conformed to the restored Church of England and remained as incumbent until his death in 1673. Together with William Southall, the Parliamentary Coroner at Penkridge he worked with Sir Edward Littleton and Richard Congreve in assessing the village for the 1666 Hearth Tax. The tax list gives us the names of the 69 Penkridge householders who were wealthy enough to pay the tax and the 55 householders poor enough to be exempt. The list is the best evidence of the individuals and families who lived in Penkridge through the troubled times of war and Interregnum.

The tax list was headed by Robert Phillipps. He had seven hearths and presumably one of the biggest houses in Penkridge. His name is accompanied by the disapproving comment " and he stopt upp 5 at Michaelmas 1662 when he was High Constable and persuaded many to do the same". Large houses were also occupied by Jeremiah Fieldhouse with six fires, Matthew Byrche with eight and William Warde with six. The other villagers wealthy enough to pay the tax were Nathanial Hinde, William Southall, Simon Woolley, William Cooke, Richard Ingram, Simon Mounford, William Tonks, Humfrey Asply, John Hicken, Ursula Grately, William Iremonger, Henry Yate, James Southall's wife, Mary Barker, Thomas Byrch, John Dickenson, John Webb, Anne Duncalfe, John Wright, John Poole, Humfrey Arcall, Thomas Collins, Widow Kinge, Thomas Lea, John Haddersich, Thomas Tonks, John Iremonger, John Cox, Edward Smyth, Simon Iremonger, Thomas Bennett, William Baxter , John Iremonger junior, George Prittland, Edward Steedman, Edward Browne, Roger Crutchly, Thomas Fletcher, Rebecca Ingram, Preston Walker senior and junior, William Reade, Edward Reade, John Woolley, Richard Asby, John Greene, William Smate, William Waller, John Stanley, William Hicken, Francis Woolley, Simon Turner, John Goodale, John Vanes senior and junior, Lewis Turner, Henry Fieldhouse, Thomas Acton, Richard Bryn, Richard Thomas, John Broome, Jane Bowre, John Fletcher, Matthew Byrche and Thomas Lynell.

The poor people of Penkridge, "certified not to be chargeable according to the Act" were John Chamley, Robert Wall, Margery Carter, Thomas Peate, John Warde, Edward Dickinson, Edward Fleming, William Ingram, Widow Lucas, John Birch, John Cotton, John Heyes, William Jenkins, Widow Poole, Mary Wright, Widow Finchley, Widow Hood, Joane Poole, John Banam, John Hadley, Robert Astley, Thomas Bannister, Thomas Poole, Joseph Cheshire, Edward Mason, Daniel Webbe, Thomas Webb, Richard Staley, John Cooper, William Hadley, Widow King, William Clarke, Joanne Woolley, Widow Worley, Edward Foster, Widow Hill, Richard Burrington, Rebecca Ingram, Richard Doughtie, James Baxter, Edward Baxter, Thomas Harvey, Richard Lome, Thomas Higgs, Widow Ingram, John Clarke, Anne Davey and John Cotton junior.

Chapter 4

Inns and Alehouses

In 1609 the enemies of Richard Blakeman, a Penkridge butcher, caught up with him at the Stafford Quarter Sessions. Originally charged with killing a tame dove with a fowling piece charged with "gunne powder and haile shott" in Penkridge on the 16th February, the details of his turbulent life in the village gradually came out in court.

A neighbour, John Iremonger, had hired a labourer to put up a fence on his land while he got on with his ploughing. When he returned from his fields he found that Blakeman had threatened the workman so that the job had not been done. He found Blakeman sitting in his own backyard and asked him to explain himself. Blakeman cursed Iremonger and his wife and said a fence should not be set up there and dared him to put the palings up.

Another neighbour with a grudge was William Humston. Blakeman had stolen "a payre of womans bodyes" from him and pawned them at an alehouse so that Humston had to redeem them with his own money. Not content with this Blakeman then assaulted Humston who was a tailor and stole his scissors. When the time came to describe the general character of Richard Blakeman it was said that he was known to be "a common frequenter of alehouses and breaker of the King's peace". Being a frequenter of alehouses was a damning charge in the sixteenth and seventeenth centuries revealing the Tudor and Stuart preoccupation with alehouses and the disturbance of good order and morals. In 1583 Stubbs in his "Anatomie of Abuses" said,

"Every village hath abundance of alehouses, taverns and inns which are so fraught with malt worms, night and day that you would wonder to see them."

From earliest times the control of the alehouses had been one of the main concerns of local government. When the Church and the Crown disputed the right to control the Manor of Penkridge during the reign of Edward I the Dean and Chapter of Penkridge made a point of claiming their right to fine people who broke the rules on the preparation of beer and bread through Penkridge's manorial court, the View of Frankpledge. It was one of the manorial court's main duties to appoint Ale Conners to assay beer and check measures.

Up to 1552 anyone could open an alehouse in the village. Then restrictions began to be imposed. The Tudor concern was with morals and order rather than the quality of the beer. As a result the county magistrates in the Quarter Sessions were given the power to close alehouses and to take recognizances from alehouse keepers that they would not allow any unlawful games or disorder in their houses. A distinction was drawn between inns and alehouses. Any inn keeper who sold ale to local people rather than genuine travellers risked three days in prison.

From Quarter Session records we can tell that by 1589 Penkridge had eleven licensed victuallers or alehouse keepers. They were Thomas Dickenson, William Broune, Henry Smyth, Thomas Fisher, Laurence Oldfeylde, William Soutton, John Buckenall, John Ley, Humphrey Smythe, Henry Bennett and Thomas Boden. They were required by law to find two people willing to stand surety of £5 for them. The publicans of Penkridge solved this problem by standing surety for each other.

By 1603 the number of official alehouses and inns in Penkridge had grown to eighteen. The magistrates recorded the main occupation of the applicants and only one of them, Leonard Pownder, was described as an inn holder (the White Hart?). John Foxe was a tanner, Thomas Hoode a husbandman, Rodger Hodgson a shoemaker, Henry Duncalfe a weaver, Thomas Till a tailor, John Baxon a collier and Thomas Ap Yeavon a labourer. No less than three of them were butchers - John Blake, John Hickin and Thomas Allin. It seems clear that the number of drinking houses was increasing mainly through workers and tradesmen using their premises to make a little extra money on the side.

If this trend was reflected nationwide it is no surprise that Parliament passed another Act "to restrain inordinate haunting and tippling in Inns, Alehouses and other victualling houses" in 1604. Landlords were fined ten shillings if they allowed locals to sit drinking. Inn keepers were forbidden to allow drink to anyone unless they were travellers, lodgers in the house, guests of travellers or labouring men in their dinner hour. This Act was an immediate failure as it drove drinkers into unlicensed houses and there was less control than before. In 1606, therefore, all alehouses had to be licensed. This had a dramatic effect on the drinkers of Penkridge. The first year of the licencing policy reduced the number of drinking places to nine. The licencees were Henry Duncalfe, Leonard Pownder, Henry Smith a husbandman, Edward Cotton a shoemaker, Henry Smith, a dyer, John Hickin, William Tonckes, a husbandman, John Reynoldes and Hugh Pynson. The control of village alehouses remained one of the irksome duties of the unpaid village officials. An Act of Parliament in 1623 charged every village official to act as a common informer against any "tipsy" man.

The licences granted for the year 1609 reveal certain trends. The number of drinking houses was held at ten. Richard Ouldfield joined his father Laurence in the business as did John Hickin junior. Skilled tradesmen like butchers and carpenters seemed to have an affinity with alehouse keeping whilst the landlords of the larger houses and inns like Leonard Pownder and Henry Smyth were able to aspire to the class of yeoman, an indication, perhaps, of large amounts of land being attached to the premises. Almost a hundred years later in 1702 the number of alehouse keepers was still only nine. Only the Tonks name seems to have survived in the trade whilst landladies in the shape of Mistress King, Elizabeth Goodwind, Mistress Muggall and Rachell Tonks had been granted licences.

During the English Civil War the excise duty on ale, beer, cider and perry was greatly increased. As a result drinkers began to look for a cheaper substitute. For the next hundred years or so the massive consumption of gin became a great social problem. In 1736 a duty of a pound a gallon was placed on gin and retailers were forced to pay £50 for a licence. This act had results similar to those of prohibition in America. The consumption of gin actually increased as the trade was driven underground in unlicensed premises and under other names. The trade of landlord in the mid-eighteenth century was clearly not always a respectable one. When John Wesley visited Penkridge in October 1745 he noted in his Journal that,

"We came to Penkridge and lit on a poor, drunken, swearing landlord, but I had spoken very little when his countenance changed, and he was so full of thanks and blessings that I could hardly make an end of my sentence."

In an attempt to undermine the economic success of the gin trade a more practical law was introduced in 1751. Distillers were banned from selling gin retail or to unlicensed houses and it became impossible to recover debts for drink at law.

From the end of the eighteenth century it is possible to identify more specifically the names of the various inns and taverns and their landlords by consulting the trade directories. The first directory to mention Penkridge was the Universal British Directory of Trade, Commerce and Manufacture which was published in 1793. In a list of the 42 principal inhabitants of the village it notes 6 inn keepers or victuallers. William Cope was the landlord at the Horse and Jockey and James Scholey ran the Fox which doubled up as the village post office. Scholey was able to act as post master since he would be meeting the mail coaches as they arrived at his inn. Landladies ran the two more prestigious inns, Nancy Wright the Littleton Arms and Ann Molineux the White Hart Inn. Nancy Anslow and John Worsey are merely described as victuallers. Their properties are clearly less important than the great inns. It becomes clear from later directories that Nancy Anslow was running the Blacksmith's Arms which was being combined with the Anslow family business of tin plate working. John Worsey's pub is not named but in later years members of his family ran both the Horse and Jockey and the George and Fox.

Penkridge had a variety of drinking places, each with a different status. At the top of the scale came the Littleton Arms Inn with its stables, courtyard and expensive lodgings. It is hardly possible to over emphasise the leading role that the Littleton played in the social, business and legal life of the village. The inn was the main auction house for the farming and business community. In the early nineteenth century the production of timber was very important in the area and the Littleton Arms was the regular auction house for its sale. An advertisement for an auction on February 6, 1813 shows the size of the business.

AUCTION OF TIMBER AND CRATE WOOD AT LITTLETON ARMS

8 ash trees lying on land at Mr. Turner's barn, in the occupation of Mr. Boulton. 12 ash trees on land at Mansty Head near Pileton in occupation of Nathaniel Worsey.
A quantity of Boat Knees - 400 doz Lock Stocks - Coal Pit posts
400 horse loads of Crate heads - 71 horse loads of Crate rods
All lying within 2 miles of the canal.
Apply to Mr. John Lewis of Penkridge.

John Lewis was a timber merchant who had his premises in Bellbrook.

At a time when local government was an unpaid social obligation and much of national taxation was farmed out to private individuals there were very few official government buildings. Inns like the Littleton with its many rooms thus became the centre of village administration. Throughout the nineteenth century it served as Penkridge's tax office. In 1806, for example the wealthier inhabitants were informed in the Staffordshire Advertiser that,

"Notice is hereby given that the Commissioners for the general purposes appointed to carry into execution 'An Act for a Tax on the Profits arising from Property, Trades and Professions' will hear appeals against assessments made under the said Act - August 4 Littleton Arms."

Other less important duties were also administered at the Inn. In 1806 Mr. Heath a collector of saddle horse duty, who would be at the inn on the 12th of August announced that,

"a saddle horse hired from one place to another, and back, is a hireling within the meaning of the Act and liable to a duty of 1½d a mile; I hereby give notice that I shall attend the undermentioned times and places to grant licences and to deliver the proper books and tickets to all such persons who apply for same."

Although attending the Littleton Estate rent days, arguing with the Enclosure Commissioners or visiting the Excise Office to sort out taxes were wonderful excuses for going to the Littleton Arms, the real glory of the Inn was to be seen on less dismal occasions. It was the natural venue for Penkridge's top social events. In 1837 the Hon. Edward Littleton, eldest son of Lord Hatherton, came of age. The Advertiser reported that,

"The ball at Penkridge to celebrate this important epoch in Mr. Littleton's life, was attended by 160 persons, comprising the most respectable residents in the neighbourhood. The ballroom at the Littleton's Arms was most beautifully decorated, and the lights were truly brilliant. The supper was most luxurious, and maintained the high reputation for excellent taste management of the Littleton's Arms."

The inns and their landlords were the prime movers in other great social events. William Cotton of the Littleton Arms organised the famous Penkridge races on, for example, 15th and 16th October 1827.

One race was restricted to horses belonging to Staffs Yeomanry. The winner was to be sold for £80 if demanded within 15 minutes. A race on the second day was for horses beaten on the first day. There was also a handicapped hunters race and races for non-thoroughbreds. No person was allowed to erect a booth, shed or stall until he had the agreement of Mr. Cotton. The Staffordshire Advertiser reported that,

"The sport at these races was of a superior description and the fineness of the weather brought together a very numerous and respectable company. The ordinaries were crowded each day and a very liberal subscription was entered into for the next year's races."

The publicity for the 1837 races makes it even more clear that these races associated with the Littleton Arms were not meetings in the modern sense but high quality events in the social calendar of the gentry.

PENKRIDGE RACES.

Stewards - J.M. Lister, Henry Critchley

Monday 16th October

The Teddesley Stakes - for horses, not thoroughbreds, who have not won £50 at one time, Two mile heats. 3 lb allowance for mares and geldings.

The Congreve Hurdle Stakes - for horses, not thoroughbreds, the property of gentlemen living within 15 miles of Penkridge, that have never been in training stables, each horse to carry 12st. The best of 2 mile heats, each heat taking in 8 flights of hurdles. Gentlemen riders only.

Tuesday 17 October

Chillington Stakes
Dunston Stakes - horses must be regularly hunted, open to gentlemen 25 miles round Penkridge.

Horses were entered at the Littleton Arms. The landlord, John Spilsbury, was the secretary of the meeting and the event culminated in a grand ball at the inn.

The Littleton Arms was more than just an inn. When it was let in 1813 two hundred acres of farm land were attached. William Cotton gave up the inn keeping business in 1837. The catalogue of his possessions at the resulting auctions reveal that he was a wealthy gentleman.

Extensive sale held at Littleton Arms Inn, 20th March. Various Effects belonging to Mr. Cotton who is retiring from the Inn Keeping business viz. 2 Post Chaises, a quantity of harness, household furniture, brewing vessels, smithy tools, 2 malt mills, bean mill, seed drill, 2 large mash tubs, 15 excellent casks, 2 cheese presses useful modern furniture - extensive assemblage of mahogany, dining and other tables, 16 excellent goose feather beds etc.

APRIL 8.

IMPORTANT SALE AT PILLATON HALL
The property of Mr. Cotton who has given up his Penkridge farm.
20 capital heifers in calf
4 capital fat cows
132 capital fat sheep
150 Leicester Ewes and lambs and farm equipment.

Judging by the social events associated with it, the George and Fox was not so highly regarded in society as the Littleton. Instead of the horse races we get,

PENKRIDGE COURSING MEETING, JANUARY 16TH 1840

Will take place on Jan 16 when a cup stake of 1 sovereign each will be contended for. Present subscribers 5.
Also a sweepstake of one sovereign each for puppies under the age of 20 months. Present subscriber 1.
To meet, with dogs, ready for the slips, at the George and Fox Inn, precisely at half past nine in the morning of the day of running.

The George and Fox did not play host to the celebrations of the Littleton estate but it did for many years entertain the leading inhabitants of the village at the annual dinner of the Penkridge Association for the Prosecution of Felons, clearly a most respectable organisation.

The posters advertising the sale of the George in 1811 show what a powerful economic grouping of property these inns were.

SALE OF GEORGE INN

George Inn and 6 acres of rich meadow and pasture land and other houses adjoining.

Auctioneer Josiah Robins
14th October 1811 3 pm

Lot 1
Inn, stables, barn, outbuildings, gardens, malthouse and 4 crofts of rich meadow and pasture land adjoining - about 6 acres.

Lot 2
All those 2 houses, outbuildings and gardens next to the Inn, in the occupation of Mr. Jones and Thomas Hillman.

Lot 3
2 cottages or workmans houses and gardens in the occupation of John Walker and Edward Simpson.
All occupied by tenants at will who have notice to quit at Lady Day next.

A Mr. Baker agreed to buy the Inn for £1,100, and paid £110 deposit. The sale took a very long time and Mr. Bennet, the Solicitor involved, had the embarrassing experience of having the property struck by lightning before the conveyancing was complete.

In 1837 both the Littleton Arms and The Boat changed hands. In the early nineteenth century The Boat was a large establishment. Despite the bravado of its description in the sale advertisement it seems to have been a victim of the opening of the railway in 1837 which necessarily reduced the amount of traffic and custom from the canal.

"All that substantially built an old established Public House known by the name of The Boat Inn situate in Husbandman St., Penkridge (now in the occupation of Mr. Joseph Dugmore, who is giving up the Publican's business) and will be found to contain strong arched cellars, two parlours, kitchen, brewhouse, pantries, commodious chambers and attics, stabling for 12 horses, granary, cottage dwelling attached; a cottage and building conveniently detached; together with several plots of rich garden ground: the whole lying contiguous with the Staffordshire and Worcestershire Canal, which has so long flourished by the transit of goods, and whose interest is not likely to be affected by railways."

In 1830 Parliament passed a new Beer Act in its continuing campaign against excessive gin and spirit drinking. From this point and until 1869 almost any householder whose name was on the rate book and was of good character could sell beer (and nothing else) without getting a licence. They were free from any control once they paid 2 guineas to the Exchequer. In 1834 "off licences" were allowed. Not surprisingly there was an immediate proliferation of beer houses across the country, Penkridge being no exception.

A review of the trade directories and censuses of the mid nineteenth century reveal a massive increase in drinking places to almost Tudor proportions. These often short-lived additions to the established inns and taverns of Penkridge could only have been tiny establishments in the halls, parlours and kitchens of people's homes. William White's History, Gazetteer and Directory of Staffordshire, 1834 notes the following new alehouses:

William Nixon, beerhouse, Clay Street
Elizabeth Cheadle, beerhouse, Market Street
Richard Boothby, beerhouse, Market Place
J. Southern, beerhouse, Mill End
William Webb, beerhouse, High Street
Samuel Bowdler, beerhouse, Wire Hall Street

From the 1841 census one can add:

Joseph Burrows, beer retailer
Robert Edwards, beer retailer
Thomas Henshaw, victualler, Lord Nelson Spirit Vaults, Market Street
John Doughty, The Star, Market Place.

The 1851 Census saw in addition George Bridgwood's beerhouse in the Cannock Road, the Old George Beer Shop run by Edward North in Market Place and the Robin Hood in Market Street. It is hardly surprising that with this massive increase in drinking premises one correspondent of the Staffordshire Advertiser in 1832 felt moved to write, about Staffordshire in general that,

"It requires no angel from heaven to tell us the wretched consequences of this most atrocious act; the effects of its poisonous and demoralizing influence are too sadly apparent ..... deluge of immorality and shameless open day impudence, and opposition to order and good government, evinced by the hordes of vagabonds who frequent the pest houses created by the act .... it is truly deplorable to witness the Sunday scenes which the bill has now introduced. Men and women drunk and fighting in open daylight."

Although strictly speaking inns and alehouses did not compete for the same customers many inn keepers felt obliged to enlarge and increase the attraction of their houses. There is evidence that in Penkridge both the Littleton and the White Hart took this course. When John Spilsbury took over the Littleton Arms from William Cotton in 1837 he announced,

"John Spilsbury (from the Trumpet Inn, Stafford) respectfully informs his friends and the public generally that he has entered on the above Inn and Posting House, and by sparing no exertions to promote the comfort and convenience of his guests and customers he hopes to receive an equivalent share of public patronage. Commercial gentlemen will find increased accommodation has been provided for them."

The sale of the White Hart two years later came after a period of expansion. It was described in the Staffordshire Advertiser as,

"All that old established PUBLIC HOUSE, called the White Hart Inn, consisting of a tap room, bar, large parlour, entrance gateway, brewhouse, cellar, 5 bedrooms, 3 attics, and store room, also large and extensive stabling for 40 horses, the principal part recently erected, gig house, large garden and pump, and other conveniences, now in the occupation of John Seaville, as tenant from year to year."

From 1867 onwards the number of beerhouses was gradually reduced. They were placed back under the control of the magistrates and had to have licences. After 1872 they were no longer allowed to stay open all night. The large Midlands breweries became involved in the ownership of alehouses and it became much harder for individual householders to get a licence. Breweries had money to invest in their houses. Butlers took over the White Hart and in 1891 completely rebuilt the frontage of the inn (though following the old Tudor lines).

By the time of the 1881 Census Penkridge had returned to a more natural number of nine public houses. Henry Anderson ran the Horse and Jockey in Market Street with his brother Joseph and nephew Henry Fiddler. The traditional link with skilled trade remained as he described himself as a sawyer and painter as well as a publican. Nearby in Market Street was the Blacksmith's Arms where the landlady, Hannah Poole, was helped by her children Isabelle and Charles Tunnicliffe. In Market Place Charles Russell ran the Star Inn and employed two servants, Sarah White and Emma Jones. The Star was put up for sale in 1883 and described as,

"The free and well frequented FREEHOLD BEERHOUSE known as the Star Inn, situate in the Market Place, opposite the National Schools, and now in the occupation of Mr. C.P. Russell. The premises comprise taproom, smokeroom, parlour, three bedrooms, pantry, with the malt room over, large brewhouse, good cellaring, with stabling, cartshed, piggeries, coal house, hard water well and pump, and large garden, which runs down to the Pinfold, and is immediately opposite to the Police Court, in the Bellbrook road from which there is an entrance as also a cartway from the road leading out of Bellbrook road into the Market Place aforesaid."

Mary Hill, a 73 year old widow, was landlady of the Railway Tavern and William Griffiths ran The Boat with one servant. Stone Cross had three public houses. At the Crown Inn William Webb continued the ancient tradition of combining the trades of publican and butcher. Richard Wright at the White Hart was a commercial traveller as well as publican and employed one servant, Maria Whilton. Timothy Riley ran the George and Fox. Thomas Robson maintained the pre-eminence of the Littleton Arms by also being a farmer. The inn housed his wife, mother and father, three sons and a housemaid, cook and boot boy.

Concern over the poverty and demoralisation caused by drinking alcohol was very strong at the end of the nineteenth century. In 1874 the government was considering extending opening hours for public houses. They felt that restrictions imposed in 1872 were deterring respectable people from entering the trade and proposed that pubs in towns with over 2,500 inhabitants should be allowed to open between the hours of 7 am and 11 pm. This horrified many in Penkridge and 156 villagers led by Mr. F. Monckton sent a petition of protest to the House of Commons. They were worried not only by the prospect of all day drinking but also increased gambling. Many of the pubs in Penkridge were allowing gambling in the form of skittle bowling. A plain clothes police raid in 1874 discovered customers illegally playing for pints of beer in the bowling alleys of the Blacksmiths' Arms, the White Hart and the George and Fox.

In February 1894 the "respectable" people of Penkridge, alarmed at the effect of nine pubs in such a small village, crowded into a Church of England Temperance meeting held at the school. They were told by Lord Hatherton that much of the crime and misery in the country was the result of the £17 per year which each family, on average, spent on drink. Before the signing of pledges Lord Hatherton bemoaned "the baneful influence of that deadly upas tree, the shadow of which was blighting the fair name of dear old England."

In Penkridge great efforts were made to keep the working class out of the pubs. In 1877 a Reading Room was opened in the Market Square. After a year it was reported that,

"There can be no doubt that the institution is proving a highly valuable counter-attraction to the allurements of the public house, by presenting to those who have not comfortable rooms of their own the means of enjoyable and intelligent social recreation."

A New Reading Room was opened in 1885 to provide a counter attraction to drinking. The first event to be laid on was a lecture on Australia and there followed a succession of concerts, lectures and tea parties. The institution does not appear to have been an immediate success since, in 1887, Mr. J.C. Tildesley expressed the hope that "its advantages would be yet more widely appreciated by the working men and youths of the parish, for whose benefit it was mainly designed." When the Vicar was forced by the magistrates to buy a 30 shillings entertainment licence for the school in 1897 he protested that "the object of providing public entertainments was to keep people out of public houses and so endeavour to make

During the celebrations to mark the 50th anniversary of Queen Victoria's accession to the throne the vicar entertained seventy members of the Church of England Temperance Society in the Reading Room whilst 350 other adults feasted in the Littleton Arms and the George and Fox. Ten years later on the Queen's Diamond Jubliee it was reported in the parish magazine that,

"In order to counteract any temptation to insobriety through the extension of time allowed to the public houses the band marched to the vicarage where they played until closing time."

By 1914 it is clear that, on the evidence of cases at the local police court, drunkenness and its consequences were the main pre-occupation of the Penkridge constabulary. In January 1914, for example, Edward Turner was charged with being drunk in charge of a horse and trap. Police Sergeant Woolley found him fast asleep on the Wolverhampton Road at 9.15 pm. He was fined 2/6d and costs. The Railway Tavern came in for particular attention from the police, associated as it was with the market at the Railway Smithfield. John Bayley Timmis, the licencee of the Tavern was charged with permitting drunkenness on his premises. PC Wallace stated that he was on duty at the Smithfield Market and visited the Railway Inn where he found a man Joseph E------, who, he noticed, looked "dozy". The constable said to the landlord, "E----- looks as though he's had enough." Timmis replied,

"He is alright, Mr. Wallace, he has had nothing to drink for the last half hour, only ginger beer," but wisely told his customer, "Come on Joe, you'd better be getting off home." Joe left the pub, staggered down the steps and went off in the direction of his home. PC Wallace followed him down the road for about a hundred yards and saw him fall into the grass by the side of the road. The policeman got him to his feet and saw him home. When Wallace returned to the pub and said what had happened Mrs. Timmis, the landlord's wife remarked, "Well, I have never known him to fall down before. He called for a gin and ginger beer. I pretended at putting the gin in but did not put any in the glass."

The locals of the Railway Tavern supported the landlord against the police charge. Charles Edwards and Harold Plant both maintained that Joe was sober inside the pub and the defending barrister said he could call many such witnesses. Only PC Wallace could testify to the drunkenness outside the pub. The magistrates on the bench were split and the charge, with some reluctance, was dismissed. Amazingly, the next case up before the bench was that of Joe. He was charged with being drunk on the premises of the Railway Tavern and pleaded guilty.

Clearly Mr. Timmis would have some explaining to do when his licence came up for renewal a few weeks later. The hearing took three hours and renewal was objected to by the police. Police Sergeant Woolley recounted the story of Joseph to which Timmis replied,

"I never served him with drink and I think it a harsh trick. If other folks let him have a drink I can't help it. I do my best."

A list of alleged offences was recounted, going back to 1912. Sergeant Woolley said that on each of these occasions he had cautioned both the landlord and his wife to be more careful in the management of the house. He said that it was common knowledge in the village that when people had had sufficient to drink and the landlord had "stopped the tap" his wife immediately supplied them. She had been warned that she risked getting her husband into trouble.

Joe then told his side of the story. He had sold some cattle at the Smithfield and had visited the inn several times during the day, drinking two glasses of hot rum and five or six glasses of beer at least. The policeman had told him that he had had enough to drink. Nevertheless he had ordered another glass but did not think he had it (laughter in court). Joe said that he had known the landlord refuse to serve people who came in and afterwards his wife would serve them.

Charles Edward, a wheelwright, recalled a disturbance outside of the Railway Tavern the previous summer. The landlord was having a row with his wife for filling glasses when he had told her not to do so. Sarah Wall said she had been to the Tavern several times for her son. On one occasion she saw that he had had enough to drink.

Mr. Timmis' barrister complained to the bench that it was not playing the game to bring up against Timmis a charge which the magistrates had seen fit to dismiss. His client was 60 years of age and had held a licence for 14 years and this was the first charge brought against him. There was not a shred of evidence that the house had been ill conducted. Mrs. Elizabeth Harvey, Edward Lyons and Joseph Holt for the defence testified that Joe was not drunk whilst they were in the house. The licence was renewed but Mrs. Timmis got a severe warning from Lord Hatherton.

Notwithstanding the evidence produced in the police courts, there can be little doubt that the inns of Penkridge played a prominent and positive role in village life. In 1914 whilst the Railway was having its problems The Boat was running a series of smoking concerts with Birmingham humourists and a Chinese conjuror, some of them in aid of Penkridge United FC. The Boat had been running a Sick and Dividend Club for three years. The George and Fox was hosting the annual dinner of the Penkridge Fire Brigade. The Littleton Arms entertained the Penkridge Branch of the Midland Farmers Association and the first annual meeting of the Penkridge Bowling Club. The landlord, Thomas Robson, laid a new green which, Lord Hatherton hoped,

"would be the means of still further promoting a feeling of good fellowship in the parish." During Queen Victoria's Diamond Jubilee the inns of Penkridge had been central to the celebrations. Mrs. Robson at the Littleton, Mrs. Richards at the George and Fox. Mr. Bird of the White Hart and Mrs. Bradford of the Star combined to feed 830 of the villagers.

Pubs in Penkridge came to be held in high regard. The Horse and Jockey was known as the "Irish House" because during most of the year, but especially at harvest time, it was used by a large number of Irish farm workers. In 1931 the police objected to the renewal of its licence because they felt that the landlady, Mrs. Billington, was not strong enough to handle the situation. The people of Penkridge rallied round the Horse and Jockey. They held Mrs. Billington, and indeed the Irish, in higher esteem than did the police. A petition in favour of Mrs. Billington was signed by 123 villagers, including the Vicar. Mrs. Billington said large numbers of Irishmen did indeed frequent her pub but they conducted themselves better than some of the villagers and had never made a disturbance.

A Penkridge pub, in the right hands, was a force for good in the village's life. This was particularly true of The Boat when run by Joseph Robert Burd. He was held in high regard and the village was profoundly shocked when his body was found in the canal by the pub in 1923. Aged 49, he had been licensee for a long time. He had served in the army in France during the war, been a member of the Rural District Council and the Board of Guardians and had been Chairman of the Parish Council. When it had seemed in doubt whether Penkridge really wanted a war memorial he had proved people did by collecting £100 in one day. He was a manager of the school and personally distributed sweets and oranges to the children when they broke up for the Christmas holidays. He was a supporter of the Discharged Soldiers and Sailors Association and Chairman of Penkridge United FC. When his funeral procession, with over sixty mourners, left the Boat the children from Penkridge School lined both sides of the road. Penkridge seems to have been well served by its public houses and publicans. The people of Penkridge truly could say, with Dr. Johnson, that

"There is nothing which has yet been contrived by man by which so much happiness is produced as by a good tavern or inn".

Penkridge Landlords

An incomplete list compiled mainly from trade directories and newspaper advertisements. It is not always clear whether the name is of the owner of the lease or of the tenant actually running the inn.

THE WHITE HART
Henry Vernon	1754
Joseph Molineux	1792
Ann Molineux	1793
Orlando Adcock	1805 - 1831
(married Ann Molineux, widow, in 1798)	
Ann Adcock	1834
John Seaville	1841
(tenant from year to year)	
Thomas Chidlow	1851 - 1872
Samuel Batte	1884
David Dagley	1885
Charles Green	1892
Joseph Bird	1900 - 1912
E.H. Brereton	1915
W. Haden	1920
H.C. Dentith	1922
Mrs. Hutchinson	1926
Harry Onions	1932
George Smith	1936 - 1940

HORSE AND JOCKEY
J. Bate	1754
William Cope	1793
Elizabeth Worsey	1806 - 1818
Edward Masefield	1834
Mr. Southern	1840
Henry Anderson	1851 - 1884
Joseph Anderson	1891
(brother of Henry)	
Henry Fidler	1892
(nephew of Henry Anderson)	
Michael Egan	1912
H. Clarke	1922 - 1926
Rebecca Billington	1930
Reginald Turberville	1932
James Caulkin	1936
Arthur Westwood	1940

LITTLETON ARMS
Nancy Wright	1793
Thomas Webb	1813
William Cotton	1818 - 1837
John Spilsbury	1837
Henry Robson	1851 - 1872
Catherine Robson	1892
Thomas Robson	1912 - 1932

THE BOAT INN
Mary Lees	1818
Joseph Dugmore	1834
Thomas Smith	1841
Eli Higgins	1851

GEORGE AND FOX
James Scholey	1793 - 1805
Joseph Smith	1805
(son-in-law of James Scholey)	
William Kittridge	1818
William Worsey	1834
William North	1840
Joseph Smith	1851
William Dyke	1870
Timothy Riley	1881
William Richards	1892
Charles Cresswell	1900
Thomas Cresswell	1912
Lillian Cresswell	1932

THE BOAT INN *Contd.*

Joseph Wood	1870
William Morris	1872
William Griffiths	1881
William Turner	1892
Edith Burd	1912
Joseph Burd	1920
Edith Page	1932

BLACKSMITH'S ARMS

Thomas Anslow	1784
William Anslow	1818
Ann Ward	1831
James Burns	1834
George Cliffe	1841
William Tunnicliffe	1851
(two daughters, Hannah and Isabella)	
George Poole	1872
Hannah Poole	1892
Isabel Tunnicliffe	1912
(daughter of Hannah Poole)	
J. Cutler	1926
Walter Adams	1932

THE CROWN

John Tomlinson	1754
Thomas Hammersley	1834
Leonard Heywood	1841
Thomas Blakeman	1851
Charles Morris	1932

THE STAR

John Doughty	1841
John Seaville	1851
(married John Doughty's widow)	
Charles Russell	1881
Thomas Evans	1891
Martha Horton	1893
John Bradford	1900

RAILWAY TAVERN

John Hill	1851
Mary Hill	1870 - 1884
Thomas Youard	1892
Charles Edwards	1900
John Timmis	1912 - 1914
Doreen Heath	1932
Ernest Davies	1936

Chapter 5

Custom of the Manor
Penkridge in the Eighteenth Century

What is it that gives a village a sense of community and its special atmosphere for the inhabitants? Interviewed in 1961 Miss Connie Hill, "Old Conn", offered a few suggestions. In a working village the interaction of working people and the tradition of family employment counted for a lot. "Old Conn" could tell the reporter that,

> "Sure it was my father's milk round to begin with, but when he died my mother kept it on. I must walk 56 or 60 miles a week. I began the milk round when I was 9 and I've been at it ever since. Used to deliver to the military in the old days of Penkridge Bank.
> I've delivered milk every Christmas Day. Never missed one."

Connie Hill's main point concerned a far less obvious factor. She recognized a decline in community spirit and put it down to a change in the nature of the ownership of property. She said,

> "Things have altered in Penkridge. At one time we were tenants, all on one level. Now every one seems as if they must own their own house. The village atmosphere has almost gone. It's more like a town now. Everyone's an owner occupier."

If such factors were noticeable and important in the years before 1961 how much more profound an effect they must have had in the eighteenth century when the bonds of tenancy were much stronger and all embracing.

In the eighteenth century Penkridge was, of course, a single parish and the village was dominated by the Church, both physically and spiritually. It was a unifying institution for the township and the outlying areas. Penkridge consisted of two manors. In the early Middle Ages this had caused some friction between the two lords of the manor but by the eighteenth century when the lordships and the ownership of the majority of the land tended to fall into the same hands the "custom of the manor" became another unifying force for the village.

Richard Clark, Nathanial Mott, John Cope, John Bate, Joseph Cooper and Abraham Duncalf knew each other. In the mid-eighteenth century they were near neighbours, owning or occupying houses in Market Place and Market Street. One day in 1758 they made their way to the manor court for one of the most important ceremonies of the year. Coming from the same place they seem to have arrived at the same time for they signed their names more or less together on the jury roll of the manorial court of survey. With thirty two other inhabitants of Penkridge they had gathered to take part as a "homage" or jury in the ancient ceremony of perambulating the bounds of the manor. In the days before there were many maps or an efficient form of land registration, proof of the ownership of land depended to a large extent on local knowledge passed down orally through the generations. As they walked around the manor they followed well known paths to well known landmarks just as their ancestors had done. If the perambulation did not take place the knowledge could have been lost forever. In 1758 four members of the jury, Matthew Webb, Richard Clark, Joseph Cooper and Lewis Simpson could not write well enough to sign their own names. In earlier years the proportion of illiterates must have been much higher so the physical perambulation was just as important as written records.

The first large scale map of Penkridge, a Littleton Estate map, was drawn in 1754 so perambulations came to have decreasing significance. When the Rural District Council suggested a revival of the practice in 1899 Penkridge Historian J.C. Tildesley squashed the idea, remarking that, "however interesting might be the revival of an ancient and picturesque observance, in these days when Ordnance Survey maps abounded, no practical results could follow." There was still a lot of life left in the custom of the manor in the eighteenth century, however. The procedure of the manorial court changed very little over hundreds of years. It followed "the custom of the manor". In 1733 the jury, "as well for our sovereign Lord the King as for the Lord of the Manor" was sworn in, in the traditional way with one person going first, then in groups of three.

"Nathanial Browne, sworn first

Edward Birch	John Aspley	John Morton	sworn
Samuel Wall	Edward Birch	William Adams	sworn
Henry Duncalfe	John Cresswell	Dennis Fieldhouse	sworn
Edward Oakley	Charles Phillips	John Padmore	sworn"

The main business of the manorial court was the ownership of land and property. Land and buildings were bought and sold, written records and deeds were exchanged. Most of the property thus exchanged, though, was held on leases from the Lord of the Manor. These leases or copyhold tenancies were established in the Middle Ages and were as good as freeholds but the ancient custom of the manor had to be followed. The court had to be informed of the sale, the new owner had to be "admitted" to the tenancy and homage had to be paid to the Lord of the Manor. In this way the ownership of land was established in open court before one's friends and neighbours and recorded on the manorial court roll in case of later disputes.

In 1733 Francis Boulton sold a piece of land to John Asprey. In the court the deal was registered following the medieval forms used in the days of the feudal system.

"To this court in his proper person came Francis Boulton one of the Customary tenants of this manor and in open court surrendered into the hands of the Lords of the Manor one acre of land in a place called Haymeadow with the appurtenances to the use and behoof of John Asprey and his assignees for and during the term of his natural life and from and after his decease then to and for the life and behoof of Elizabeth his wife for and during the term of her natural life and from and after the decease of the survivor of them then to and for the use and behoof of the heirs of the body of the said John Asprey upon the body of the said Elizabeth lawfully begotten or to be begotten and for want of such issue then to and for the use and behoof of the right heirs of the said John forever and so to remain in the hands of the Lords. Whereupon to this court in his proper person came the aforesaid John Asprey and prayed to be admitted tenant to the premises aforesaid. To whom the said Lords by their deputy steward aforesaid granted and delivered seisin by the rod TO HAVE AND TO HOLD all and singular the premises aforesaid with the appurtenances to the aforesaid John Asprey and his assignees for and during the term of his natural life at the will of the Lords according to the custom of the manor aforesaid therefore due and of right accustomed and the aforesaid John hath given to the Lord for his fine three halfpence did his fealty and was admitted tenant."

The manorial court, called the Court Leet and also the Court Baron was held before the Steward of the Lord of the Manor and retained many important powers in the eighteenth century. In 1735 the Lord of the Manor was the infant Lord Brook and his steward was William Dixon. Once the jury was sworn in much important business was transacted. In 1735 the manor court was still responsible for law and order in the village. It did not act as a court of law, judging and sentencing those breaking the law of the country but it was responsible for appointing the constable for the manor. Each year the court appointed one constable and two headboroughs to assist him. The offices were unpaid and only for a year at a time. Between 1751 and 1755 the following law officers were appointed,

1751 - John Collins, gent. Constable
1752 - Wm. Potts, Constable, Thomas Spooner, Walter Ellis, Headboroughs
1753 - Thomas Spooner, Constable, Wm. Pitts, Joseph Rudge, Headboroughs
1754 - Walter Ellis, Constable, John Brown, Matthew Webb, Headboroughs

1755 - John Brown, Constable, Joseph Bannister, Thomas Smith, Headboroughs

This seems to show that very few gentlemen were willing to undertake the irksome task of being constable. Constables were not trained professionals but appeared in Penkridge, at least, to serve a year's apprenticeship as a headborough.

The manorial court was a very convenient place for proving legal documents. People brought wills into court to make sure that they were accepted as the true heirs to property. In property deals, contrary to our usual impression of eighteenth century life, the court seems to have taken some care to see that the property rights of wives were protected. Whenever a married couple were involved in the sale of land the ritual of surrendering it first to the Lord of the Manor allowed the custom of the manor to exert its influence. In 1735 the court roll recorded that,

"To this court came John Cotton and his wife Ann in their proper persons (the said Ann being first solely and secretly examined by Stafford James, Deputy Steward of the said manor in the absence of her husband and confessing that she joined in the passing of this surrender freely and voluntarily without the compulsion of her husband)."

It was realised that the property rights of married women were fragile and cautious husbands made sure that their widows did not have to rely on the protection of the custom of the manor, in the event of their re-marriage, by carefully wording their wills. In 1793 John Hinckley of Penkridge protected his wife, Elizabeth, by stipulating,

"I hereby will and direct that all the property, benefit, interest, estate, effects and premises whatsoever which my said wife shall be entitled to, shall be had, held and enjoyed by her independent of any after taken husband for her own sole and separate use and benefit and at her own sole disposal and free from the control, debts and engagements or intermeddling of any future husband so that she may have, dispose of or enjoy the same as if she was sole and unmarried."

In the absence of maps and the detailed addresses of modern times, the deeds to land in the eighteenth century were very vague. The documents could have been useless without the local knowledge of the manorial court jury. In 1736,

"John Woolsey surrendered a parcel of land containing in length from a street called Mill St. to a Pear Tree growing upon the land of said John Woolsey, nineteen yards and in breadth five yards."

If ownership of that land was to be disputed in future years, after the pear tree had been grubbed up, the collective knowledge of the court would have had to be called upon.

Apart from property matters and the appointment of constables the most important task of the court leet in the eighteenth century was the regulation of agriculture in the village. In the Middle Ages, when much of the village was farmed under the open field system and land was held in small scattered strips in large hedgeless fields, co-operation and co-ordination at the court leet was essential. By the eighteenth century, when most of the land had been enclosed, co-ordination was far less important but the question of the use of common land remained. Penkridge retained two large blocks of common land on the Marsh and at Penkridge Heath. Used mainly for grazing, the common could be a source of irritation and conflict as villagers tried to abuse the custom of the manor by putting more animals on it than they were entitled to or even building homes upon it. The court rolls in the eighteenth century record the same misdemeanours and the same names year after year.

1709 - Fine William Perry for oppressing the common with sheep. Ambrose Phillips for a nuisance laying his muck in the street. Also presented William Aspinall for laying dung in the street.

1711 - William Wright fined 4d for a cottage on the Lord's waste.
Ambrose Phillips for laying his muck in the street to the great nuisance of his neighbours.
William Perry for digging and getting marl in Penkridge .... to the foot road there and in making a marl pit which is very dangerous to passengers.
William Perry for oppressing the common. Fines of 2d on cottages on lord's waste.

1716 - William Perry for grazing the common with horses and cows and sheep having no right to pasture them there.

Fining villagers for building and living in cottages on the common was a round about way of allowing the poorer villagers to have a place to live whilst retaining the legal rights of the land owners to the common. When enclosure of the remaining common land happened in the early nineteenth century the cottages and crofts could be easily cleared.

The custom of allowing villagers to use the common land for arable farming or building is most clearly seen in the records of the Deanery Manor Court which was called "The View of Frankpledge and Court Baron". In 1749 the jury was Edward Read, gent., John Turner, John Smart, Richard Asprey, John James, Henry Duncalfe, John Heath, Orlando Arkoll, Edward Day, Edward Crowder, Francis Chambley, Richard Clarke and James Southall. Mr. Southall was made constable for the Deanery Manor and John Heath headborough. Seventeen villagers were brought before them for abusing the common land. Such a large number shows that the action was in fact tolerated and that the fines were really a form of rent. It is clear that the old concept of the common land was out of date and that there was great economic pressure to convert it into arable land. By 1749 a formula had been arrived at to allow this. The court roll records that,

"We present all persons that live in the township of Penkridge for breaking up the Lord's waste upon Penkridge Heath at or upon Midsummer Day and we amerce in two pence each."

Outsiders were charged 2/- for the same privilege. Richard Clarke was presented for encroachments and "for not scouring his ditch and water course" and he was a member of the jury.

A near neighbour of Richard Clarke in 1754 was Samuel Hinckley. He lived in a good house in Market Place and was clearly one of the wealthier villagers. In such a small village the rich and the poor clearly lived very close to each other. We can imagine that a poor farm labourer owned next to nothing. What did a reasonably well off villager living in Market Place in 1754 have to his name? In 1765 Samuel Hinckley died and an inventory was made of his goods and chattels. It consisted of,

1 brass furnace	£1	0s	0d
2 cast metal brass pots		14s	
1 brass pott kettle		4s	
1 maslin brass kettle		1s	
2 barrels		4s	
1 oval table		6s	
1 square table		2s	
2 joint stools			8d
2 baskets			6d
1 ash chair			6d
2 bedsteads and hangings		15s	
2 feather beds	£3	3s	
3 bolsters, 1 pillow	£1	6s	
6 boxes		6s	
Several pieces of linen cloth	£3		
5 pewter dishes and 7 pewter plates		17s	
1 pewter chamber pott		1s	
1 pewter tankard			8d
1 pair of *** inglos			6d
Cash	£135		
Total	£147	1s	10d

In eighteenth century Penkridge it seems that the property of even quite a well off man was fairly basic. A high proportion of his wealth consisted of cash, only £12 being in the form of property. True wealth came with the ownership of land and buildings. Since so many villagers, farmers and tradesmen alike, were tenants of the Littleton family and did not own land, a strong community spirit could have existed.

Old traditions and country sports certainly helped to keep the community together. The Lord of the Manor was something more than just a landlord. Being a tenant of Sir Edward Littleton in 1775 often meant that you were involved with him and his estate in more positive ways. Sir Edward's foxhunting diary makes clear that his tenants looked after some of his hounds when they were not hunting. This was a relic of the feudal services of medieval times. It had survived whilst most of the rents had long been paid in the form of money. Sir Edward records that Charlotte was kennelled with J. Fieldhouse, Buxom at the Crown, Bellman with Ironmonger of Pileton, Stroller with Thomas Fellows, and Rookwood with Henry Duncalfe. In 1777 the Penkridge people who took in the hounds were recorded as Fieldhouse, Keeling, Chambley, Worsey, Haddersiche, Baker, Tomlinson, Hickin, Cotton and Hodson. At this time Sir Edward had a pack of 50 hounds and he reported the fate of some of them that year.

"25 couple, *NB* those dashed with red ink made off in the end of the season (viz) Bellman died, Dido, Vernon and Rookwood hanged, Pleasant and Bonylass to Mr. Barret; Charmer and Painter to Baron Bode."

Sir Edward Littleton was not the only owner of land in Penkridge, of course. At the end of the eighteenth century there was a land property qualification of £40 to serve on the jury at the county court. In 1784 eleven villagers, William Hodson, Thomas Pool, Thomas Watson, William Riley, Joseph Rudge, Robert Adams, Simon Glover, John Moore, Dunstone Clark, William Brookes and Joseph Devey passed this test. The picture of a quaint, rural village encumbered with medieval institutions is also far too simple. In the eighteenth century Penkridge could be viewed as a bustling and dynamic place. The old Georgian houses of the conservation area were once brand new. In 1799 the Advertiser described,

"A large commodious modern built house with a good garden, Bakehouse, Malthouse, and other outbuildings, situate in Penkridge; the building is entirely new, the malthouse large, with 3 floors, and patent kiln. Further particulars may be had of Mr. Duncalf, of the above place."

The Universal British Directory of Trade, Commerce and Manufacture, published in 1793 recorded that "No material trade is carried on in this place", but its list of the principal inhabitants of the village seems to indicate quite a varied and thriving trade, servicing mainly, but by no means exclusively, an agricultural economy.

GENTLEMEN

Hodgson John, Gent.

CLERGY

Slaney Rev. Richard   Stafford James, M.A. Vicar and Official

PHYSIC

Lewis Augustus Francis, Surgeon

Perren William, Surgeon

TRADERS, &c.

Akers Isaac, Taylor
Barnfield Joseph, Butcher
Botton George, Sadler
Chamley Joseph, Carrier
Cheadle Henry, Smith
Cope William, Victualler, (Horse and Jockey)
Cotton Mrs., Farmer
Devie Joseph, Tanner
Duncalfe Abraham, Grocer and Mercer
Duncalf Abraham, Hatter
Eaton Thomas, Gardener
Finey John, Carpenter and Joiner
Groves Joseph, Baker
Hanslowe Nancy, Victualler
Harrison Philip, Cooper
Hordern Sarah, Draper
Jackson Mary, Grocer
Keller Richard, Ropemaker
Kirk William, Peruke -maker

Lewis John, Carpenter
Maiden Joseph, Glover
May Robert, Taylor
Molineux Ann, White Hart Inn
Onslow William, Tinman and Brazier

Onslow George, Butcher
Preston William, Turner
Scholey James, Victualler (Fox)
Sothern John, Bricklayer
Tomlinson Joseph, Baker
Turner James, Farmer
Walker George, Maltster
White Mrs., Huckster
Webb Thomas, Tanner
Wise William, Smith
Withams Owen, Taylor
Worsey John, Victualler
Wright Nancy, Littleton's Arms Inn

Chapter 6

Wakes, Fairs, Festivals and Fetes

It was the habit in the Middle Ages to mark the passage of time by reference to the feasts and holy days of the Church. As a result the records of the law courts make strange reading, linking the descriptions of many horrible crimes with the Feast of St. Clement, the Feast of St. John the Baptist and other religious occasions. In Penkridge much of the serious crime and turbulence happened on church holidays and the greatest trouble occurred on the village's greatest feast day, that of St. Michael, to whom the Church was dedicated. The Penkridge Wakes, the holiday on September 29th linked to St. Michael's was, in the Middle Ages, a market day and a time of crowded streets and much drinking. The Royal Charter for a yearly fair dated from 1312 and was granted in perpetuity for the "vigil and feast of St. Michael and the three following days". During the first fair held under the Royal Charter violence broke out.

> "John de Kneclet feloniously killed Thomas de Blythefeld at Penkridge on Thursday, the Feast of St. Michael and John the Taillour of Penkridge aided and abetted the said John in committing the said felony."

This was merely the first of many examples of violence at the Penkridge Wakes and Fair. In 1324 the jury of the Cuttlestone Hundred complained that,

> "William de Stretton and Thomas his brother, the chaplain, are common malefactors, going about in the society of other malefactors, armed to the fairs and markets, to the great terror of the people, and that they had beaten John Balle and Ralph de Grendon at Penkridge on the Feast of St. Michael."

Not surprisingly the idea of the Wakes eventually lost its religious significance much as did the idea of the "holy day". In 1617 James I allowed the Fair to be extended to a period of eight days, six before the Feast and the day after. The Penkridge Wakes became associated in villagers' minds with the excitement of markets and fairs and in time moved from Michaelmas to the days of the two great horse fairs on April 30th and October 10th. Without a shadow of doubt the great horse fair of October 10th and the following days became the most important event in the Penkridge calendar.

In about 1724, Daniel Defoe, the author of Robinson Crusoe, passed through the village. His description of Penkridge during the great horse fair is well known but bears repetition.

"We were much surprised in a most agreeable manner passing through a small but ancient town called Penkrige (vulgarly Pankrage) where happened to be a fair. We expected nothing extraordinary; but was I say surprised to see the prodigious number of horses brought hither, and those not ordinary and common draught-horses, and such kinds as we generally see at county fairs remote from London. But here were really incredible numbers of the finest and most beautiful horses that can any where be seen; being brought hither from Yorkshire, the bishopric of Durham, and all the horse-breeding countries. We were told that there were not less than a hundred jockeys and horse-copers as they call them here, from London, to buy horses for sale. Also an incredible number of gentlemen attended with their grooms to buy gallopers or race-horses, for their Newmarket sport. In a word I believe I may mark it the greatest horsefair in the world, for horses of value, and especially those we call saddle horses.

We stayed 3 days here to satisfy our curiosity, and indeed the sight was very agreeable, to see what vast stables of horses there were, which were never brought out or shown in the fair. How dextrous the northern grooms and breeders are in looking after them and ordering them. These fellows take such indefatigable pains with them, that they bring them out like pictures of horses, not a hair amiss in them; they lie constantly in the stables with them, and feed them by weight and measure; keep them so clean and so fine that in short nothing can be more nice. Here were several horses sold for 150 guineas a horse; but they were such as were famous for the breed, and known by their race almost as well as the Arabians know the genealogy of their horses."

The huge number of visitors and horses must have swamped a village of about two thousand people and generated great excitement. As "jockey" was the usual term for a horseman or horse dealer it is probable that the "Horse and Jockey" Inn was named for this great event rather than the very small scale annual races on Preston Hill.

By the nineteenth century many people were beginning to regret the passing of the link between wakes and religious festivals. The celebrations staged to mark the defeat of Napoleon in 1814 led one Yoxall man to comment that,

"These rural scenes put some of the inhabitants in mind of what tradition says the wakes used to be in former times; a festival of great joy kept up in commemoration of the dedication of the Church and which if properly conducted might still be very useful in exciting gratitude in the people, for the benefit of good instruction received through the medium of her clergy; it grieves me sir, to see not only this but other great festivals of the church, such as Christmas, Easter and Whitsuntide so much neglected and the festive part gradually declining: because they are abused is but weak reason why they should be abolished."

It seems that the religious wakes declined because of the uproar associated with them. It is easy to understand the attitude of religious people to wakes in the early nineteenth century. Descriptions of the Penkridge Wakes in 1823 make it seem a particularly unprepossessing event. The Advertiser reported that,

"This ancient festival was this year more than usually brilliant; in addition to the customary amusements of bull baiting, cock fighting and other gentlemanly sports, there was horse and ass racing. The first contest was between Mr. Cotton's Black and all Black, Mr. Boothby's Challenger, and Mr. Bowker's Bother'em which was won in high style by the former. On Tuesday a match between Mr. Boothby's Arabian and Mr. Tatlor's Grey Long Ears, was won by Mr. Boothby, but a dispute arising the stakes were withdrawn. A match between Mr. Harper's Bay and a mare from Stourbridge was severely contested, the bay had the advantage but this was in a great degree compensated by the agility of the rider who contrived to have five falls during his ride round the course."

As the country moved into the Victorian era the forces of respectability began to catch up with the Penkridge Wakes. Positive efforts were made to reduce the hold the Wakes had on the village. In the early 1850s more controlled and edifying entertainments were put on for the people in the form of Rural Fetes held at Teddesley Park. These were well organised and ambitious events. In 1853 special trains from Stafford and Birmingham brought hundreds of visitors to the fete. Over three thousand people crowded the streets of Penkridge on their way to the park. At the fete there were many marquees, a circus, a fun fair, three bands and a cricket match. The fete was regarded as an experiment. Could large crowds of working class people be trusted in the gracious surroundings of Teddesley Hall? Would they appreciate the efforts that had been made to entertain them? The organisers were gratified when, at the end of the day, they discovered that there had been "not a single breach of decorum" and that not a single flower had been damaged. The county police had been present but did not have to do anything.

The 1853 fete was such a success that it was prolonged so that local school children could attend it, without paying the shilling entrance fee. On the following day 317 children from Penkridge, 95 from Cannock, 95 from Acton and Bednall and 25 from Lord Hatherton's Farm School were brought by waggon to the park. "They entered the park about 3 o'clock, cheering at the top of their voices. Their appearance was that of health and happiness. Accompanied by their teachers they promenaded the pleasure grounds and gardens." The children were given tea in a marquee, being waited upon by Lady Hatherton and other members of her family. Footballs, battledores and skipping ropes were provided for sport. An inspector of schools who was present said he had "never witnessed a more agreeable or interesting sight."

After initial success the Penkridge Rural Fete went from strength to strength. By 1857 the event was so large that the Mayor of Stafford organised half day closing in the town so that workers could attend the fete. The train from Stafford carried 1,000 people to Penkridge and 3,000 people attended altogether. Lord Hatherton was proud to have his most distinguished guests witness the holiday. In 1857 the great French historian and statesman Alexis de Tocqueville strolled round the park, rubbing shoulders with Penkridge people on the day of the fete.

By 1858 the Rural Fete was so well established that not even heavy rain could harm the occasion. On the day of the fete "a vast crowd" gathered on Stafford station for the 9.30 train to Penkridge. One thousand passengers were seated but many had to be left behind. When the fete ended "the press of people at the Penkridge station was so great that very serious inconvenience was experienced, and it was necessary to engage three special trains to convey them to their destinations". The main attraction in 1858 was the presence of several large hot air balloons. Although the fun fair was an important ingredient the fetes had a serious social purpose, described by the Advertiser as "removing the barriers which once too much separated the aristocracy of England from the people". Lord Hatherton never lost sight of the educational and improving purpose of the fete, compared to the often dissolute wakes. The fete was part of his campaign for "the elevation of the working classes, in their respective spheres". It was hoped that the festivities would give "a healthier tone to the tastes and pursuits of the community".

In this improving atmosphere disgust with the activities of the wakes grew. Other traditionally robust and uproarious celebrations were also being discouraged. In 1881 the Bishop of Shrewsbury came to Penkridge and congratulated the parish on the "sober and religious form" of its harvest festival which contrasted with the carnival nature of former festivals which were "often disgraced by an excess of conviviality". In 1887 a tea party and concert were staged on Wakes Monday as a counter attraction to the cruder amusements of the day. One of the older inhabitants of the village observed that "some three score years ago the wakes of Penkridge would have been considered a failure unless a bull had been baited on the Horse Fair and a bear had been tormented on Dunston Heath."

By the second half of the nineteenth century the chief area of respectable concern about the wakes was excessive drinking. The recently formed police force were not willing to turn the blind eye to drunken and rowdy behaviour that had been traditional with the old manorial law officers. In 1851 the Vicar warned the people of Penkridge that the magistrates "understand it is the intention of the police authorities to make no distinction between wakes and any other time, but all parties will be summoned before the magistrates."

Some reports of the village on Wakes Monday create a dark picture of respectable and sober citizens being virtually under siege during the holiday. By 1881 this was persuading Anglicans and Methodists to forget their religious differences in the face of what they saw as a rising tide of ungodliness. On Wakes Monday in 1881 the vicar went to a meeting in the Wesleyan Chapel. This was a very unusual occurrence and he explained himself, saying that,

"I have no doubt that before noon tomorrow it will be generally known that I have been present at a meeting in the Wesleyan Chapel. Soon after I became your Vicar I received anonymous and other letters requesting me not to persecute poor Methodists. I am present, therefore, to convince you I am not a persecutor, but that I hold out the hand of fellowship to other sections of Religionists who hold the faith in the Truth. I am also present to make a protest against the drunkenness and wantonness incident to the Wakes which are now being celebrated in the town, the whole proceedings connected with which tend to the demoralization of the people."

By the end of the nineteenth century the main location of festivities was the Stone Pits field off the Wolverhampton Road. Fetes and sporting events were held there at the beginning of August. There is evidence that these could be unruly affairs. In 1896 George Johnson was running a coconut shy. When local stonemason, Albert Faulkener, arrived he aimed, deliberately, at George's head rather than at the nuts. In 1900 the fete was the scene of a dangerous argument between local postman Edward Brookes and hairdresser Walter Steele. Steele was sending up "fire balloons" using wadding saturated in methylated spirits. Brookes felt that Steele was deliberately sprinkling the meths in his eyes. They struggled over a piece of wadding, which ignited, and Walter Steele's hands and face went up in flames. The postman was committed for trial.

All the reports of the Victorian Penkridge Wakes describe a holiday that invariably was a Monday in the early part of October. Interestingly, the memories of the old inhabitants of Penkridge quoted in more recent times refer to the Wakes as having happened on April 30th, the date of the other great Penkridge fair. In 1961 Mrs. A.H. Rudge, born in 1881 and a member of the ancient Wall family of Penkridge recalled a cattle fair in the street by the church. "All down Church Lane", she remembered, "with horse driven merry go rounds. They used to call it Gorbymarket."

After the First World War the main parish fete was safely in the hands of the Vicar. They were splendidly ambitious affairs, resembling the great days at

Teddesley Park and held in the vicarage grounds. When three thousand people attended in 1923 it was regarded as a disappointing turn out. Two hundred tables were set up to provide teas. Eight hundred visitors came from Wolverhampton by train. There was a horse show, a horticultural show and dancing late into the night. These were very well regulated events, conducted under the stern eyes of the vicar and the schoolmaster. The money raised went to Penkridge Church and to poorer, surrounding parishes. In 1924 the local MP, Captain Ormsby Gore, recognised that they retained their earlier social significance. He said that "these shows brought people together and it helped them to realise that in life they got along much better by pulling together, than by pulling against each other."

Chapter 7

Peace and Plenty?
1800 - 1830

In the last week of December 1813 news reached Penkridge that the war with France that had lasted for over 20 years had come to an end. Mail coaches out of London had reached Birmingham covered with ribbons and laurels and bearing flags inscribed with the word "PEACE". Three coaches came to Penkridge from Birmingham every day, the "Bang-Up", the "Eclipse" and the "Regulator" so the good news travelled fast.

Unfortunately, as is the way with news, the tidings were rather inaccurate and the celebrations a trifle premature. Napoleon replied evasively to peace proposals after his defeat at the Battle of the Nations on October 19th and the war did not end until the allied invasion of France forced him to abdicate on April 14th 1814.

When the fact of peace was established, however, there was no doubt in peoples' minds that they were living at a momentous time. A combination of patriotism and civic pride ensured that the joyful event was celebrated across the country. It was expected that villages like Penkridge would make a great effort to mark the event and report the details of the celebrations to the newspapers.

The high point of Penkridge's celebrations came on Saturday July 16th 1814. A huge dinner was held in the field which joined the west side of the church yard where over 1,400 people enjoyed a meal of roast beef, plum pudding and ale. After the meal and singing of patriotic songs the large group lined up and marched through the streets led by a band and three flags, one displaying "GR", another the lillies of France and the inscription "Vivent les Bourbons" and the third "Peace and Plenty". The procession returned to the field where a dance was held until late into the night.

Tremendous efforts had been made by some of the ladies of Penkridge to decorate the field. The rows of tables were marked by arches formed by wreaths of evergreens and flowers from which hung ribbons and gilded ornaments. The entrances to the field were similarly festooned, with particular attention lavished on the entrances from the church. The posts of the gates and the trunks of the trees in the church yard were dressed with moss so as to resemble rocks covered with seaweed and flowers. An archway carried the words "Peace - Britons Rejoice".

The main streets of Penkridge boasted similar decorations. At the Littleton Arms there was a very large triumphal arch whilst the bridge over the canal by The Boat Inn had a large arch and an effigy of Napoleon, hanging from a tree, "dancing on nothing".

The local pride is easily discernable in the descriptions of these events as reported in the Staffordshire Advertiser. The organisers of the celebrations were expected to send in their own account for publication. Near the end of the article Penkridge's unnamed reporter glows with justified satisfaction. He writes,

"Upon the whole we do not recollect to have heard of or seen rejoicings at any place on this occasion having exceeded those of this small town, and very few have equalled them".

It would be a mistake to assume, however, that the great success of this one day meant that Penkridge, and villages like Penkridge were living out some carefree idyll. The columns of print devoted to these celebrations, the insistent tone of goodwill and happiness are fuelled by an underlying tension which, in fact, made them newsworthy.

The hidden concern, the spectre which, happily, did not arrive at the feast was revealed in the article on Penkridge which ended with the statement that,

"Every person, rich and poor seemed happy and the whole concluded without any accident or unpleasant occurrence happening to interrupt the harmony of the day."

Here we have a society that is unsure of itself, aware of the tensions between rich and poor and fearful of disorder just at the moment when its army and navy had given the country its greatest ever victory.

The sense of relief that the victory celebrations had passed off peacefully was probably heightened by the awareness that 1814 had been a very bad year for the poor of Penkridge. The winter had been unusually severe. In January prolonged frosts and temperatures of 22 degrees below freezing were experienced. The rivers Penk and Severn froze over and no mail came from London because of deep snow.

More significantly, on the very day that the poor were enjoying their unaccustomed roast beef and plum pudding came the official notification that the common lands of Penkridge were to be enclosed by Act of Parliament. The long process of surveying and mapping and establishing ownership of the land was to begin at the Littleton Arms at 11 am on the 28th July. The Commissioners appointed by the Act of Parliament were to begin walking the boundaries of the common fields, common meadows and waste, particularly Broad Moor Common, Bosco Moor, Marsh Common, Beacon Hill Common and Dunston Heath. Most of the arable land of Penkridge had been enclosed for a long time. The enclosing of the marsh, commons and waste represented a marginal increase in efficiency for larger tenant farmers and the Littleton estate. For the farm labourers and other poor of Penkridge, however, it meant the loss of their last few rights, the chance to graze a few animals, collect firewood or glean grain. By October 1815 land on Penkridge Heath that used to be common land had been divided into lots of up to 5 acres and was being fenced and auctioned off in order to pay the preliminary expenses of the enclosure process.

In the nineteenth century two strong themes developed in the Littleton stewardship of Penkridge: a genuine concern for the welfare of the people and the sponsorship of efficient and scientific farming methods. When it came to enclosing the remaining common and waste land these two ideals clashed. It had been part of the Littleton philosophy to maintain a prosperous peasantry and this required common and waste land. In 1817 William Pitt's History of Staffordshire warmly recommended Sir Edward Littleton's attitude, saying,

"The worthy gentleman, with great humanity turned his thoughts to the comforts of the labourer, by erecting upon his estate warm and comfortable tenements for their use. His idea was, that for the sake of economy three dwellings should be put together, with a room to serve them all for washing, baking etc. and an oven large enough to bake for all three at once, the occupiers heating the oven in rotation, and giving notice of it to their neighbours: if by the side of a common the better, as the furze will supply the oven with fuel and a few sheep or geese may be kept. Every labourer (he said) should have keep for one cow, with meadow ground for winter keep, and a garden of one third of an acre for vegetables, fruit trees and hemp; and where it can be done, it will be desirable to have them near a pool of water."

A village where all the common land had been enclosed could be a harsh place for the labouring poor. The farm labourer who previously had some rights and economic independence became totally dependent on wages. The poor of Penkridge lost their common rights on Penkridge Heath and the Marsh as well as smaller pockets of common land at Woodbank, Quarry Heath and Boscomoor. The ancient right to pasture animals, after mowing, on the Hay Meadow between the Penk and Pinfold Lane was also lost. Up to thirty small crofts, gardens, cottages and intakes were cleared from the Marsh. Symbolic of the loss of independence and freedom for most villagers was the disappearance of over 50 footpaths which were "stopped up" by the commissioners. In their place a few private carriage roads were built, cutting through the old common land, leading to the larger farmhouses.

Contemporary observers noticed the connection between the enclosure of common land and the demoralisation of the working class. The Annals of Agriculture protested,

"Go to an ale house of an old enclosed country, and there you will see the origin of poverty and poor rates. For whom are they to be sober? For whom are they to save? For the parish? If I am diligent, shall I have leave to build a cottage? If I am sober, shall I have land for a cow? If I am frugal shall I have half an acre of potatoes? You offer no motives; you have nothing but a parish officer and a workhouse! Bring me another pot."

The problem of a demoralised working class which lacked motivation and its connection with public disorder was recognised in Penkridge. When the Penkridge Savings Bank was founded in 1818 its prospectus contained the following improving words.

"A Few Words On the Use and Advantages of Banks for Savings

A bank for savings enables a poor Man to help himself honestly, and to save himself from the disgrace of being a burthen to the Poor's Rate or any public charity.
One shilling a week saved and put into this bank becomes £20 in 10 yrs.

(This is) the way to avoid, not only want or begging, but many sins which are followed by many sufferings; the Sin of drunkenness with the brutish blasphemy that attends it; the sin of wastefulness; the sin of misspending time; the sin of neglecting wife and family.

'Go to the ant, thou sluggard; consider her ways, and be wise; which having no guide, Overseer, or Ruler, provideth her meat in the summer, and gathereth her food in the Harvest. Proverbs of Solomon VI.6,7,8'."

The bank was clearly a charitable venture designed to improve the character of Penkridge people. It was a non-profit making organisation set up at a "Respectable Meeting" held at the Vestry. It had 43 directors, the leading members of Penkridge society from Sir Edward Littleton and the vicar down. The bank had no staff as the directors themselves took turns in accepting deposits. No one was allowed to deposit more than £100 a year. Although the scheme was an example of nineteenth century condescension it also introduced the more democratic idea of the queue to Penkridge with the prospectus explaining that "the business of each person to be transacted according to his or her priority of attendance."

The attitude of the middle and upper classes of society towards the poor, patronising yet fearful, was deeply ingrained and widespread. At the Staffordshire General Agricultural Society, amongst the prizes for the best pigs and cattle in 1814 came the following.

"To the day labourer in Husbandry, who has maintained himself and family, and brought up the greatest number of children (born in wedlock) without Parish Relief (except in illness) a reward of £5. *NB* The candidates will (in addition to the usual certificates from the persons they have served) be required to produce one from the clergyman or some respectable householder of the parish in which they reside, not only of good character but of the cleanly state and condition of the cottage and garden they occupy."

The enclosure of the commons and waste was a very contentious and time consuming process. The poor had no voice in these matters, however, and the bitter arguments were between Mr. Littleton and the enclosure commissioners. There should have been little trouble. Robert Harvey Wyatt knew Penkridge well, having compiled rate books for the parish and tithe lists for the Littleton family. Unfortunately Mr. Littleton, the nephew of the previous Sir Edward, found Wyatt a little more independent than circumstances would suggest when he would not allow a new road in Teddesley Park to be paid for out of the common fund for enclosure expenses. When the first allotments were sold to pay for preliminary expenses Mr. Littleton, who bought them, thought the prices were far too high. The whole process was slowed down by Littleton buying, selling and exchanging plots of land in order to reap the greatest benefits from enclosure. The first survey was found to be inaccurate and the land had to be remeasured. Many Penkridge landowners employed lawyers to represent them and as a result meetings with the commissioners at the Littleton Arms used to stretch into the early hours of the morning.

When Mr. Littleton employed Wyatt's former surveyor in 1823 a very annoying story emerged. Davenport, the surveyor, had been earning £170 a year yet Wyatt had charged £5,160 for his services. Davenport also recounted how Wyatt and his partner had "overcharged, greatly overcharged and fraudulently overcharged in their attendances as commissioners". They were allowed a maximum of 4 guineas travelling expenses but amassed 8 guineas per meeting by arriving late the day before and leaving early the day after. The meetings occupied 115 days in 1816, 42 in 1817, 165 in 1820 and so on until 1827 when the award was finally made.

In 1829 Mr. Littleton took Wyatt to court and charged the commissioners with being "persons of wicked and fraudulent minds and dispositions and disregarding their duty, unlawfully, wickedly and deceitfully did conspire, combine and confederate to cheat and defraud." The trial was held on neutral ground at Gloucester Assizes. The prosecuting lawyer introduced the case by describing Penkridge as "a place where probably my lord will recollect, in travelling from Wolverhampton to Stafford, where I believe my Lordship has changed horses, and where I hope he will often change horses again." The effort to ingratiate himself with the judge failed as Wyatt produced evidence of how hard he had worked and eighteen character witnesses including Lord Anson. He was found not guilty and when he returned home to Barton-under-Needwood he was greeted as a conquering hero with church bells being rung, guns being fired and the street being lined with supporters.

For the poor of Penkridge a more pressing concern at this time would have been the level of wages. At the end of the war with France the pressure on wages was downwards as the farmers faced increased competition from cheap foreign imports. It was vital for the labourers that the tenant farmers who paid their wages had a sympathetic landlord to whom they paid their rents. In 1815 Edward John Littleton contributed £52.10s to help the wounded after the battle of Waterloo, the battle which proved the 1814 celebration, like those of 1813, to be, again, a trifle premature. Fortunately for the people of Penkridge he was as generous to his own people. On March 25th the Staffordshire Advertiser announced that,

> "Edward John Littleton Esq, MP for the county, attained the age of 24 on Saturday last at which time came into possession of his estates; and on Thursday last great rejoicing took place at Teddesley Park where an ox and three sheep were roasted whole, which, with a profusion of plum pudding and 12 hogsheads of excellent ale upwards of 3 years old, regaled a numerous populace; and nearly 200 of Mr. Littleton's tenants and neighbours and families dined at his house, where most of the gentlemen sacrificed "to the rosy God" until the effects were very visible.
>
> The tenantry were delighted by the assurance given by Mr. Littleton that he should take an early opportunity of evincing to them the interest he felt in their welfare, and his determination to regulate his rents to the times."

On December 2nd 1815 the paper announced,

> "We have great pleasure in announcing that E.J. Littleton Esq at his rent day on Tuesday last, at the Littleton Arms, Penkridge, made a deduction in his rents of his immense estates by which £15 per cent was taken off the shoulders of his tenantry."

Chapter 8

The Churchwardens
1799 - 1840

When Horatio Nelson won a great victory over the French Fleet at the Battle of the Nile in 1798 the people of Penkridge turned to William Riley to celebrate the event. He duly organised the ringing of the church bells and later paid the ringers five shillings for their efforts. His next item of official business was to count six dozen sparrow heads and pay their executioner one shilling. Such were the wide ranging duties of the Churchwarden who, with the Overseer, Beadle, Constable, Clerk and Parish Vestry played a large part in the lives of most people in the village.

The office of Churchwarden was an ancient and honourable one. The Church defined them as "The proper guardians or keepers of the parish church" and they existed in the twelfth century when they were known as church reeves. Originally their most important task was to give to the Bishop information on the disorders of the clergy and people in their parish but gradually over the centuries additional civil duties were imposed upon them. Penkridge followed the usual pattern of having two wardens, the Minister's Warden nominated by the vicar and a People's Warden chosen by the parishioners at the Easter meeting of the Vestry.

To most people the Churchwarden and the other parish officers embodied authority. In the days before the police force and government agencies these men represented the law and the state for the great majority of villagers who would not come before the magistrates at Stafford. If times were harsh actually knowing the wardens and their personal failings was an added irritant which could produce a jaundiced view of village government such as that held by the poet John Clare who declared that,

"Churchwardens Constables and Overseers
Makes up the round of Commons and of Peers
With learning just enough to sign a name
And skill sufficient parish rates to frame

And cunning deep enough the poor to cheat
This learned body for debatings meet."

In 1779 William Riley paid 7/6d for a new accounts book. It sits today in the County Record Office at Stafford and is one of Penkridge's most precious historical documents. The record for the first year of the book gives an indication of the work of the village's Churchwarden.

THE ACCOUNTS OF WILLIAM RILEY 1779

Spent when elected	6d
Ringers	2/6d
Wine	5/3d
Cleaning flags and walks	1/6d
Spent on Mr. Wood	1/-
Paid at the Visitation	4/-
Spent giving the dole	6d
Spent copying indentures	6d
For oyl for clock	6d
For a new book	7/6d
Paid for wine botels	7/6d

The first item of annual expenditure throughout the accounts invariably covered the cost incurred when a representative of the Bishop arrived to swear in the Churchwarden. This event, together with a customary dinner held at the end of the previous year of office could sometimes be controversial and was indeed to cloud the end of William Riley's long period of service in 1808. It is clear that the warden was responsible for the provision of wine for the communion services.

The most persistent items of expenditure throughout the accounts are concerned with maintaining the fabric of the Church. The flags and walks were cleaned annually with sometimes the added expenditure of clearing snow off them. A recurring item is "bearing the big ladder" and "bearing the big ladder to put in a piece under ye beam". In 1784 five shillings was spent "examining the lead and roof of the church before it was taken down", weighing the old lead and "gave man getting up the roof of the Church".

In 1830 the wardens had to make a special effort to raise enough money to re-cast the five church bells and buy three new ones. They encouraged 95 parishioners to pay £246 in sums ranging from the £70 of Edward Littleton to the 2/6d of Richard Adams. The structure of Penkridge society is reflected in the list of subscribers written in the warden's accounts, the large landowners being followed by the gentlemen and tenant farmers, the business men and then the artisans.

The list begins with the undoubted leaders of society: Edward Littleton, Earl

Talbot, the Reverends Slaney, Stafford and Salt, Mrs. Miss and Colonel Walhouse are followed by Edward Monckton, Richard Croydon of Rock House and John Hodson. Gradually the names on the list change in nature, being made up of the lesser gentry, farmers and owners of businesses. These names include Mr. Cotton, farmer and landlord of the Littleton Arms, Mr. Miller of Pileton, James Turner, gentleman farmer, Mr. Bartlam, gentleman, and Thomas Croyden senior and junior, who were millers and farmers.

Eventually the list moves on to tradesmen and shopkeepers with victuallers and beer sellers being particularly well represented: Thomas Cope, plumber, Humphry Devie, tanner and farmer, Mr. Hazeldine, grocer and chandler, Mr. Mason, draper and druggist, Mr. Anslow, tin plate worker and victualler at the Blacksmith's Arms, Richard Adams, a coal and lime merchant, Orlando Adcock, victualler at the White Hart and Richard Bannister, grocer and flour dealer.

Maintaining and reflecting the structure of village society was an aspect of another of the churchwarden's important duties, that of allocating pews in the Church. The occupation of a particular pew in church was not a matter that was taken lightly. Pew rights were attached to certain properties and they were obviously highly desirable. In July 1818 when Rodbaston Hall was for sale it was advertised thus:

> " The estate abounds with game, being surrounded by the preserves of the Hon. Edward Monckton, E.J. Littleton and Lord Willoughby de Brooke. There is a good Pew in the principal aisle of Penkridge Church, in front of and near to the reading desk and another Pew for servants."

When the Church was repaired and completely repewed in 1831 it was a very serious matter for the churchwardens John Hazeldine and William Taylor who inserted a notice in the Staffordshire Advertiser informing the public that,

> "The Commissioners for allotting the Pews in Penkridge Church will meet at the Littleton Arms Inn, Penkridge, on Friday morning next at ten o'clock when all persons interested are requested to attend."

The Churchwardens drew up plans of the Church, numbered the pews and allocated them to people and properties. There was clearly a distinct pecking order in the position of the pews, with free pews for the poor and children situated in the corner and the back of the church. The structure of village society was visible and affirmed each Sunday morning. In the early nineteenth century rights and privileges came with the ownership of property, and rights and privileges were regarded **as** property.

William Riley's accounts for the year 1779 indicate the important role the wardens played in dealing with the problem of the poor. His expenses of 6d spent giving the dole show that the warden was responsible for dispensing the village's charities. Throughout the accounts there are instances of the giving of charity to individuals. "July 28th 1788, Gave Samuel Gibbon in need 1/-" is one example. The receipt of charity, however, meant surrendering one's freedom into the hands of the wardens. The parish refused to support the sturdy children of paupers and it was the warden's task to find work for them. In 1780 Riley spent sixpence "fixing masters for Prentices". In 1783 he spent time "signing indentures" and in 1779 "copying indentures".

When crimes directly affected the Church the wardens assumed the powers of the modern police. In 1784 the Penkridge Church plate was stolen. Riley went to Stafford and paid for 500 posters to be printed. When a suspect was found he paid for two warrants to be issued for the arrest of James Slenger. He paid for two men to be present at his arrest and personally took him to Stafford for questioning. Unfortunately for Riley the venture was unsuccessful and a later entry in the accounts reads, "Paid James Slenger for lost time, 7/-".

One of the more unpopular tasks that the wardens undertook was the collection of money for deserving causes that lay outside the boundaries of the parish. In 1783 the accounts read, "To briefs Upton Warren Church, Bagnal Chapel, Talk on Hill Fire all 2/6d". Church briefs were royal mandates for collections for particular causes. They were addressed to the minister and wardens. They were read from the pulpit and the parish clerk took a collection at the church door. Church briefs were unpopular as appeals were sometimes made weeks in succession. In 1754 the whole process was farmed out to private enterprise which made it even less endearing. One of the main agents for the country was Messrs. Byrd, Hall and Stevenson of Stafford who retained control of the business until 1828, running up high administrative costs.

In 1532 every parish was ordered to provide itself with a net for the destruction of sparrows and other birds. In 1566 the churchwardens were told to assess the holders of land for a contribution to a fund for the destruction of vermin. The heads of birds were to be shown to the wardens and then destroyed. It has been estimated from other records that from the late eighteenth century onwards this system accounted for about 10,000 hedgehogs and several million sparrows in Bedfordshire alone. When one looks at records of Penkridge's wardens one is not surprised at these totals. The first mention of the practice in 1790, "December 11th pd for sparrows heads 2/-", gives little indication of the slaughter that was to follow. By 1793 William Riley was inspecting and paying for 26 dozen heads, in 1788 55 dozen heads, in 1800 97 dozen heads, in 1801 163 dozen heads and in 1804 245 dozen. After Riley died in 1808 the new wardens spread their activities to include hedgehogs. During the period 1810 to 1812 they paid for the destruction of 3,631 sparrows and 107 hedgehogs.

In 1807 William Riley's accounts for the year were rejected by the Vestry for the first time in 29 years' service. He was forced to pay back the sum of 5/-, spent when he was elected. He died a year later. In Penkridge a sharp eye was kept on public spending. There is no doubt that much invaluable work was done by the wardens. The problem was that the good works had to be paid for and it was the wardens who had to supervise the raising of the money in levies and rates. The churchwarden had the unenviable task of raising money to sustain the poor of the parish from many people hardly above the breadline themselves. John Clare describes the warden and the clerk,

> "Carrying the parish book from door to door
> Claiming fresh taxes from the needy poor".

As the nineteenth century progressed and the problem of the poor increased, hearts hardened and the system was to be changed in 1834. The poor of Penkridge would, perhaps, look back with nostalgia to the time when they dealt with the local man and local charities and even the local workhouse.

Chapter 9

Roads And The Canal

In 1698 the great traveller, Celia Fiennes, recorded in her diary that, "I went to Panckeridge Race over the Kankwood, 7 mile, where were most of the Gentlemen and Ladies of the Country, severall coaches and six horses; indeed the miles are long and the wayes bad in the winter that obliges them to drive more horses". Celia had made a 14 mile round journey but "there appear'd only one horse to run for the plaite". Travel around Penkridge could be very difficult at the end of the 17th century despite Staffordshire having a rather good reputation for its roads.

Long before 1698 the traffic on the roads produced by increasing commercial activity was creating problems of wear and tear. The Highways Act of 1555 placed the responsibility in the hands of the parish vestry. An unpaid Surveyor of Highways was elected annually to supervise the annual stint of 4 to 6 unpaid days work of the parishioners on the roads. By the 18th century this unfair and inefficient system was clearly failing as a memorandum to the Surveyors of the Cuttlestone Hundred shows.

"Memorandum for ye Surveyors

That you give notice in ye church that all persons without delay do scour their ditches, clear their drains, brush their hedges, and that in a little time after, you do appear before some one justice to give an account who are defaulters that warrants may be issued out against them.

That you make a list of all the teams and labourers within your Liberty thereby to set them ye more equally to work and make your presentment with greater certainty.

That you begin to set the teams and labourers to work as soon as the season will permit.

That you mend only one track and where there are ridges by no means to dig them down into the rutts but throw them out.

That you set those persons soonest to work who did not so much as the rest of their neighbours the last year; and that you duly present to some one justice those persons who refuse or neglect to do their work as the law requires that warrants may be issued out against them.

To present those who throw the soil out of the ditches into the roads."

Clearly only the most basic road repairs were being carried out and with some reluctance. It was an unwieldy system involving unpaid labour, the Manor and Hundred courts and Justices of the Peace. It is little wonder that Penkridge followed the national trend and turnpiked its most important road to Stafford and Wolverhampton.

Although the Turnpike Trusts were fiercely independent and often financially inept, if not corrupt, by the 1830's they controlled about 22,000 miles of road and constituted a national network, of sorts, of trunk roads. Penkridge, strategically placed between Birmingham and the north, enjoyed a great increase in traffic and therefore business in the first half of the nineteenth century. Penkridge's entry in the 1793 Directory of Trade make the village's links with the outside world seem fairly sparse.

" No material trade is carried on in this place. The post office is at the sign of the Fox. Letters are dispatched to Wolverhampton (and thence to London) every morning at ten; brought to Penkridge at three in the afternoon. Dispatched for Stafford at three in the afternoon. A coach goes through this town every day for Birmingham and Manchester."

By 1834 there had been a massive increase in traffic bringing lucrative business to the Littleton Arms, the George and Fox and the White Hart. The Littleton played host to the Mail, Traveller and Eclipse stage coaches which ran from Birmingham to Manchester and The Bang-Up which linked Cheltenham, Birmingham and Liverpool. Between half past seven in the morning and four in the afternoon it dealt with eight coaches with paying customers to be refreshed and horses to be changed and stabled. The George and Fox specialised in coaches running between Birmingham and Liverpool namely the Mail, the Erin-Go-Bragh and the Rocket. The dark and quiet streets of the farming village would have echoed to the rattle of these coaches as they made for the bright lights of the Fox at 2 and 4 o'clock in the morning. The White Hart, which had stabling for 40 horses, entertained only one stage coach, the Hark Forward which went from the Potteries to Birmingham. At the less glamorous end of the transport business local people would have been more familiar with the local carrier, Humphrey Webb, who provided the necessary slow heavy wagons which linked the village with Wolverhampton on Wednesdays and Fridays and with Stafford on Saturdays.

The Turnpike Trusts set up toll gates and houses on the turnpike roads but early nineteenth century notices appeared in the Staffordshire Advertiser declaring,

"Notice is hereby given that Tolls arising at the several gates upon the Turnpike road leading from Cannock to Penkridge, called the Mansty Head and Penkridge Town End Gates
WILL BE LET BY AUCTION
to the best bidder, at the Littleton Arms, Penkridge ..... which tolls are let for the current year for the sum of £123. The bidder must pay 1 months rent in advance."

The toll gate keepers made their profits through the efficiency with which they collected the tolls from travellers. They were not allowed to set the level of the charges themselves. This power was retained by the Turnpike Trusts. In 1837, for example, in response to the new competition from the railway the Stone, Stafford and Penkridge Turnpike Trust announced that,

"Notice is hereby given that a meeting of the Trustees will be held in the Grand Jury Room, Stafford on Friday 24th March for the purpose of reducing the tolls taken at Burton Gate on the road between Stafford and Penkridge."

The job of toll gate keeper with its provided house and about 10 shillings a week wage was a good one in the poverty stricken countryside of post Napoleonic war Britain. A man of some character was needed to be trusted with varying amounts of money collected and to withstand the hostility of local travellers who would resent paying tolls to use "their" roads. Another reason why toll gate keepers might have been unpopular is revealed in the first advertisement for the Penkridge Association for Prosecuting Felons in 1795 which cast them in the role of informers, stating that,

"For the more effectual discovery of every offender, all Gate-Keepers and others are desired to take notice of what horses pass through their gates (especially at night) ..... 5g reward."

Some of the leading inhabitants of Penkridge, however, clearly felt that they were not blessed with a toll gate keeper of sufficiently high character. Michael Causer was forced by Penkridge butcher John Spilsbury to make the following cringing announcement in the Advertiser.

ACKNOWLEDGEMENT

Whereas, I Michael Causer, keeper of the Turnpike Gate near to the Spread Eagle in the parish of Penkridge, did on Friday last, illegally break into the Public Pound, situate in Penkridge, and take thereout a Mare of mine, which has been justly impounded by Mr. John Spilsbury of Penkridge, butcher. And the said Mr. Spilsbury having threatened to proceed against me for the same, but he being willing to forego such proceedings on condition of my paying all expenses, paying him reasonable damages and making a public acknowledgement of my offence.

Now I do hereby humbly ask pardon of the said Mr. Spilsbury for such offence and do promise that I will never in future be guilty of like misconduct: And do further return Mr. Spilsbury's thanks for the lenity he has shewn me. And do agree that this Advertisement shall be inserted in the Stafford and Birmingham (Commercial) Papers.

Witness Thos. Hart   The Mark X
Michael Causer, jun.

Although the improvement of the roads would appear to be a less dramatic development than the building of the canal and the railway it contained the seed of possible social disruption. Almost any improvement in transport would be bound to bring this farming village into closer contact with the industrial areas of the Potteries and the Black Country. A correspondent of the Staffordshire Advertiser in 1839 shows how sensitive the religious public could be to the intrusions of road transport on the Sabbath.

"Watch the arrival of the Newcastle Mail cart, and view the unloading of its cargo: contemplate for a few moments the nature of its contents, and its effects upon the minds of hundreds in that place and its populous neighbourhood. Among a number of bags from Liverpool, Manchester and Birmingham you may view a large white sack, called the London bag (containing newspapers and letters). If these newspapers were examined I have no doubt that they would be found to consist principally of such as are organs for information on sport, gambling, racing, pugilism and other demoralizing exercises, and stories of licentiousness; some of them also having an exceedingly democratic and seditious tendency."

Concern about this in Penkridge surfaced in a controversy about keeping the Sabbath holy in 1818. The arguments began in the county magistrates court when the chairman of the Epiphany sessions George Chetwynd Esq. referred to the "increasing immorality and depravity of the lower classes in society and to the decay of that genuine feeling and spirit of independence - those habits of industry, and that aversion to idleness - which formerly distinguished the English peasant", and wanted "every endeavour to enforce a due observance of the Sacred duties of the Sabbath". Overlooking the fact that the mainstay of the sturdy, independent English peasant, the common land, was at that moment being taken away from him by enclosure, a resident of Penkridge who signed himself XYZ rushed out a letter agreeing with the chairman of the magistrates saying,

"Sir
The remarks of your worthy Chairman at the Sessions, on the profanation of the Sabbath and other evils connected therewith were become highly necessary; and while it is earnestly to be hoped that some vigorous measures will be adopted to prevent the travelling of Crockery and other carts through this place on that day, the instances of this are become very numerous, and call for the interference of Magistrates of this district in particular."

This letter stirred, another Penkridge inhabitant, ABC, to pen a barbed retort which aimed quite high on the social ladder.

"Sir,

I am not at all disposed to cavil at the proper and very pertinant remarks of the respectable Chairman of the Sessions, or to sanction any profanation of the Sabbath, but I must beg leave to ask XYZ in your last of the "travelling of crockery and other Carts" through this place on that day how much greater is the want of observance of that day in the poor "Pot seller" who having disposed of his load of Ware on the Saturday "travels" through this place with his unladen Cart or Carriage on the Sunday to procure a fresh load on the Monday than is that of the Nobleman, Gentleman or (softly be it spoken) "Magistrate of this district" who in pursuit of pleasure, profit or other worldly affairs travels through here on that day in his carriage, mostly accompanied by servants etc? The former has in general the decency to delay his journey during Divine Service - The French proverb "Precepte commence, exemple acheve" might be applicable here.
ABC Penkridge, January 30 1818".

The argument ended, at least in the correspondence columns of the Staffordshire Advertiser, with another letter from ABC two weeks later. He wrote,

"Sir,

I should not have troubled you with any further observations relative to the complaint of XYZ against the sellers of Pots travelling on the Sabbath day .... ought the crockery seller be punished for this offence while "Stage coaches and post Chaises" are constantly travelling on that sacred day and not only with impunity but even without a remark from XYZ.

I have already stated that I do not wish to sanction in any wise the profanation of the Sabbath; but I cannot say I wish that if "Drunken Barnaby" should again travel through the kingdom, he should describe this town as he has done another, thus -

'Thence to Penkridge, oh profane one,
Where I saw a Puritane one,
Hanging of his cat on Monday
For killing of a Mouse on Sunday'

ABC Penkridge February 10"

The charging of tolls on the turnpiked roads continued long after the coming of the railway in 1837. The accounts of two local farms in the 1860s, for example, show the advantages and disadvantages of having a local turnpiked road. In June 1861 the Deanery Farm sold 16 loads of stones from the fields to the turnpike road. On the other hand the Preston Vale Farm accounts have regular entries like, "April 1867 - Acton Tollgates 7/6d, tolls on every load of soil, 2 loads 4/8d". The Turnpike Trust took every opportunity to raise money even from the most unlikely of sources. In November, 1839, for example, it advertised that,

"Persons desirous of purchasing the Scrapings of the road, for 1 year, from the Spread Eagle to Dunston are requested to apply to the Trustees".

Nevertheless the days when the road was economically supreme were over, at least for a time. The 1851 Trade Directory entry for Penkridge makes a stark contrast with 1834 as far as transport is concerned. The village's most important links with the outside world are noted as being,

"RAILWAY
Trains six times a day each way
CARRIERS
Railway Company to all parts
Hmphy. Webb to Stafford, Saturday, and to Wolverhampton, Wed.
VESSELS from the Wharf; Thos. Boyd, wharfinger."

Although the carriers provided a necessary and important adjunct to the national railway system the romantic days of the long distance stage coach which brought so much business to the local inns were clearly gone completely. Even before the railway was opened, it was announced, in April 1837, that

"The parties interested in the horsing of the London and Manchester mail, have, we understand, received an intimation that their services will not be required after the 5th June next. It is supposed that the mail will, after that period be conveyed over the line of railway from Birmingham to Manchester."

The building of the Staffordshire and Worcestershire Canal between 1767 and 1772 was obviously a disruptive event, being the biggest example of civil engineering since the building of the Church. Although Penkridge did not have the industry to benefit from opportunities offered by the canal there is no doubt that the area did gain from its construction. An important part of the rural economy was the timber trade. In 1816 an auctioneer's advertisement highlighted the importance of the good communications. On January 20th, 80 oak trees from Mr. Crockett's land on the turnpike at Ivetsy Bank were to be auctioned at the Littleton Arms, and,

"A quantity of very prime oak trees growing in Mansty Wood within a very short distance of the canal at Penkridge, particularly well adapted for boards, or coopers' stuff, being little inferior, if any, to Spanish boards. Apply Mr. Hodson, Penkridge".

Despite the economic benefits of the canal it remained unpopular and controversial in some quarters long after the navvies who had built it had left. Unease at the alien traffic through Penkridge, especially on the Sabbath came to a head when the whole county was shocked by the sensational and lurid murder of Christina Collins at Rugeley by three boatmen in June 1839. The execution of two of the boatmen drew an estimated crowd of 10,000 at Stafford Gaol in 1840.

The priest at the hanging said that,

"I do not think there can exist in the world a more wicked and profligate set of men than those who are employed on the canals".

Every parish along the line of the Staffordshire and Worcestershire Canal sent a petition to Parliament asking for traffic on the canal to be stopped on Sundays, to give the boatmen an opportunity to attend church. The Vicar and Churchwardens of Penkridge signed a letter by the Archdeacon of Stafford calling for similar action. Lord Hatherton chaired a committee in the House of Lords which looked into Sunday working on the canals and put pressure on the canal company to voluntarily cease Sunday traffic. Lord Hatherton felt unable to support stronger action because the railway companies would not suffer from similar restrictions. At Gailey Wharf, however, a mobile church was wheeled down to the canal on Sundays and apparently attracted a good congregation.

By 1832 the people of Penkridge were aware that another system of transport would be making its appearance in the parish. The bill for the establishment of the Grand Junction Railway was making its way through Parliament. Although the bill was being held up by the convulsions caused by the Reform Bill, Penkridge was allowed a foretaste of the age of steam and the horseless carriage. Early on the afternoon of Monday 17th September a steam carriage on a journey from Southampton arrived in the village. It had the frame of a large gentleman's coach but with a coke boiler three feet six inches high and four feet wide. It had steel springs which gave it an exceptional smoothness for the day and on the open road it could complete a mile in a minute and ten seconds. The carriage must have been a sensation as it stayed in Penkridge until the following Friday for repairs and improvements. When it left for Stafford on Friday afternoon it carried several women on the inside and ten men, including two engineers, on the outside. By the time it reached Stafford the streets were lined with spectators to greet it.

Chapter 10

The Poor

"On Wednesday last, about five o'clock in the afternoon, Hannah Cliff of Boscomoor, aged seventy, was found dead in a ditch near Penkridge - where she had been to receive a donation of bread".

Thus the Staffordshire Advertiser reports the main event in Penkridge on the first day of 1800. The condition of the poor was to be a major national concern in the nineteenth century and this small news item tells us much about the problem in Penkridge. It is important to note that the death of one poor person did make the news. The poignancy of the situation was recognised. People did care. It is significant that the dead woman was 70 years old. By far the biggest problem for the labouring class before the 1908 Old Age Pensions Act was falling into poverty when they became too old to work. The report highlights the separateness of Boscomoor. It seems cut off from the rest of the village not only by distance but because as one of the last remaining areas of common land in the village it had a higher proportion of poor people who needed its advantages. We also glimpse the traditional way of helping the poor, the piecemeal gifts of various charities and individuals.

In 1703 Widow Backhouse was the first person to be described as a pauper in the Parish Register when her burial was recorded. She was to be the first of many. In 1727, for example, there were 76 recorded Church of England burials and 21 of the deceased were described as paupers. Obviously we are not dealing with one or two unfortunate individuals but a whole class of people, sometimes amounting to 25% of the sick and the old.

That there was a large class of people who could be described as poor was openly accepted. The word "poor" was used without blushing. Even so the upper classes could be embarrassed by the sheer numbers involved. To mark the coronation of George IV in 1821,

"E.J. Littleton Esq. regaled the poor people in the vicinity of his seat for which purpose 12 cwt of beef, besides mutton, veal and 13 cwt of bread was provided but so great was the influx of persons, not only from the immediate neighbourhood of Teddesley, but from nearly every town and village within the circle of 10 miles that the fare provided was insufficient for their supply and all the bread at Teddesley and the Farm House was brought and distributed with upwards of 2 cwt of cheese, in addition to the provisions purposely prepared. English stingo, 5 years old, circulated freely and 8 hogsheads were emptied.

Nearly 3,000 people took part. The Penkridge band attended and at 9 o'clock everyone sat down to the enjoyment of a hot supper and plenty of ale; punch had been prepared for them, but with true British feeling, they preferred the National Beverage. Country dances commenced about 4 o'clock and were continued with great glee and animation until about 9, after which reels were the order of the night."

Bread and circuses had been the traditional and cynical way of keeping the poor happy since Roman times. By the nineteenth century, however, England had developed a far more logical and systematic method of dealing with the problem. The local government of the parish was intimately concerned with the problem of the poor. The first law concerning the poor in 1388 forbad vagrancy and ordered sick and disabled beggars to return to the parish of their birth where they could be supported out of the church tithes. Little mercy was shown. In 1624 one Robert Hill died and was buried in Penkridge. He was described as "a poor craple sent from Wolverhampton and being carried to Eccleshall". By the sixteenth and early seventeenth centuries the giving of relief had become institutionalised and centred on the parish. The individual giving of alms was condemned as "foolish pity and mercy". In 1601 the churchwardens and substantial householders nominated each year as Overseers of the Poor were charged with maintaining and setting the poor to work and taxing every inhabitant of the parish to pay for it. In 1609 it was ordered that Houses of Correction be build for vagrants, rogues and "lewd women who have bastards".

Churchwardens were central to the relief of the poor in Penkridge. They tended to remain in office for much longer periods than other parish officers and so would, presumably, build up an expertise in this difficult area. They gave sums of money up to a shilling to individuals when they were "in need". They distributed much more money on regular, fixed occasions like Candlemas and St. Thomas' Day and seem to have been entrusted with the task of administering private charities. In 1809 the warden "gave the poor Mr. Clarke's dole £4/10s/-" and in 1836 gave" to twenty poor widows agreeably to Mrs. Constance Groves wish £2."

In an attempt to keep a check on the amounts of money being given to the poor the office of Overseer was created in 1572. The overseer was elected each year by the vestry. It was an unpaid, unpopular and time consuming post. The overseer had to put the poor in receipt of relief out to work and then supervise the work done.

The work chosen was often pointless and badly done and the overseer could easily fall foul of many government regulations. Because of this and the ever growing work load, Penkridge like many other parishes, illegally appointed a professional "standing overseer" to do most of the work. They placed an advertisement in the Staffordshire Advertiser saying,

"WANTED
A Standing Overseer for the Parish of Penkridge. Whoever is desirous of undertaking the office must signify his intention at the next Vestry meeting, the 7th March 1814."

This practice was made legal in 1819. Penkridge also got volunteers for the job of overseer by combining it, logically, with the post of Governor of the Workhouse or House of Industry or Poor House as it was sometimes called. Penkridge's Workhouse was on Cannock Road, or Husbandman's Street as it was known in 1805 when the building was up for sale. It was described as,

"A large dwelling house (now used as a workhouse) together with a yard, barn and piece of land behind the same, the breadth of the said barn, from front to bottom of the croft containing 3/4 acre or thereabouts, situate in Penkridge, in the holding of the Overseer of the Poor. Mr. Philip James at the Workhouse will shew the premises."

Philip James was Penkridge's acting overseer and Governor of the House of Industry. Thirty years later in 1834, when the Cannock Road was called Wirehall Street, James Nixon combined the two posts. As can be seen from the advertisement the number of paupers in Penkridge's workhouse could not have been too great since a normal, if large, house was sufficient. The workhouse was more or less opposite to the Haling Dene site and, before the enclosure of 1827 had a garden on the Marsh common land in the vicinity of the modern Grosvenor Close and Haling Road.

Because care of the poor was the duty of the parish its officers took a great interest in that behaviour of its inhabitants which was likely to result in increased expenditure. An important concern of the parish was the paternity of illegitimate children. In 1594 William Birche of Penkridge appealed to the justices of the peace to save himself and his parish from future expense saying,

"that he is still (as hee hath heretofore signified at sundrye times) wrongfully charged, troubled and molested with one bastarde childe keeping, in that case provided wheere one Edward Wood of Cotshall, yeoman, is the reputed father of the sayed bastarde childe, the which bastarde childe was neither gotten nor born within this parish of Penkridge and therefore he supposed that he the sayed William Birche nor any other within the sayed parish of Penkridge ought not to be troubled with the keeping of the sayed bastarde."

If a husband left his wife and family it became the concern of the parish and it had the powers to deal with the situation. In 1814 Penkridge put a notice in the Advertiser saying,

"Left his wife and two children chargeable to the parish of Penkridge, James Whistance, labourer, 32 years of age, black hair, sallow complexion and stout made, about 5ft 8ins. Any person who will take the said James Whistance into custody, and conduct him to the Overseer of Penkridge shall receive 1 guinea reward and all reasonable expenses."

If the parish failed to make your father face up to his responsibilities or if you were an orphan it was possible that you would be apprenticed off by the parish so as to avoid further expenses. In 1711, for example, Francis Royby and Thomas Lynton, the churchwardens of Penkridge and overseers Thomas Steedman and Thomas Parton apprenticed William Haynes alias Bartly "a poor child of the said Parish" to John Potts of Whiston,

"with him to dwell and serve ... until the said apprentice shall accomplish his full Age of twenty four years .... During all which term, the said Apprentice his said Master faithfully shall serve in all lawful Business according to his power, wit and ability; and honestly, orderly and obediently, in all things demean and behave himself towards his said Master and all his during the said term."

In return John Potts promised to teach William Haynes the "art of husbandry" and "find, provide and allow sufficient Meat, Drink and Apparel, Lodging, Washing and all other things necessary for an Apprentice. And also shall so provide that he be not anyway a Charge to the said Parish and at the end of the said term will make, provide, allow and deliver unto the said apprentice double apparel of all sorts, good and new, (that is to say) a good new suit for the Holy-days, and another for the Working-days".

In this way poor and orphan children were consigned to years of unpaid labour with little to show for it except two suits of clothes. William Haynes was fortunate, however, that he was apprenticed near to home as a farm labourer. By the end of the century other parishes were using this method to send their unwanted charges to the dreadful cotton mills of Lancashire.

Although this treatment of the poor seems harsh and oppressive today, by the standards of time the parish was taking its responsibilities seriously. The parish did look after its own. The churchwardens undertook their unpaid work, the tradesmen certainly wanted the poor to have some money in their pockets and the farmers benefited from a source of cheap casual labour. there is little reason to doubt the truth of comment written in pencil in the Churchwardens' Account Book that,

"The Rev. J.C. Stafford succeeded the Rev. Richard Slaney in March 1830 and resigned December 1833 during which time he exerted himself so much for the poor and to the satisfaction of the inhabitants generally that a subscription was set on foot to purchase ... (a tea and coffee pot) ... what was subscribed to by many of the poor people".

The celebrations that marked the coming of age of the Honourable E.R. Littleton in 1827 were sharply divided along class lines but the poor were included and we should not disregard the beneficial effects of the local patriotism of the Littleton family. At his party E.R. Littleton declared that,

"the happiest moment of a man's life was not that in which it was most easy to describe his feelings. The manner in which they had received his name had almost overwhelmed him. He had been born and reared amongst them. The names of most of those by whom he was surrounded, and the localities and interests of the neighbourhood, stood associated with many of his earliest recollections."

Although parishes like Penkridge accepted the duty of looking after their own poor they tended to draw the line at accepting those from other areas. Since 1662 the Law of Settlement and Removal meant that any stranger settling in a parish could be removed by the justices unless he rented a house or land worth £10 a year. Casual workers or poor travellers had to carry a certificate of settlement or pass from their original parish saying that they would be taken back if they proved to be chargeable on the rates. Since 1685 strangers had been required to give churchwardens written notice of their arrival in a village.

Penkridge saw many poor travelling people over the years because of its location on a main road. In a twenty year period the parish register records that five of them actually died here.

"1677 Jan 9th A poor travelling woman

1680 Mary Cooper, a travelling woman

1860 Jan 5 a child of a wandering woman

1685 August 7 A travelling man who dyed in Wm Baxter's barn.

1695 a wandering woman who died at Isaack Forshoos".

If the wandering person had a pass the churchwarden did not mind helping him on his way. In 1785 William Riley noted, "September 30 gave a man with a pass 2d". Otherwise strangers were treated with the gravest suspicion. Even the most deserving cases were treated harshly. On the 30th September 1837 the Staffordshire Advertiser carried the following disgraceful story.

"DEATH FROM STARVATION AT PENKRIDGE

An inquest was held Tuesday last at the Fox Inn on the body of an unknown female who died on the preceding Saturday from actual starvation. Sarah, the wife of John Anslow stated that at 7.30 Saturday evening the unfortunate deceased passed by her door and fell down near the step. She immediately procured assistance and raised the poor creature from the ground; but her exhaustion was so great that she sank down again and the witness laid her under the window where it seems she lay for five hours without the slightest attention.

During the time she lay in that position, a woman named Margaret Mapp went to the Overseer and made him acquainted of the situation, but he believing her to be drunk did not go for some time. When he arrived he found her in a state of great exhaustion and wretchedness and applied to a lodging house keeper, Mrs. Biddle to take her in but she refused; and she was ultimately conveyed to the house of Margaret Mapp. Mr. Lister was called in; he found her extremities cold and her teeth fixed. He ordered her a little warm brandy and water and prepared some medicine. She died shortly afterwards. On a post mortem examination the stomach and bowels were quite empty, except a few bits of apple."

Sarah Anslow lived at the bottom of Market Street. Mrs. Biddolph (the actual name of the lodging house keeper) lived half way up the street. Thus the people of Penkridge allowed a stranger to lie dying in the centre of the village for five hours.

The cruelties of the Poor Law in the nineteenth century did not go uncriticized at the time. During the harsh winter of 1814 the Staffordshire Advertiser satirised the attitudes of parish officers.

"PARISH BUSINESS

In consequence of the inclemency of the weather and the consequent hardships experienced by the poor, a meeting of the Churchwardens, Overseers etc. of the Parish of _____ in this county was lately held.

MR. FAIRPLAY opened the business by stating that he had called the meeting for the purpose of proposing that the poor in the parish should be regaled with plum pudding on the ensuing Sunday, cold, benumbed and pined as they were.

MR. PAUNCH was surprised at the motion, a most important question left undecided, namely what they themselves should have for dinner.

MR. RAISIN thought the poor ought to be regaled with plum pudding and very generously offered to supply the fruit at a farthing a lb, cheaper than any of his neighbours.

MR. SOAK thought it would be cruel to give the poor plum pudding now, as they would miss it all the year afterwards.

Mr. Fairplay's motion was lost by a large majority."

The paper then went on to quote approvingly the words of the author Tobias Smollett who had said concerning the previous hard frost of 1739 -40 that,

"Nothing can redound more to the honour of the English nation than did those instances of benevolence and well conducted charity which were then exhibited. The liberal hand was not only opened to the professed beggar and the poor that owned their distress, but uncommon pains were taken to find out and relieve those more unhappy objects that from motives of false pride or ingenuous shame, endeavoured to conceal their misery. They were assisted almost in their own despite."

Other, stronger voices were being raised, however, protesting at the growing cost of the Poor Law and the effect it was supposedly having upon those it was designed to help. In 1819, ABC, who in the previous year had admitted a Penkridge address, wrote to the Advertiser complaining that,

"Being the occupier of a considerable farm in a somewhat extensive parish it has been my business occasionally to attend the stated meetings of the parishioners held for the purpose of examining and giving relief to the poor. I have had on these occasions frequent cause to lament the depravity accompanying many of the applications for relief. Indeed it is a notorious as well as a melancholy fact that the spirit of independence which formerly pervaded the lower classes has almost entirely disappeared; so that now not only the really needy apply for parochial assistance, without the least sense of shame, but even those whose earnings are comparatively great think this is no reason why they should not share the common bounty provided they can but find the means to impose upon the credulity of those whose business it is to dispense it."

It was this attitude that was to prevail and the poor of Penkridge were to feel its full effect in 1836.

Chapter 11

The Workhouse

In 1834 the Poor Law Amendment Act introduced the principle of "less eligibility ". The Government were determined that anyone accepting poor relief would be worse off than an "independent labourer of the lowest class". Outdoor relief, money given to people living in their own homes, was to be severely restricted. Able bodied poor were to be taken to the workhouse which was to be made deliberately unpleasant as a deterrent. From that time on people would accept relief only as a last resort, when all else had failed.

The leading inhabitants of Penkridge began to feel the effect of the Act in 1836. The parishes of Penkridge, Brewood and Cannock were formed into a Union with a central workhouse in Brewood. The Poor Law Guardians led by Lord Hatherton began holding meetings in October 1836 at the Lion in Brewood. They appointed a Relieving Officer for the Union, three Medical Officers of Health for the three parishes and appointed a Governor and Matron for the Workhouse. The workhouses in Penkridge and Cannock were closed down and their iron bedsteads were transferred to Brewood Workhouse, which was rented for £25 a year.

The first task of the Poor Law Guardians was to discover the number of paupers being relieved under the old system, and at what rates, for the previous 20 years. This information came from the parish churchwardens. The respective parishes handed over the balance of their Poor Law money to the Guardians. For Penkridge this amounted to £98.

The poor of Penkridge began to notice changes when the Guardians, using the new harsher guidelines swept the parishes and brought paupers into the Workhouse. One of their first decisions was made when in November 1836 it was resolved

"that the Bastard children ordered to be brought into the Workhouse of the Union at this and the former meeting of the Board, be ordered into Brewood Workhouse."

Nobody was allowed to dodge the new system by moving out of his home district. In January 1837 the Governor of the Workhouse was sent to Birmingham to enquire into the cases of all Penkridge Union paupers living there. If paupers refused to return to their parish the Guardians used the law. In November 1837 the Overseer of Penkridge was ordered "to apply to the Bench of Magistrates in Wolverhampton and take measures to remove Frederick Oldbury, a lunatic, now residing at Calf Heath to his own parish". The Guardians sometimes used the opportunity to deal with paupers who had been awkward customers in the past. In June 1837 they explained a particularly harsh decision to the Poor Law Commissioners in London saying that,

"The Board have heretofore carefully considered the case of Sara Bennet and that they have decided that she should only have relief in the union workhouse having been for a long time very troublesome to the Parish of Penkridge".

For paupers a visit from the doctor became a tense occasion. It could be very bad news to be getting better. In February 1839, for example, the Medical Officer of Penkridge was "directed to visit Mary Buckley and report to the Board as to whether she is fit to be removed to the Workhouse".

The workhouse regime was designed to be harsh and unpleasant. This led to difficulties when employing the staff. The Governor and Matron of the workhouse were offered £60 a year plus rations from the workhouse kitchen. The first Governor of the workhouse, Henry Addenbrooke, who was to last only eight months and leave abruptly without giving notice, was dismayed at this and asked the Board of Guardians to,

"Write to the Assistant Poor Law Commissioner Mr. Eade to enquire from him if the rations of the Governor of the Workhouse are to be limited both in quantity and quality according to the Diet Table of the Paupers."

Eventually it was agreed that the Governor and Matron should be allowed to draw six rations daily from the workhouse stores according to the Diet Table. This seems to indicate that Penkridge paupers were being given a third of a normal, acceptable diet. Sometimes the tradesmen who won the contracts for supplying food to the workhouse tried to take advantage and the paupers would suffer even lower quality food for a time. In February 1837 notice was given to a Mr. Lilley to terminate his contract "in consequence of his having sent meat of objectionable quality to the workhouse". In the early days of the workhouse the diet for the paupers seems to have been particularly tedious. In February 1839, for a four week experiment, the Governor of the workhouse was,

"Directed to make an alteration in the Diet of the paupers by giving a dinner of fresh meat and a dinner of soup instead of their present dinners of bacon and by giving potatoes with their soup instead of bread."

To conform to the spirit of the Poor Law Amendment Act it was necessary to cut down on the pleasures of life in the workhouse. In March 1837 it was decided that no able bodied man should be allowed to smoke in the workhouse. In the following year one of the softer-hearted Guardians proposed that aged and infirm paupers should be allowed to have a pint of beer with their supper each night. The proposal was lost by 7 votes to 4. By the standards of the time, the Penkridge Poor Law Union was an outstanding success. In their first year of operation the Guardians cut Poor Law costs from £4,771 to £2,964.

It is difficult to tell from the surviving records which of the paupers in the workhouse actually came from the village of Penkridge. We can be fairly sure that Elizabeth Webb lived in the immediate area, however, because of her dispute with the Penkridge Officer of Health, Mr. Lister. The sad record of her dealings with the new Poor Law reveal some of the indignities that could be heaped upon a poor, if spirited, personality. She first appears in the records in February 1837 when she made some unspecified complaint against her Poor Law doctor, Mr. Lister. The Board of Guardians decided in favour of the doctor. Elizabeth Webb then fell foul of the particularly objectionable rule that all paupers must give up their money and private property before receiving relief. In April 1837 it is recorded that,

"Elizabeth Webb, a pauper from the workhouse having been called before the Board to account for some property she had disposed of, and having behaved insolently orders were issued to the Governor of the Workhouse to put her in solitary confinement for 24 hours and feed her upon bread and water only for 1 week."

The dismal record of Elizabeth Webb shows how the lives of paupers could be made miserable until their spirit was broken and they were brought into line.

"4 Sept 1837

Elizabeth Webb, an able bodied pauper applied for leave to quit the workhouse for a few days to see her children; which the Board refused, but permitted her children to visit her in the workhouse.

Jan 1 1838

The Governor of the Workhouse made a complaint of the refractory conduct of Elizabeth Webb and Mary Toft. Ordered that the Governor keep each of the paupers in solitary confinement for 24 hours and diet them both on bread and water only for 1 week; and that they be brought before the Board on Monday next.

Jan 7

Elizabeth Webb was brought before the Board. The Governor reported that her behaviour had been very blameable during and since her solitary confinement. Ordered that she be kept on bread and water till Friday next. Mary Toft also appeared and the Governor reported that her behaviour had been quite correct since her solitary confinement - punishment remitted.

Jan 15

Elizabeth Webb's behaviour had been correct."

The records of other inhabitants of the workhouse give some indication of its harsh environment. Hard working, law abiding and Christian villagers who had fallen on hard times could find themselves in an institution designed to deal with the anti-social and recalcitrant members of society.

"22 May 1837

A complaint having been made by the workhouse visitors of the filthy habits of Ann Felkin, Ordered that her allowance of tea, sugar and butter be withheld for 1 week.

17 July 1837

The Governor reported that he had confined Mary Toft in the strong room for 24 hours in consequence of her being found in the Men's bed room contrary to orders and the Board approved of the same.

7 August

The Governor of the Workhouse made a complaint against William Owen, Thomas Hyde and Mary Toft for refractory and violent conduct and also against William Owen for swearing, cursing and assaulting the Governor; that the Governor take William Owen before the magistrates and obtain for him the punishment his offence deserves.

That Hyde and Toft having been reprimanded by the Board, no further notice be taken of their case.

4 September

Mary Toft, an able bodied pauper, applied for leave to quit for a few days which was refused.

4 April 1839

Mary Marshall applied for permission to see her daughter in the workhouse who is there with a Bastard child; which the Board refused."

The Poor Law Guardians at the workhouse continued the practice of apprenticing the children of paupers and orphans. Younger children were at first given an education at the local National School but arrangements were soon made to set up a school within the workhouse. In December 1838 a schoolmistress for the Workhouse was appointed. The children were to be instructed daily from 9 to 12 and 2 to 4, and on Saturdays 9 to 12. Most elementary schools for the poor at this time had limited ambitions but the curriculum of Penkridge Union Workhouse School was remarkably narrow. "The boys and girls (were) to be taught Reading, Knitting and the girls plain sewing, but not writing."

Even young people who accepted the philosophy of the Poor Law and were trying to better themselves were treated in a shabby way. In June 1843 the Guardians discussed the case of Thomas Poole. The minutes record that,

"Thomas Poole, a pauper in the workhouse, having only one arm, applied to the Board for permission to attend the National School for the purpose of qualifying himself to fulfil the duties of a National Schoolmaster. The Board granted the permission but ordered that if Poole on any occasion omitted to come direct from the school to the workhouse, the Governor should not permit him to go again until the case had been reported to the Board."

As numbers in the workhouse increased to about 200 the problem of public health arose. The old cess pit could not cope and a new water supply was needed. Separate small buildings were considered for use as fever and receiving wards. A certain Mr. Morgan must have been quite pleased when he was given the contract for workhouse coffins in 1837. Even if a pauper managed to escape the clutches of the Poor Law and leave the workhouse there could be one final indignity. In April 1840 the Secretary to the Board of Guardians noted that,

"The Overseer of Penkridge directed to obtain from James Smith the repayment of the sum expended on his maintenance while he was in the workhouse".

Viewed from the late twentieth century the attitude of the Penkridge Poor Law Guardians is appalling. How severe were they, however, when compared to the other unions in the county? Certainly the Penkridge Poor Law Guardians were ruthlessly efficient in making sure that no one fit to work received charity. According to the Assistant Poor Law Commissioner Penkridge was the only union in his district that did not have a single able bodied pauper in the ten years between 1842 and 1852. When the Staffordshire Advertiser reviewed the Poor Law statistics for the last week of 1859 it put the position of the Penkridge Union into perspective as well as outlining the philosophy of the Workhouse Test. The paper published a table comparing the number of outdoor paupers receiving relief at home with those in the workhouses. A soft-hearted union would have a high proportion of people getting outdoor relief compared to those in the workhouse. A strict union would have few "outdoor" paupers since, as the newspaper said,

"The Poorhouse is a test, and only a small proportion of the applicants for relief will accept an order to enter it. Hence by offering the House and refusing outdoor relief the number of paupers is kept down. In some cases this may be done with cruel strictness, while in others there may be a facility in granting outdoor relief of which the increase in expenditure is the smallest evil; the spread of a spirit of dependence among the poor being a far more serious one.

Glancing at these returns it appears that in the Seisdon Union there are more than 14 outdoor paupers in receipt of relief to one in the workhouse whilst in the Newcastle Union there are less than 3 outdoor to 1 indoor.
Between these two extremes almost every proportion obtains.

Dudley 10 -1
Tamworth 9 -1
Leek 8 -1
Lichfield 7 -1
Penkridge 6 -1
Stafford 4 - 1."

From this account it seems that Penkridge, even by the standards of the day, was running a strict Poor Law regime.

It was seen as an intractable problem that generosity towards the "deserving poor" encouraged pauperism in others and attracted vagrants from other areas. In 1869 it was calculated that there were 40,000 British vagrants "in perpetual motion". Sometimes the Penkridge Union had to cope with over a thousand vagrants a month. In the harsh winter of 1861 Lord Hatherton gave generously to the poor of Penkridge. Two paupers, later bitterly described as "worthless vagabonds" arrived, were given dinner, bread, meat, a bag full of provisions and orders to the shops in Penkridge to provide them with goods. Other tramps made a practice of arriving at the workhouse, destroying their own clothes and asking for a new set to be supplied.

The workhouse was designed to stop this type of indiscriminate charity which made vagrancy possible. When tramps arrived at the workhouse in Brewood and asked for a new set of clothes the Governor, therefore, supplied them with ones made out of old sacks and stamped with the words "Penkridge Union". This practice had been made illegal in 1815 but continued in Penkridge until the 1870s.

The harsh attitude of the Penkridge Union was condemned by the Poor Law Board in London. They said that turning out vagrants in sacking was "repugnant to feelings of common humanity". The views of the Poor Law Board could be ignored but not those of Lord Hatherton. He disliked the practice as sacking gave no protection against wind and rain. In deference to his views the other guardians made two grudging concessions. The words "Penkridge Union" were taken off the clothes and the sacking was lined with flannel.

The strict rules of the Penkridge Union eventually succeeded in deterring vagrants. The guardians introduced a "fair and just" ticket system of relief. Instead of being given indiscriminate alms each tramp had to break stones for four hours to earn a ticket that entitled him to "a proper amount of wholesome food and a warm comfortable bed" in the workhouse. When the system was introduced in 1869 the number of vagrants fell from 6,615 of the previous six months to 2,680 in the following six.

By 1869 it was clear that the workhouse at Brewood could not cope with the growing numbers of paupers and that a new one would have to be built. A workhouse generated a lot of business and the guardians could not agree whether Brewood, Cannock, Four Crosses, Gailey or Penkridge should benefit from providing the new site. The sometimes bitter argument had lasted for four years when Lord Hatherton and his supporters forced a decision on the rest of the guardians. The alternative was that "the Board would go on carrying and then rescinding motions and continue, as they had become, the laughing-stock of the whole country". In 1869 logic prevailed and the large rise in the population of Cannock was recognised as having shifted the centre of gravity of the union to the mining area. A piece of land, three furlongs from the Crown Inn, on the west side of the Cannock to Wolverhampton turnpike road was bought from the Marquis of Anglesey.

The decision had not come a moment too soon as the old Brewood Workhouse was declining rapidly. In 1869 a Poor Law Inspector found the female receiving ward in a dirty and improper state. It was damp and no nurse was on duty. The night commode had not been emptied and was very dirty. Most of the adults had to sleep two to a bed. There was no mortuary and bodies were kept in the clothes store, being covered with clothing that was liable to be used at any time. Boys in the workhouse were under the unsupervised control of an ex-pauper who constantly thrashed them with a belt and a stick. The old workhouse building in Bargate later became a Dominican convent and then a girls' school.

The new workhouse was a huge building, reflecting the continuing huge problem of poverty. It consisted of offices, a vagrants' ward, kitchens, a general school, boys' and girls' day rooms and playgrounds, dormitories, an infirmary with sick wards and detached fever wards, a laundry and wash houses, infirm and aged men's and women's day rooms and dormitories, and a dining room divided so different classes of paupers and men and women were separated.

In 1877 the name of the Union was changed from Penkridge to Cannock so ending a chapter of Poor Law history that had lasted forty three years. The Guardians continued to meet at Cannock and maintain the workhouse until 1930. Over the years the attitude to the poor gradually softened and conditions in the workhouse improved. The Local Government Act of 1929, introduced by the Minister of Health, Neville Chamberlain, abolished the 635 Poor Law Unions and transferred their powers to the County and Borough Councils. Cannock

Guardians had their last meeting on March 21st 1930. The Union had lasted 94 years. For 84 of those years a Lord Hatherton had been their chairman. Lord Hatherton was too old and frail to attend the last meeting. The other Guardians complained that the Act was a blow against local democracy but prided themselves in handing over modern buildings in perfect condition.

Chapter 12

The Railway

The coming of the railway to Penkridge brought disappointment and danger as well as economic benefits. The subdued opening of the line on July 4th 1837 seemed to foreshadow a rather half-hearted contribution to the life of the village by the railway companies. Having survived the presence of the railway navvies for about three years towns along the line of the Grand Junction Railway anticipated grand opening ceremonies. Unfortunately, the directors of the company feared a repetition of the accident which marred the opening of the Liverpool - Manchester Railway and used the excuse of the recent death of William IV to make the occasion a low key one.

The first train passed through Penkridge at 8.30 am and the first to stop arrived at 10.15 am. This must have been an exciting sight but the great event for Penkridge came on the following day when the railway engineer Thomas Brassey held a huge auction of the company's construction equipment in the village. Up for sale were 30 workhorses, 280 tons of wrought iron railway bars, 167 railway waggons, 2 moveable cranes and a vast selection of wheelbarrows, planks, blacksmith's tools and ropes etc.

In the years immediately after 1837 the people of Penkridge made good use of the railway. The two trains a day in each direction were well patronised and several jobs for labourers, like platelaying, were created. The railway station was regarded as an asset when houses and businesses were put up for sale. In 1839 the Teddesley estate utilised the segment of land caught between the railway viaduct, the Penk and the turnpike road by building houses. They were advertised as,

"Two newly erected houses, beautifully situated on the banks of the river Penk, between the railway viaduct and the bridge over the river; with a southern aspect, and commanding a beautiful view.
These villas are built in a most substantial manner and each house contains an entrance, dining and drawing rooms, kitchen, back kitchen and offices, in an enclosed yard with five bedrooms and a closet."

The proximity of the line and railway station were a positive selling point. In 1840 "eligible residences" with orchard gardens were advertised with the recommendation that "a station on the Grand Junction Railway lies within two hundred yards of the premises at the back".

As the century progressed and passenger and goods traffic increased, the people of Penkridge began to display more enthusiasm for their station than the directors of the railway. An almost constant battle began to encourage the company to improve its service and facilities. One of the main problems was that the farmers and the passengers used the same platform at the same times of day. The railway line was of enormous benefit to the local farmers. One of the great sights in a normally peaceful village was to see the milk waggons converge on the station to deliver their churns or collect their "empties". Local waggoners, already notorious for "furious driving" could not resist the temptation to race each other when they met on the narrow road leading to the station. In 1897 a Mr. Bewley of Penkridge was strolling to the station when he saw two waggons racing towards him. He had to throw himself into a holly hedge to avoid being run over. When George Stanley, from Deanery Farm, claimed he was only doing 4mph Lord Hatherton remarked that he had "never come across a milk cart that goes at the rate of 4mph."

By 1902 the dairy farmers of Penkridge were sending over 100 cans of milk a day by train. Both the road leading to the station and the platform itself were inadequate for the task. The steps leading to the platform were narrow and steep and the cans, each weighing about 120lbs., had to be manhandled up and down. The farmers suggested that since their business more than covered the entire expense of running the station the least they could expect was a new road, sloping up to the level of the platform. In 1903, when the congestion caused by milk traffic began to delay the trains, the LNWR took the logical decision of moving it to the Goods Station. The problems of the station, however, were far from over.

The paucity of stopping trains was an irritation. In 1895 the farmers and traders of Penkridge complained that there were no trains to Wolverhampton in the middle of the day, between 10.30 and 3 except on two days a week. The milk traffic caused "inconvenience and discomfort". The station was not raised to second class status by the LNWR until 1903 and the approach road was muddy. All these were minor issues compared to the dangerous problem of public access to the "down" platform.

The railway had brought danger and tragedy to the village since its earliest years. One of the first local men to get a job on the railway was Henry Mapp, a platelayer who lived on Pinfold Lane. In 1845 he decided to walk to Dunston along the line, rather than the road. He was hit by a mail train and killed instantly. Penkridge engineer Edward Dugmore was hit by a train at Birmingham in 1849 and had both his legs severed. In 1896 Penkridge platelayer Alfred Powell was one of dozens of men placed along the track to ensure the safety of Queen Victoria as her train passed through Penkridge one midnight in September. He had already worked twelve hours that day and was hit and shockingly mutilated by the Royal pilot train which travelled one mile ahead of the Queen's. Queen Victoria sent Alfred's widow £20. The greatest danger to members of the public, though, was that they had to get to the far platform by walking over the rails at a level crossing.

The first person to die near the station was porter John Capewell in 1881. He was chatting to a signal man and saw the train approaching. He decided that he had time to cross the track but he was caught by the buffer plank of the engine and killed. The Parish Council began a long campaign to persuade the LNWR to build either a subway or a footbridge to replace the level crossing. As a tunnel under the line already existed, the council could see no reason for the delay. The railway company promised action but did nothing. Almost twenty years later, in August 1900, the Staffordshire Advertiser reported,

> "At Penkridge station a few days ago a railway porter named James Bellingham performed a very plucky act. An elderly woman whilst crossing the line became confused and within a hundred yards of her an express train from Stafford was rushing along and she must inevitably have been killed had not Bellingham dashed onto the metals, lifted her bodily and deposited her on the platform. It was a remarkable escape and the incident should suggest the need of abolishing the level crossing at such an increasingly busy station".

This incident spurred the council once again to write to Euston to urge the LNWR into action. The company said that they were conducting a survey into the possibility of a subway but a year later the issue was still "under consideration". This was too late for Samuel Smith in March 1902. The 91 year old man was crossing the line from one platform to the other when an express came into view. The driver blew his whistle but the old man did not hear it and was caught by the buffer plank of the engine as he was about to step on the platform. He was shockingly mutilated and died instantaneously.

The station master at Penkridge, Mr. A.J. Buckley, told the inquest at the Littleton Arms that 120 trains passed through the station every day. There was only one booking office, on the "up" line and so all the "down" passengers had to cross the track. He said that he had seen the company's plans to build a subway and a booking office at ground level. The down side platform had already been lengthened to cope with the increasing number of passengers. The company's district inspector claimed that the work planned for Penkridge was "marked urgent" but that delays might be caused since all level crossings were under review. The jury returned a verdict of accidental death and pleaded that the subway be built and the platforms widened. They expressed regret that the railway company had done nothing despite many representations from the Parish Council and other individuals.

After this verdict the LNWR decided to build a footbridge across the line but in September 1902 the council was complaining about the long delay in starting work. Safety standards at the station still left much to be desired. In 1904 an inquest on a man who fell from the platform and died came to the conclusion that the platforms were too narrow and improperly lit, with only half of the lamps on. In 1905 the Parish Council complained that "the inadequate flight of steps leading to the station were much too narrow and in a press of traffic absolutely dangerous". Eight months later the LNWR promised to start work on a new flight of steps. Seven months after this declaration, in April 1906, "a handsome flight of stone steps" was built.

Relations between the village and the railway company remained cool. In 1914 the council was still asking them to build a subway rather than a footbridge. There were by this time signs that the economic tide was about to turn against the railway and that the years of neglect and delay would be costly for the company. At the annual meeting of the Penkridge branch of the Midland Farmers Association, held at the Littleton Arms, a debate was held on whether to send their milk churns by road or rail. James Heath pointed out that a motor van could be run 80 miles a day at the cost of only £10 a week, much less than the railway rates. The meeting then heard a flood of complaints against the efficiency of the railway. E.R. Holmes had lost many churns on the railway. If they were sent by van he would at least know who to blame! James Heath estimated that farmers who sent milk by rail lost £5 annually in churns that were never returned. Henry Heath claimed that one of his churns stood on Stafford station for three weeks before it was returned to him. Thus even by 1914 the supremacy of the railway, which had lasted only eighty years, was being challenged.

Chapter 13

Surgeons, Apothecaries and Druggists
1793 - 1841

The epitaph of Thomas Ecclestone reads, "To the memory of Thomas Ecclestone of Penkridge, Surgeon and Apothecary he died April ye 8 1793 aged 31 years". Coincidently 1793 provides us with the first printed record of Penkridge's doctors. The Universal British Directory of Trade, Commerce and Manufacture notes, under the heading PHYSIC, the names of Augustus Francis Lewis and William Perrin, both described as surgeons. Notwithstanding the respect granted surgeons today, in the eighteenth and early nineteenth centuries they constituted, with the apothecary, the lower rungs of the medical profession. The most eminent medical men were the physicians who were university graduates and as a rule only attended rich patients. Physicians were few and far between. Most ordinary people, having failed to cure themselves with traditional herbal remedies relied on the surgeon and apothecary. Both these professions had lowly social origins. Up to 1616 apothecaries, who made up prescriptions, were in the same guild as the grocers and, more famously, up to 1745 the surgeons were linked with barbers. Nevertheless, with only vague apprenticeships and obscure exams behind them these medical men could only succeed if they won the confidence of their patients and built up a good reputation in the village. Events in Penkridge were to reflect the growth in the prestige and power of doctors generally and answer the question of when did it start to matter how well qualified was your doctor.

Before the medical revolution begun by Louis Pasteur's Germ Theory of Disease doctors, however well qualified, could do little for their patients. As so few medicines actually worked, much must have depended upon the personality of the doctor. In trying to reach a conclusion about the state of health in Penkridge in the seventeenth and eighteenth centuries study of the burial records in the Parish Register gives a necessarily pessimistic outlook. A few selected entries, however, help to form some sort of balanced picture.

> "1654 Widow Lees, aged well nigh hundred years
> 1655 Old Stanley of the Heath, eighty years
> 1666 William Tonck, well nigh a hundred years
> 1672 Widow Hood, aged a hundred years

1684 James Southall, almost 82
1686 Steven Nicholls, aged nr. hundred
1694 Mary Smith, widow 100
1699 Widow Stanley, aged nigh 100 years."

Although these figures may be prone to an exaggeration possible in the days before the compulsory registration of births it seems that once people survived into adulthood they had a reasonable chance of living into old age despite poor medical care. More tragic entries reveal that the real costs of poor medical knowledge were dangerous childbirth and infantile mortality.

"1660 Elizabeth, widow of Sampson Turner with her two children, twins, being all in one coffin. She died in child bearing.

1679 A child of Thomas Harryman of Dunston, twins, (followed by another child of Thomas four or five days later)."

In 1656 a quarter of the year's twenty burials were of children. In 1658 it was one fifth. Another example of the poor state of medical knowledge is revealed in the aftermath of an eighteenth century traffic accident.

"1730 William Allen, coachman to Sir Edward Littleton who was killed from a fall from the coach.

1731 Francis Corbett, coachman to Sir Edward Littleton, who died of mortification, having broke his leg by a fall from the coach box."

Faced with being in a trade or profession in which the tangible proofs of success must have been quite rare and so much therefore depended on the reputation they could acquire, the doctors in Penkridge developed a characteristic sensitivity and combative nature. Their outrage could spill out into the newspapers when they felt that their business was under threat. On April 11 1807 Augustus Francis Lewis, nearing the end of his career, wrote to the Advertiser that,

"Whereas a report has been circulated probably for interested purposes that Mr. Lewis of Penkridge has declined the practice of a surgeon and Man - midwife he finds it an incumbent duty to himself and his friends to give the public information of his having entered into partnership with a gentleman of the town and that he still attends in every branch of the above profession notwithstanding moving to Preston Hill.

He likewise takes this occasion of returning his most sincere acknowledgements to his numerous and respectable friends for the very flattering proofs he has ever received of their confidence ..."

The second paragraph of his letter is a blatant advertisement, taking a form designed to appeal to the literate and the gentry of the area and being indistinguishable from the advertisements of grocers, saddlers and private schoolteachers of the day.

In the early nineteenth century surgery was a trade, albeit a lucrative one. It is unlikely that the doctor or his family were regarded at this time as being gentlefolk. When William Perrin died in 1816 his widow put the following notice in the paper, revealing the close relationship between medicine and ordinary trade.

"All persons indebted to the Estate of the late Mr. Perrin of Penkridge, surgeon, are requested to pay their respective debts to Mrs. Perrin, his widow, and sole Executrix immediately. And the several creditors of Mr. Perrin are desired to send the particulars of their demands to Mrs. Perrin, that they may be discharged in due course. Mrs. Perrin takes this opportunity of informing her friends that she intends to carry on the business of Draper and Grocer, in the shop so long occupied by her late mother and herself, and that she is about to lay in complete a new stock of articles in each business, which she will sell on the lowest terms."

After the death of William Perrin the medical practice was kept in the family. Perrin's former partner and prospective son-in-law Thomas Sanders took over and shared the profits with the widow. In such a small village, however, doctors attracted gossip and scandal. In order to protect his reputation Sanders put the following extraordinary notice in the Advertiser.

"It having been industriously reported that a certain yearly allowance only is to be made by Mr. Sanders to Mrs. Perrin out of the profits of the business in which Mr. Sanders succeeds the late Mr. Perrin (we state that according to) the agreement entered into by us, subsequent to the death of Mr. Perrin, the profits of the business are divided according to their amounts, and in the proportions agreed between us.
M. Perrin
T.A. Sanders"

Having few drugs that were actually effective the doctors in Penkridge faced far sterner competition from patent medicines than do their modern successors. These were sold from the shops of grocer/druggists like Cornelius Cox in Stone Cross in the 1830s. They had the advantage of years of unrestricted and unregulated advertising by the makers of these medicines. If the following outrageous claims were made week in, week out for years surely there must be some truth in them?

Mrs. Johnson's American Soothing Syrup	for teething
Wessel's Jesuit Drops	for kidneys
Blair's Gout and Rheumatism Pills	prevents the disease flying to the brain

Powell's Balsam of Aniseed	for coughs, asthma
Ashley Cooper's Botanical Purifying Pills	the only certain remedy for Gonorrhoea, Gleets, Strictures all other venereal diseases and scurf and pimpled faces. Works in days.
Dicey and Co.'s True Daffy's Elixir	immediate relief in the most painful fits of colic.

In a largely unregulated and ignorant profession the standards of the grocer/druggists stand out as being particularly low if, as the Staffordshire Advertiser seemed to imply, they needed to heed the following advice printed in the paper in 1837.

"Hints to druggists - a plan worthy of imitation. It is to have a separate shelf apart from the rest, appropriated to poisonous drugs, with the word POISON printed over it in large letters so that a mistake could hardly be made, even by the youngest apprentice employed in administering drugs."

By the beginning of the nineteenth century, however, standards and qualifications in the medical profession were becoming a matter of great public concern. An act for "the better regulating the practice of Apothecaries throughout England and Wales" passed in 1815 caused a great deal of tension and political in-fighting when it came to be implemented in Staffordshire in 1820. The leading apothecaries and surgeons of the county were suspected of holding a series of secret meetings in order to create a "closed shop", keeping out "those whom they consider as intruders in the profession and of giving such information to the Apothecaries Co. as may enable them to institute legal proceedings against such offenders". An outraged correspondent of the Staffordshire Advertiser accused them of hypocrisy since "some of these very gentlemen are known to employ their servant boys in the compounding and dispensing of medicines". It was just as well that the new act instituted a five year apprenticeship which included several courses of lectures and an examination which covered business and medical matters.

There can be little doubt that being a successful doctor was a lucrative profession and Penkridge doctors were substantial citizens. In 1840 William Scarlett sold his house. He had clearly been doing very well.

"Eligible Residences, orchard garden
Pleasantly situate at Penkridge.
A commodious family house, formerly called "Deanery Hall" comprising 2 front parlours, kitchen, 2 rooms now used as front and back surgeries, and six bedrooms, with cellar and pantry over it; detached wash house, containing brewing conveniences, and dairy; a pump of excellent water in the inner yard, and shed, piggery etc in the outer yard to which there is a separate approach; together

with a large flower and kitchen garden and spacious orchard, well stocked with excellent fruit trees, containing in the whole about 1 acre.

The whole are now in the occupation of Mr. William Scarlett, surgeon, the owner, and are copyhold of the Manor of Penkridge, not inferior to freehold."

Occasionally the poor of Penkridge did not have to pay for a medical opinion. In 1834 a visiting doctor went to the trouble of advertising in the paper that,

"Mr. W.A. Hubert, Surgeon, Member of the Apothecary company and Externe to the Hotel Dieu, in Paris, begs leave to inform the Inhabitants of Penkridge and its vicinity, that he will give advice, gratis, to the poor, at his residence in the Market Place, Tuesday and Friday mornings, from nine to eleven o'clock".

The most significant change in the relationship between the doctor and many of his patients came in 1834 with the passing of the Poor Law Amendment Act. In an attempt to reduce the high level of public spending on the poor, severe prison-like workhouses were established to deter them from claiming relief. It became the duty of the doctor to decide which of the paupers were genuinely sick or disabled and therefore eligible for dole payments at home and which of them were able-bodied and destined for the dreaded workhouse. It was an important job and carried for the Penkridge district the salary of £40 a year. Dr. Lister was appointed Penkridge's first Medical Officer of Health in 1836. He was soon to find that he was no longer an independent professional with a business relationship with his patients but was answerable to the powerful Poor Law Guardians led by Lord Hatherton. Perhaps even more irritating was the fact that his pauper patients, right at the bottom of the social pile, came to expect a standard of service for which they had not paid and were ready to complain to the Guardians if they did not receive it.

Dr. Lister, who in a long career was to develop into one of the strongest and most prominent personalities in the area, had a stormy relationship with the Poor Law Guardians. One of the earliest entries in the Minute Book of the Board of Guardians is a note that he be requested to attend the following board meeting to answer a complaint of a pauper, Elizabeth Webb. In the book the word "requested" is crossed out and the word "directed" is substituted. Dr. Lister was always able to defend himself strongly and the Board later agreed that "there appears to be no foundation whatever for the charges made against Mr. Lister." A pattern, however, had been set and complaints mounted against the doctor. In October 1837 the Clerk to the Board was instructed to "write to Mr. Lister and explain his duties as to attendance on non settled paupers and also to inform him that he must pay Mr. Herbert for his attendance on a Traveller whom Mr. Lister objected to attend." In February 1838 Lister had to appear before the Board "to answer a complaint of neglect made against him by William Myatt, a pauper of Church Eaton". In 1840 he had to answer a complaint that "he neglected to attend Mary Hadley when ordered to by the relieving officer".

John Matthews Lister, 29 years old when he took the post of Penkridge District surgeon, was undoubtedly an awkward character. His behaviour eventually came to the attention of the Poor Law Commissioners in London when in 1841 the Reverend A.C. Talbot complained to them that the doctor had been neglecting some pauper patients in Church Eaton. Lister explained to the Board that he had been visiting his sick sister in Broseley and had arranged for Mr. Bond of Brewood to attend to his patients. Apparently unwilling to take Lister's word as a gentleman the Board asked to interview his housekeeper to see if she had been given instructions to send for Mr. Bond in cases of emergency. Mr. Lister did not take this affront lying down and refused to allow his housekeeper to appear before the Board. He placed the blame on the churchwarden at Church Eaton who had sent a verbal request for help rather than a written one which his housekeeper could have forwarded to Mr. Bond. Once again Lister successfully argued his case. The Guardian's Minute Book records, "Resolved unanimously that the Board was perfectly satisfied with Mr. Lister's conduct. No just cause of complaint."

Despite this brush with authority Mr. Lister continued to live dangerously as the following three extracts from the Minute Book of the Guardians show.

"Aug 19 1841
Read a letter from Mr. Jones, surgeon of Penkridge requesting payment of 21/- for attendance on the wife of Thomas Oakley in labour. Mr. Lister was twice sent for and refused to attend the case.

Sept 2 1841
Mr. Jones, not attending before the Board this day as requested to substantiate his charge against Mr. Lister. Resolved unanimously that in the opinion of this Board Mr. Jones' charge was falsely made and the board hereby express their strongest disapprobation of Mr. Jones' conduct and refuse to pay his bill.

Jan 20 1842
Read a letter from Mr. Lister stating his inability to attend the Board and expressing his regret for having omitted to send his (account) book on the day appointed by the auditor. Ordered that the clerk write to Mr. Lister stating that the Board is much dissatisfied with his letter and that a repetition of his neglect will subject him to the severest displeasure of the board."

John Lister was leading a charmed life. He was upsetting some patients, offending fellow doctors and irritating important figures like Lord Hatherton and the Poor Law Guardians yet seemingly escaping the consequences of his actions. Despite this he must have been recognised in the village as being a very good doctor as his practice flourished over the years. He started at Gable End House in Clay Street, moved on to Ivy House and ended his days at St. Michael's Lodge where he died in 1887. By 1854 he was a prominent figure in village life, a successful doctor and was strong enough to oppose head on Lord Hatherton's pet scheme for the reform of the village's health care.

Chapter 14

Three Doctors

In the early 1850s Lord Hatherton came to the conclusion that Penkridge families were so frightened by the spectre of the Workhouse that hardly a week went by without one of them accepting "protracted illness and even the possibility of death" rather than risk calling in a doctor whom they could not afford to pay.

Lord Hatherton was on the horns of a dilemma. He did not believe in indiscriminate charity. He was proud to be chairman of the Penkridge Poor Law Guardians who had eliminated able bodied paupers in the Penkridge Union. He thought that charity demoralised the poor, undermining their independence. He believed in "Self Help". His experiences in Penkridge taught him, however, that the Poor Law could not cope fairly with illness and epidemics. A better, more positive way had to be found to support the poor when illness threatened.

In 1853, under pressure from his wife, Lord Hatherton discussed the problem with the Duke of Rutland who told him about the Self Aiding Medical Club he was running on his estate at Grantham. Lord Hatherton decided to introduce a similar system in Penkridge and called a meeting at the Littleton Arms to rally support for the idea. One hundred and twenty people attended the meeting including most of the gentry and all the doctors of the area.

Fully prepared with facts and figures Hatherton proposed that married couples in Penkridge should pay 7 shillings a year to a club, single adults 3 shillings and sixpence and children under 16 one shilling. In return the doctor would come free of charge and most of the cost of the treatment would be found. The basic nature of medical treatment for the poor in the 1850s is shown in some of the rules of the proposed club. The major concern seemed to be the fracture of arms and legs and attendance at births. Doctors were to receive 10 shillings and sixpence for mending a broken arm and 21 shillings a broken leg. They were to be paid 10 shillings and sixpence for acting as midwife or 15 shillings if they had to travel more than a mile. "Trusses to be provided by the society, leeches by the medical officer at 4d each." Clearly blood letting was still a common practice. The sick patients had to provide their own bandages and their own bottles for medicine.

The early Victorians had an acute awareness of the different layers of society. This club was for the benefit of those lower classes who were always on the fringe of pauperism and no one else. The rules on those eligible to join, borrowed from Grantham made this quite clear.

1. Only labourers in agriculture and trade, servants and journeymen strictly belonging to the working class.
2. Any man or woman keeping 1 cow to be admissible on paying 6d extra.
3. All entitled to vote, excluded anyone owning property £5 annual value.
4. Gentlemen's domestic servants excluded, also most handicraftsmen, grocers, drapers and shopkeepers.

Victorian liberals believed that much poverty was self-inflicted and this part of their moral code was reflected in rule 5 which ruled that "Habitual drunkards excluded, those receiving injury whilst in a state of intoxication."

When he had finished speaking Lord Hatherton was probably not surprised to see Mr. Lister rise to his feet. The medical grapevine was just as strong as the aristocratic one and Lister had come prepared with information from a doctor working under the Duke of Rutland's scheme. Lister maintained that he was not against the club in principle but objected to the rates of pay for doctors. This claim for a pay rise really irritated Lord Hatherton and he hit back, saying, rather unwisely,

"I must repeat that this institution is not established for the benefit of medical men, but for the benefit of the poor and it will be the duty of the committee to obtain at the lowest terms they could an efficient attendance on the part of medical men. All the receipts could not be divided up among the doctors - there were other expenses to be provided for."

Faced with an organisation determined to force down their rates of pay Penkridge doctors launched a most vigorous campaign against the proposed Medical Club. Once again doctors resorted to the power of the press and on December 31st 1853 placed the following notice in the Staffordshire Advertiser.

TO THE COMMITTEE of the PROPOSED SELF AIDING MEDICAL CLUB OF THE PENKRIDGE UNION.

My Lord and Gentlemen, We the undersigned Medical Practitioners of the Penkridge Union ..... most respectfully request that you will call a Public Meeting of the Subscribers to the proposed scheme, and allow us an opportunity of laying before them the course we have taken in the matter and explaining our reasons for the same.

John M. Lister, Penkridge
J.W.H. MacKenzie, Penkridge
Charles H. Green, Brewood
J. Blackford , Cannock
J.J. Sparham, Brewood

The campaign against the club was well organised. As well as notices in the press the doctors had posters printed and placed in the tavern windows of Penkridge to attract the attention of the villagers who might have supported the club. John Hay, secretary to the proposed club, wrote to Lord Hatherton expressing his concern at the strength of the opposition. He gives every indication of being outmanoeuvred by the wily John Lister and losing touch with the situation especially after falling out with the Brewood doctor John Sparham. He warned Lord Hatherton that "this looks like serious alarm - but it cannot be a politic measure. I read it in a tavern window. I have unfortunately quarrelled with my old acquaintance Mr. Sparham about his pothouse style last Friday; so I know less than ever at the moment."

The doctors had three reasons for opposing the proposed club. One was the level of pay. John Hay dismissed this argument since the club intended to pay the doctors at a higher level than other similar clubs and the Poor Law Guardians. Another, stronger argument concerned the qualifications of the doctors accepted into the scheme. The issue could no longer be avoided since vaccination against smallpox had been made compulsory in 1853. The Registrar General had ordered that lists be drawn up of those legally qualified to practice. These were medical graduates of a university, members of the British or Irish College of Surgeons, Licentiates of the Society of Apothecaries and apothecaries who were in practice before 1815.

The doctors opposed to the scheme objected to the inclusion of a Brewood doctor, Thomas Crean. Crean was a Member of the Royal College of Surgeons, Dublin and evidently another colourful character. In describing him to Lord Hatherton, Hay said that,

"He (tho' a Papist) attends all the clergy in Brewood. He has lately won a Fame (!) by his quarrel with Mr. Edwards of Wolverhampton which led to a mutual horsewhipping. He will act with us cordially."

Other doctors in the area, however, were unwilling to accept qualifications from Ireland. Mr. Wheatcroft, a Cannock doctor, referring to Crean said that, "I will not be associated with Quacks". This problem was solved by Crean re-qualifying in England by taking an examination at Apothecaries Hall in London.

With the question of money and qualifications out of the way Hay came to the crux of the issue which he recognised to be "one of feeling". The doctors were disgruntled that they had not been consulted and wanted a far greater say in the running of the club. Not surprisingly John Hay identified John Lister as the ring leader of the opposition. He had experienced Lister's forceful personality at first hand when he had been secretary to the Poor Law Board of Guardians and now described with feeling the nature of Lister's opposition to the club in a letter to Lord Hatherton.

"In the first place your Lordship must look upon the objections stated as belonging entirely and solely to Mr. Lister. Mr. Sparham dislikes the thought of the Club and will probably refuse to take any or many members as Patients, and he has promised unconditionally to "back" Mr. Lister.

Mr. MacKenzie I believe is satisfied with the terms; of course he would gladly get better ones, and joined the party in the hope that the Club cannot go on without them.

Then I think your Lordship will see that in spite of what has been said Mr. Lister disliked the Club from the beginning and for this reason - that he not only makes larger bills against the poor, but by some means gets them paid better than, perhaps, any other doctor in the Kingdom.

As to admitting the Doctors to be lawmakers for the Club, I am sure it would be bad in practice - I think, indeed, utterly impossible.

I cannot help at this particular period recalling the great trouble we had with Mr. Lister for the first few years of the formation of the Union - and no one but myself knows the full extent of that trouble: - If he is permitted in the present affair to suppose that he has an authority, I should certainly be alarmed."

John Hay did not have a high opinion of the other doctors who supported Lister. In a series of character assassinations he noted that,

"Mr. Blackford and Mr. Greene have not (I believe) 10 patients in the district and are unknown to the poor.

John Sparham M.R.C.S.L. and L.A.C. His practice is not so great as it has been - it is principally in Brewood but some in Lapley and Wheaton Aston. Mr. Wiggin is his patient. He is a favourite Accoucher. His habits are rather peculiar and he is not generally popular.

Charles H. Green L.A.C. and Member of the Faculty of Medicine at Glasgow. I know of no practice that he has or can have - He keeps a Retail Druggists Shop in Brewood - I do not suppose we should ever find 6 poor people who could wish him to attend them."

Eventually Hay and Lord Hatherton realised that they could not overcome the opposition of the doctors. It had been a striking early example of the power of the profession wielded against an earlier type of authority. The Littletons had been the leading family in Penkridge for generations and Lord Hatherton was still the major landlord and employer in the village, yet Lister exploiting professional unity and his close contact with the poor won the struggle easily. He was prepared to use modern tactics like an extended newspaper campaign which Hay and Lord Hatherton considered improper and probably ungentlemanly. In January 1854 a notice in the Advertiser said that the club was being withdrawn "having failed to procure that extent of medical support which was anticipated".

John Matthews Lister, however, was to live a long life and to become eminently respectable. He was one of a very few Penkridge people to gain an obituary in the Staffordshire Advertiser when he died in 1887. They reported the death of Dr. Lister,

"Who for many years conducted an important practice in the medical profession in the village and surrounding district where he was well known and deeply respected. He retired from active business about 13 years ago. The funeral took place on Wednesday. A number of influential parishioners attended the ceremony as a mark of respect to the deceased, among whom were the Hon. Algernon Littleton and the Hon. William Littleton. The coffin was covered with floral devices and a beautiful cross of Eucharis lilies sent by Lady Hatherton."

John Lister's successor as doctor of Penkridge and occupier of Ivy House was Dr. Frederick Boldero. He came to Penkridge from Suffolk in the 1860s and became a leading personality in the village. He was a long serving member of the parish vestry, looked after the church yard for years and organised the great village celebrations such as those for Queen Victoria's jubilees. In 1887 he acted as chairman at the annual dinner of the Teddesley Lodge of Oddfellows. The Oddfellows enjoyed the patronage of Lord Hatherton and were very strong in Penkridge. They marched through the village on this and other festive occasions often with a brass band. They had 294 local members and 130 of them attended Boldero's dinner at the George and Fox. Dr. Boldero praised the Society as a safe mode of investment for the working class and a promoter of self reliance. He announced that the Lodge had £7,392 in its Sick Fund. It seems that Lord Hatherton's dream of a self-aiding medical club had come to pass in a different form, helped by John Lister's colleague and successor.

The work of Dr. Boldero in the 1880s and 90s was important and often grim. There was still a large well of ignorance and disease amongst the working class brought about by poverty, poor sanitation and a poor water supply. In January 1887 for example, the Advertiser reported,

"Death of a child. A caution to mothers. An inquest was held on Tuesday last at the Boat Inn on the body of Louis Roberts, aged 6 months, son of Frederick Roberts, a labourer living at Wolgarston Lodge.
On Sunday morning his mother fed him with some chewed bread and sausage. He suddenly went black in the face and died in his mother's arms. Mr. F. Boldero

surgeon, who attended after the death said he found some of the sausage just over the glottis. Death was due to suffocation and he considered such food as sausage was improper for a child of the deceased's age. He found continually in his practice that among the labouring class mothers would give their children improper food. The usual excuse was "we give it the same as we have" and then they wondered why the child was sick and didn't get on. The inquest was held as a warning to mothers."

Despite all the advances in medicine and surgery in the second half of the nineteenth century and the missionary work of local doctors, some of the oldest practices and superstitions survived in Penkridge. In June 1891 Henry Fiddler was found drowned in a ditch leading from a spring on Wolgarston Farm. The reason Fiddler was wandering around the fields of the farm derived from perhaps medieval times.

"The deceased had gone to the place for water to bathe his grandchild's eyes, the water there being supposed to have curative properties, hence the spring is known by the name 'Holy Water'."

Doctor Boldero retired in 1908 and died in 1914. He was succeeded in 1908 by Dr. Nock who attended his funeral. Blessed with the longevity also granted to his two immediate predecessors, he was interviewed by a reporter in 1961. He remembered that Penkridge in 1908 was little more than "a very narrow street and we had comparatively little traffic". Having seen the village into the era of the welfare state he commented that "Everybody is fat".

So many people remember Dr. Nock, even in 1993, that it is true to say he is part of Penkridge folklore. Cyril Felthouse collapsed with appendicitis in a field at Pillaton farm in 1915 when he was 14 years old. He was taken upstairs and Dr. Nock was called for. Through an open window Cyril heard his parents, Dr. Nock and a specialist from Birmingham discussing what to do. When he heard the trestle table being carried up the stairs he knew he was in for an operation. His appendix was taken out in the spare room. A mask was put over his face and the anaesthetic was dripped on to it from a bottle.

Before Penicillin almost any infection could be deadly. During the harvest in 1928 Cyril Felthouse used to grease his binder at tea time. For the rest of the day he wiped the back of his neck with his gritty, oily hands. He had a carbuncle there which soon became infected. Dr. Nock came and decided to cut it out. After the operation the wound became septic and the poison spread to his head. Cyril was nearly at death's door. The wound "stunk the house out". He was rushed to Dr. Cookson's Nursing Home, next to the Sun, in Stafford where they operated. Dr. Nock came with him and administered the anaesthetic. During the operation Dr. Nock dropped the bottle of anaesthetic which shattered on the floor. Cyril woke up in the middle of the operation to find the doctors and nurses in a panic, "running around and cussing".

Chapter 15

The Select Vestry
1832 to 1894

When William Scarlett and Thomas Saunders, surgeons, Francis Mason, Overseer of the poor, Thomas Miller, Thomas Aston, William Taylor and Thomas Kent met John Hazeldine, Churchwarden and J.C. Stafford, the minister, in the church vestry on August 27th 1832 they had sombre business in hand. Together they composed a letter to the Central Board of Health in London.

"Gentlemen,
    We the undersigned members of the Select Vestry, and principal inhabitants of the Parish of Penkridge are deeply impressed with the necessity of guarding against and the prevention of that dreadful disease, the spasmodic cholera. For that purpose we humbly but respectfully solicit the advice of your honourable board, for the establishment of a Board of Health in this town."

Throughout the previous year the literate inhabitants of Penkridge could have followed the devastating path of cholera across Europe in the columns of the Staffordshire Advertiser. Now this terrifying disease was much closer to home. Ten days later a large public meeting of Penkridge ratepayers passed the following resolution,

"That this meeting learns from public and private account, that the spasmatic cholera is making dreadful havoc and devastation amongst the inhabitants of Bilston and its environs:-

That it has already swept away 600 of its inhabitants which is more than one twenty seventh part of the whole population.

That connected as Penkridge is with Bilston, both in a local and public point of view, it is become imperative on the inhabitants of Penkridge to exercise every means in their power to prevent as much as possible so fearful and awful a Pestilence from visiting the neighbourhood; for this purpose they most gladly avail themselves of the advantage and opportunity offered by the Central Board of Health, and especially by the Lords of the Privy Council to confirm the resolution that, the following inhabitant ratepayers be formed into a Local Board of Health.

Rev. J.C. Stafford, Chairman	John Hodson Esq.
John Hazeldine	William Scarlett
Francis Mason	William Cotton
William Taylor	Thomas Saunders
Charles Keeling	William Holland
James Turner"	

Luckily for Penkridge the cholera did not spread this way. The powers given to Local Boards of Health - the compulsory removal of nuisances like slums and filth- would have done little to protect the village with such a poor water supply from this water borne disease.

Nevertheless this was a significant and revealing episode in the history of Penkridge. It is clear that the Vestry and the new Local Board of Health were composed of virtually the same people. It was becoming clear that the local government of the village had insufficient powers to deal with the growing problems of the nineteenth century. How extraordinary it is to modern eyes that a major public health crisis should be dealt with by a small group of prominent ratepayers led by the vicar and his churchwarden.

The Parish Vestry was a sixteenth century institution dealing with nineteenth century problems. It had risen to prominence when the old manorial courts of the feudal system began to decay. Facing a more complex society, the Tudor governments realised that the Church Vestry, with its power to levy rates for the repair of the Church, was a convenient vehicle for local government. Gradually more and more duties had been placed upon the Vestry. They were to supervise the repair of the highways and look after the weapons needed by the militia. The Vestry supervised the actions of the churchwardens, waywardens and constables. As the Vicar, by common law, was the Chairman of the Vestry it assumed his responsibilities for the vexed question of relieving the poor.

Initially the Vestry had been a meeting of the whole community, open to all those who had an interest in its decisions. As their powers and duties increased, however, vestries began to restrict their membership. Although it was a breach of common law, many vestries began to find it too dangerous to leave the levying of rates and the relief of the poor in the hands of the majority of the citizens. In many villages the meeting of the inhabitants became a meeting of the "chiefest" or "most substantial" or "most discrete" inhabitants and the Select Vestry was born. The Vestry became an unelected and self perpetuating oligarchy acting on behalf of the village.

There can be no doubt that Penkridge's Vestry had taken this route. In May 1827 the following notice appeared in the Staffordshire Advertiser,

"Wanted. A middle aged man and his wife, without incumbrance, to reside in the Poor House, as Governor and Matron. Candidates are required to meet the Select Vestry at 11am on May 28th." Further information was to be had from William Southern, the Assistant Overseer of the poor. The whole mechanism for dealing with the poor was under the Vestry's control. In 1814 they advertised for "a standing Overseer for the Parish of Penkridge. Whoever is desirous of undertaking the office must signify his intention at the next Vestry meeting, the 7th March 1814".

It became clear in 1832 that the Vestry could not deal with major public health problems without being converted into a Local Board of Health. In 1834 the vestries lost direct control of the intractable poor relief problem when the Poor Law Amendment Act created Unions of Parishes. By the late eighteenth and early nineteenth centuries it also seems that the leading members of society had lost confidence in the Vestry to maintain law and order in the community. In June 1795 the leading inhabitants of Penkridge set up an Association for the Prosecution of Felons in order to detect and deter crime.

By the time we come to 1853-4 we can be more confident in describing the work of the Church Vestry since the Minute Book survives in the County Record Office. The business of the meeting of March 28th 1853 would not greatly surprise the modern reader.

"A meeting of the ratepayers of this Parish was held in the Church Vestry for the purpose of examining the present churchwardens' accounts, and appointing churchwardens for the ensuing year.
Also resolved that a meeting of ratepayers be called for the 25th of April to consider the propriety of amalgamating the Penkridge and Dunston Church rates and expenses.
Agreed that the Clerk's salary be raised from £5 to £7..10s. in consideration of his giving up the collection of Christmas Gifts.
Resolved that Mr. Jos. Hood's two sittings in Pew 56 allotted to house situated at the Foxholes be restored to him.
Also resolved that Messrs. Thos. Cope, Wood, Bannister be requested to attend at a Vestry meeting to account for the money received by them for the heating of the Church and at the same time that the meeting pay the expenses incurred in removing the heating apparatus."

A few eyebrows would be raised at the idea of the Church Vestry coming round to collect money for the repair of the Church as discussed on April 25th.

"That a rate of 1¼d in the pound for the necessary repairs of the church be granted. That a collector be appointed to collect the church rates and the churchwardens be allowed £3 per cent towards the expenses of the same."

What would be astonishing, however, was the business of September 22nd 1853 when "at a Vestry meeting held Thursday to appoint a collector of income tax, Mr. Oakley having resigned that office, Mr. Mason was unanimously appointed to fill the aforesaid office." Thus what has now become the province of a vast department of state was, in 1853, in the hands of an unpaid group of farmers, doctors, innkeepers and the vicar.

The minutes of the meeting of March 25th 1854 show us the still extensive powers and duties of the Vestry in the mid-nineteenth century.

"........Saturday morning for the purpose of appointing Overseers of the Poor and Surveyors of the Highway for the ensuing year.
Resolved Mr. Higgins and Mr. Robson appointed Overseers. Mr. Keeling and Mr. Mason continue the office of Guardians of the Poor. J. Croyden and Mr. Eli Shaw appointed assessors and collectors of taxes."

By the late nineteenth century the pattern of Penkridge's Vestry meetings was for the first meeting in March to be chaired by a prominent lay Vestryman such as Charles Reynolds Keeling at which the officers of the Vestry were appointed. In March 1887, for example, George Nagington and Joseph Smith were appointed Overseers of the Poor. Richard Bennet Jones was appointed Surveyor of Highways and Alfred Gilbert and Mr. Keeling became Collectors and Assessors of Taxes. By this time a number of the officials were being paid. The Overseer appointed an assistant at £10 a year and the Surveyor of Roads employed a collector at £5 per cent. This meeting was always followed by the annual Vestry meeting at Easter with the Vicar in the chair at which the main business was the appointment of churchwardens and the auditing of their accounts.

In these and subsequent meetings throughout the year much secular business was transacted. Every year inspectors had to be appointed to carry out the provisions of the 1833 Lighting and Watching Act and sums of around £55 a year were raised to pay for the gas and maintenance of the street lights. The Vestry in Penkridge was directly responsible for the state of the roads. Although by trade Richard Bennet Jones was a baker and grocer he was given permission each year to use his own team of horses to draw materials on the highways of the parish. In 1887 the Vestry considered the advisability of straightening part of Pinfold Lane next to the George and Fox subject to conditions offered by the Lichfield Brewery Company.

The minutes of the church business of the Vestry highlight a tradition of continuity of service among certain Penkridge families. In 1887 Mr. Biddle resigned as Beadle and his son was appointed in his place. In 1888 the Vestry passed a vote of regret at the loss sustained by the death of Mr. W. Cheadle who had served the office of parish clerk for 44 years. He was succeeded by J. Cheadle as clerk and A. Cheadle as deputy clerk. In 1888 the parish clerk was paid £8 a year for his duties in church on Sundays, £5 a year for attending to the heating apparatus and £2 extra for services connected with the firing and lighting on Tuesdays.

Other salaried posts that came up for discussion were those of verger (Mr. Plant), organ blower (Mr. J. Davis) and bell ringers. In 1890 it was resolved after discussion "that owing to the repeated misconduct and negligence of the sexton Mr. R. Doughty and that after having been previously cautioned by the Vestry, notice should be given him that his tenure of office will cease on November 29th. An application from Mr. John Rostance for the office was accepted".

By 1893 the authority of the Vestry was coming to an end. They remained a narrow and homogenous section of Penkridge society. Of the seventeen members of the Vestry the Littleton family, in the form of the vicar and Lord Hatherton were supported by the Rev. J.W. Payton, the curate and Mr. Foden who was Lord Hatherton's agent. Mr. G. Brown of Wolgarston, one of Lord Hatherton's long standing tenants headed a group of farmers including Mr. Nagington and Mr. Smith. Mr. Tildesley was a manufacturer of locks and was the most prominent of a group of tradesmen including A. Gilbert, builder and stone mason, W. Hill, draper and grocer, and Mr. Pearson, saddler and harness maker.

When the business of the last Vestry meeting of 1894 was completed Lord Hatherton explained to them that democracy, in the shape of the 1894 Parish Councils Act, had arrived to deprive them of all their secular powers. Rev. Ticehurst Corfield, Dr. Boldero and Mr. Foden had already discussed the likely passage of the Act at a Ruraldecanal meeting of the church in Penkridge and had decided that "churchpeople at present taking an interest in parish affairs should equally endeavour to do so under any new regime." The intrusion of democratic politics into the local government of so small a community was obviously distasteful to the members of the Vestry and steps were taken to try and avoid its more unpleasant consequences. The Parish magazine reported that,

"An adjourned meeting of parishioners was held at the schools for the purpose of discussing some means of forming the first Parish Council without the need of a contested election. The Vicar presided."

It seems clear that a contrived and smooth succession from the Vestry to the Council had run into opposition. The report continues,

"After some discussion Mr. Tildesley proposed that the nominations of persons to serve on the Council at the last meeting be rescinded and that the meeting should decide on the proportional representation of farmers, tradesmen and working men, and ask those three bodies to nominate their chosen candidates at a meeting to be held a fortnight hence."

Eventually a compromise was achieved. The men nominated to the Council consisted of three workmen, Smith, Palin and Core, two farmers, Brown and Stubbs and two tradesmen, Nagington and Jones, a system of representation hardly proportional to the number of workers, business men and farmers in Penkridge. The first three Chairmen of the Parish Council up to 1914, the Rev.

Ticehurst Corfield (who of course had been chairman), J.C. Tildesley and G. Brown had all been members of the Vestry.

The Parish Councils Act ruled that for every rural parish there would be a Parish Meeting and for every rural parish which according to the 1891 census had a population of 300 or upward there would be a Parish Council, elected by Parliamentary and County electors. Most of the powers of the Vestry, other than ecclesiastical affairs were transferred to the Parish Council, and churchwardens also ceased to be overseers of the poor. For every existing rural sanitary district there was to be a Rural District Council.

The parish of Penkridge was allocated three seats on the Cannock Rural District Council. The Parish Council was given the power to hold and manage village property like park land, walks and allotments and could take over any well or stream for a water supply, yet many people doubted if there would be enough work for a Parish Council to do. The early experiences of the Parish Council seemed to suggest that, much like the Vestry, "the extent of their functions depends in some degree on the public spirit of the people who constitute them".

Chapter 16

Who Lived in Penkridge?
1841 - 1881

In the spring of 1841 the Registrar of the parish of Penkridge, John Lister, received his instructions for the taking of the decennial census. The parish was to be divided into districts of between 50 to 80 houses. He was to appoint intelligent tradesmen living in the neighbourhood to make inquiries in these districts and record the age, sex and employment of the residents.

Every effort was made to ensure that the census would be accurate. The enumerators were well paid, ten shillings for every 50 houses with an additional shilling for every extra 10 houses. A blank form was left in every house with instructions that the occupants must fill in the names and details of all who slept there on the 6th June. The enumerator collected it on the 7th and immediately entered the details on to a blank schedule. Although the census had been carried out every ten years since 1801 this was the first one that would record actual names and personal details rather than just numbers. A certain discretion was therefore allowed. The Staffordshire Advertiser reported that "to facilitate the enquiries with respect to age, and to meet the reluctance of those who may be unwilling to declare their exact age, it is provided that the enumerator shall enter the ages of all those above 15 at the multiple of 5 below their real age". The penalty for giving false answers was between £2 and £5.

The "intelligent tradesmen" chosen by John Lister for this task were Joseph Burrows, a beer retailer and William and Thomas North who were builders and joiners in the Market Place. The picture of Penkridge that they record, a picture of one day in June, is of a small but crowded village. The main occupation of the men of the village is overwhelmingly agricultural especially in the streets leading out to the fields. There is a large number of skilled craftsmen and, in the central part of the village, tradesmen.

The village was much smaller in 1841 than today but would present the modern witness with a picture of a crowded and bustling community. An astonishing 68 people lived on Woodbank, for example. Of these 45 were either agricultural labourers or members of their families. Another eight people belonged to wood-cutting families. The families of the agricultural labourers, especially in the more isolated areas, tend to have the older and longer lasting family names in Penkridge. On Woodbank the main families were the Thatchers, Reynolds, Copes, Birds and Rileys. The Wall family comprised 11 people of three generations. William Dean, a carpenter, was the only skilled worker and Edward Bush was a woodcutter.

Mill Street was a well populated and busy street in 1841. Fifty six people lived there. Nine men were agricultural labourers but one of the leading artisan families of the village was also represented, by Thomas Cope who was a glazier and plumber. The main part of the family business was run from Park Gate by his father, also Thomas Cope. The business of plumbing and glazing went back at least as far as 1818 when a William Cope had premises in Market Place. Apart from three women of independent means and two female servants the only other occupations mentioned were fell monger, boat builder, farmer and shoemaker. Henry Bate was the fell monger in Mill Street which had, even in the twentieth century, an area called the Tan Yard. The centre of the smelly and unpleasant business in 1841 was located on New Road where Henry's father, Francis Bate employed William Capewell in the trade. The split in the family business had been recent, public and acrimonious. In April 1839 Francis Bate had published a notice saying,

> A CAUTION
> Whereas I, Francis Bate, Fellmonger and Tanner, am
> informed that my two sons, John and Henry, lately
> employed by me to buy and collect skins and pelts for
> the purpose of my trade, have represented themselves
> as being in partnership with me therein; now I do hereby
> give notice, that neither of my said sons is or ever was in
> partnership with me. And I do also give notice that I have
> now ceased to employ my sons to buy or collect skins. I
> shall not after this notice be answerable for any debt they
> may so contract in my name.

The 56 people counted in Mill Street did not include the occupants of Mill House, where John Croyden and his brother Daniel supervised the running of the mill, nor Mill End where there were 24 people in five households. The heads of the families were Henry Bloxham, miller; Thomas Wall and Thomas Woods, agricultural labourers; Edward Riley, blacksmith and Thomas Price, woodcutter.

The Cannock Road has been known at various times as Husbandman Street, Wyre Hall Street and, in 1841, Wire End. At the time of the census it had 156 inhabitants living in about 30 households. Of the 46 occupations recorded half were agricultural labouring. The others included builder, boatman, rat catcher, tailor and dealer in earthenware. Some of the richer inhabitants of Penkridge lived at Wire End including Joseph Roberts, lawyer and farmer Joseph Adams. Once again it is the family names of the farm workers that seem most familiar, including George and Elizabeth Plant, John Wall, John Rostance and Randle Bagnall.

Before the enclosure award of 1827 Boscomoor had been common land. Fourteen years later it was still thoroughly agricultural and sparsely populated, having 56 inhabitants in about 16 households. Most of the population were dependent on the wages of agricultural labour including the Chettoe, Rochell, Woollain, Gibbon, Lonne and Gregory familes. Undoubtedly the moor was dominated by the Hough family of blacksmiths and wheelwrights who had three houses. William Hough was a repository of ancient farming wisdom, being Penkridge's "cow doctor" and having inherited the secret recipes for medicines from James Rostance who had practiced in the 1780s. The other area of common land, the Marsh, was divided into Great Marsh and Little Marsh by the canal. Thirty four people lived on Great Marsh. They were mainly working class families with the four agricultural labourers having platelayers, bricklayers and general labourers as neighbours. Fifty seven people lived on Little Marsh in twelve houses, most being farm workers.

In 1841 Market Street was a crowded, bustling street from first light to night time. One hundred and thirty nine people lived there, forty seven of them under the age of fifteen years. At the crack of dawn the 15 farm labourers would make their way to the fields. The youngest was the 14 year old William Smith, the oldest Edward Oakley who was at least 75. He was a near neighbour of William Parkes, an 80 year old general labourer. In the days before the Old Age Pension there was often a stark choice between pauperism or working 'till you dropped.

Whilst the younger children played in the street the shops and workshops would open for business. Although the Northampton shoe factories had been advertising for labour since 1831 shoemaking was still, in Penkridge, largely a skilled craft. There were three shoemakers or cordwainers in Market Street - William Lee, William Rostance and William Smith. Altogether there were eleven shoemakers in Penkridge in 1841. There were two tailors and three dress makers in the street; Henry Thrustance, Philip Mulagan, Charles Cooper, Louisa Parker, Maria Smith and Jane Perry. The two main food shops were the bakery run by Charles Cliffe and William Whilton's butcher's shop. Other tradesmen in the street included a plumber, two potters, Humphrey Webb, who was Penkridge's carrier, and a cooper. When the work of the day was over the inns and beerhouses would come into their own. Sarah Cheadle ran a beerhouse, Thomas Henshaw the Lord Nelson and there were the Horse and Jockey and the Blacksmith's Arms. Apart from butchers and bakers there seem to be few shops dealing in specific lines that we would recognize today. Owning or renting premises was an economic opportunity to be exploited in many ways. The grocery shop was very likely to double as a drapery and a chemist's.

Fifty six people lived on Bridge Street in about 15 households. They included Joseph Hales, a butcher; John Bannister, a miller; William Thrustance, a tailor,

George Jones, a grocer; Thomas Timbs, a saddler; William Adams, a coal dealer and George Boulton, a farmer. Henry Holt ran a school for boys in Bridge Cottage. The main private girls' school was owned by Mary Ford, over the road at Ivy House. With the help of a teacher, Elizabeth Rostron and two servants, she taught six pupils and three of her own children. It was a household of fourteen people.

Between the Littleton Arms and the Railway Tavern were the homes of ninety eight people. The most distinguished inhabitant was the surgeon, John Lister, who was the registrar for the census. Forty people lived on the High Street and fifty two at Stone Cross with its three inns, the White Hart, the George and Fox and the Crown. Stone Cross was also the home of two large and important families, the Cheadle family of blacksmiths and Cornelius Cox's family of grocers.

Market Square was home to forty seven people. There were six agricultural labourers, four carpenters and a joiner. William North ran the carpentry business with the help of his sons and Richard Doughty. John Doughty combined the running of the Star with the trade cordwainer. Also living in the square were Eli Shaw and his wife Susan who ran the National School.

The occupations of people living in Penkridge on 6th June 1841 were as follows:-

Agricultural labourers	132	Bakers		3
Servants (mostly female)	60	Saddlers		3
Independent means	44	Coopers		3
Carpenters (and joiners)	13	Fell Mongers		3
Cordwainers	11	Boatmen		3
Tailors	10	Wheelwrights		3
Farmers	8	Locksmiths		2
Inn Keepers	8	Drapers		2
General Labourers	7	Maltsters		2
School Teachers	7	Woodcutters		2
Blacksmiths	6	Potters		2
Dress Makers	6	Wool Staplers		2
Plumbers	5	Platelayers		2
Grocers	5	Hairdressers		2
Millers	5	Excise Officers		2
Hawkers	4	Doctors		2
Bricklayers	4	Lawyers		2
Butchers	3			

and one builder, rat catcher, railway porter, clerk, gardener, vet, parson, carrier, milliner, coachman and coal dealer.

The list shows clearly that in the first half of the nineteenth century most boys born in Penkridge could expect to become farm labourers and most girls became domestic servants or the wives of labourers. Later censuses which record birth places reveal that most labourers were born in the village whilst shopkeepers, professional people and those of independent means were likely to have come from outside the village.

By 1881 the number of people living in Market Street had increased to 187. The street was home to a mixture of social classes, mainly labourers, craftsmen, shopkeepers and some farmers. The craftsmen included Samuel Powell, cooper; Henry Hill, wheelwright; John Davies, blacksmith; Thomas Davies, saddler; George Woolley, plumber; Thomas Burns, shoemaker; James Woollans, joiner; Robert Dent, tailor; Joseph Anderson, sawyer and Henry Fiddler, painter, both of whom lived at the Horse and Jockey; William Simcox, blacksmith; Richard Doughty, joiner; Benjamin Peake, shoemaker and William Wood, carpenter.

The labouring classes of Market Street were mainly made up of farm workers and servants. Sixteen people worked as servants. They were Emma Noble, Mary Whitehouse, Fanny Emery, Ellen Jones, Jane Stone, Beatrice James, Harriet Shilton, Phoebe Sharrat, William Blake, Albert Burns, Lucy Belcher, George Smith, Mary Smith, Ann Saunders, Harry Fletcher and Jane Wood. The farm workers consisted of Samuel Powell, John Doughty, James Cunniffe, William Brookes, John Thrustance, Joseph Cresswell and William Bradbury. The other working men were William Adams, carter; James Rostance, railway plate layer; John Wallace and Aaron Hodgkiss, both besom makers; John Tooth, labourer and platelayer and John and William Davies, general labourers.

There were only four shopkeepers in Market Street. They were Joseph Smith, a butcher and farmer; William Edkins, baker; Richard Jones, baker and grocer and William Hill, baker, grocer and draper. Hannah Poole ran the Blacksmith's Arms and Henry Anderson was landlord of the Horse and Jockey.

The rest of the population of Market Street was made up of the professional classes, the well-to-do and pensioners. Harriet Phillips was a governess looking after four children who were boarding with her. Joseph Cresswell was a farmer with 23 acres. Thomas Croydon was a retired farmer who lived next door to Eli Shaw, the relieving officer and registrar.

By 1881 the population of the Cannock Road had declined slightly to 149. This was not the fault of Charles Rodwell, chimney sweep who was the first name on the road to be registered. He and his wife Elizabeth lived there with eight children. The other adult inhabitants of the street were Joseph and Mary Amuson, hawkers of crockery; John Pool, farm labourer; Charles Cooper, tailor; Alfred Onions, groom and gardener; William and Eliza Cox, grocers and drapers lived at Wyre Hall with their servants Elizabeth Bill and the twelve year old Fanny Hinton. Fanny's mother and father, a laundress and bricklayer respectively lived nearby with three other children.

Cannock Road was dominated by Haling Grove, occupied by Haden Corser, a barrister, and his wife, Mary. They lived there with two children, a German governess, a cook and two housemaids. Other inhabitants of the road include George Nock, saddler; Leah Sergeant, needlewoman; Charles Ault, bricklayer's labourer; Jane Jones, laundress; John Bloor, farm labourer; Samuel Pearson, builder; Edward Ward, launderer; Joseph Bagnall, woodman; James Biddulph, bricklayer's labourer; Joseph Adcock; William and Sarah Griffiths at the Boat; William Bond, carter; Thomas Chetter, agricultural labourer and his wife Fanny; Mary Delbridge, charwoman; Nathan Doughty, gardener and his daughter Emma, a dressmaker; William Bond, labourer; John Cecil, carpenter; Joseph Clarke, a farm labourer with a splendidly named family - wife Sophia and daughters Penelope and Lucchrita; Thomas Oakley, farm labourer; Edward and Samuel Whitehouse, farm labourers; Hannah Billingsley and her granddaughter Annie who was a pupil teacher; Patrick Gibbin, farm labourer; William Dyke, ale merchant and George Wincer, his groom; Thomas North, carpenter and Thomas Stringer, wharfinger.

The other adult inhabitants of Penkridge in 1881, too numerous to comment upon, follow in list form.

MARKET PLACE:
Thomas Cox (Mary)	farmer
Joseph Beswick (Sarah)	farm labourer
William Beswick	blacksmith
Thomas Hodgetts (Mary)	grocer, tailor
Charles Russell (Annie)	Star Inn
Louisa Cox	dress maker
Sarah Whitehouse	servant
Emma Jones	charwoman
Frederick Smith (Anne)	school teacher

BELL BROOK ROAD:
John Boon (Elizabeth)	police sergeant
Henry Hill	police constable

FRANCIS GREEN LANE:
George Bradley (Selina)	buster?
Henry Wassell	postman
Zacharia Boyden (Ann)	general labourer
Andrew Oakley (Elizabeth)	agricultural labourer
Thomas Evans (Penelope)	agricultural labourer

NEW ROAD:
Mary Holdford	Alms House

Sarah Billingsley	charwoman, Alms House
George Core (Mary)	bricklayer
John Davison (Sarah)	gardener
Edward Huntly (Jane)	railway agent
Richard White (Louisa)	bricklayer's labourer
William Adams	agricultural labourer
Alfred Gilbert (Francis)	farmer of 96 acres employing 15 men and 5 boys
Sarah Wood	domestic servant
Mary Smith	domestic servant

CLAY STREET:

Thomas Fiddler (Sarah)	wheelwright
Thomas Fiddler	painter
Joseph Fiddler	baker
John Fiddler	agricultural labourer
Ellen Rushton	charwoman
Thomas Rushton	cowboy
Jabez Rushton	waggoner's boy
Harry Scott (Ann)	railway porter
Enoch Bott (Sarah)	sawyer
Charles Bott	waggoner
Ann Wincer	
Richard Wincer	apprentice
Benjamin Lowe (Eliza)	general labourer
Samson Lowe	general labourer
William Lowe	general labourer
Francis Lockley (Elizabeth)	road labourer
Kate Riddington	farm servant
Thomas Riddington	agricultural labourer
George Ingland (Caroline)	postman
Thomas Allen (Emma)	insurance agent
William Butler (Emma)	general labourer
Robert Williams (Mary)	agricultural labourer
Emma Wincer	
William Wincer	painter
Henry Wincer	bricklayer
Edward Wincer	gardener
John Gretton (Hannah)	fish and fruit dealer
Charles Hale (Ellen)	White Lodge, poulterer
Caroline Bastone	domestic servant
James Westbury (Mary)	painter
Arthur Webb (Elizabeth)	railway clerk
Joseph Dyke (Leah)	agricultural labourer
Thomas Haycocks (Emma)	tailor

Emma Baker	dressmaker and newsagent
Fortune? Weatherer	wheelwright
Sarah Weatherer	dress maker
Matthew Shutt	machinist
Ann Riding	
Fanny Riding	
Helen Masfen	
Alice Baldwin	cook
Mary Westbury	housemaid
Charles Day (Jane)	income from dividends
Mary Aspley	domestic servant
Annie Dyke	domestic servant
Sarah Dale	milliner, haberdasher
Benjamin Lawrence (Elizabeth)	chemist
William Lawrence	railway clerk
Henry Lovatt (Rosa)	clergy without cure of souls, schoolmaster
Richard Parr (Martha)	waggoner
George Webb	baker, confectioner
William Evans	agricultural labourer
Elizabeth Foster	
Eleanor Foster	domestic servant
Mary Hill	Railway Tavern
Emma Hill	domestic
Frances Hill	domestic

ROCK HOUSE:

Richard Croydon (Mary)	yeoman of 34 acres, employing 1 man, 1 boy
Anne Croydon	
Martha Smiegswood	cook
Elizabeth Follows	housemaid
William Davison	servant for house and land

WOLVERHAMPTON ROAD:

Thomas Adams (Anne)	gardener
Clara Sanders	domestic servant
William Lane (Hannah)	gardener's labourer
Ann Thursfield	
Frances Thursfield	dressmaker
Louisa Thursfield	cook

HAMPTON COTTAGES, BUNGHAM LANE:

William Crutchley (Emma)	agricultural labourer
Sarah Crutchley	general servant
Thomas Winsor	agricultural labourer
Joseph Horton (Mary)	agricultural labourer
Charles Horton	agricultural labourer

GUARDSMAN COTTAGES, CONGREVE ROAD:
John Evans (Eliza)   agricultural labourer
John Evans   agricultural labourer
Elizabeth Evans   servant
John Podmore (Ann)   agricultural labourer

VICARAGE:
Cecil Littleton (Catherine) vicar of Penkridge
M. Shirer Brown   curate
Sarah Walters   domestic servant
Annie Taylor   servant
Mary Haywood   servant
Fanny East   servant

THE FIRS:
James C. Tildesley (Fanny)   merchant and manufacturer
Mary Butcher   domestic servant
Harriet Powell   domestic servant

STATION ROAD:
John M. Lister (Harriet)   surgeon, retired
Mary Miles   cook
Elizabeth Turner   servant
Ann Rushton
Emma Adams

CUTTLESTONE HOUSE:
Henry Jevons (Sarah)   retired coal proprietor
Theresa Ford   domestic servant
Emily Terry   domestic servant

IVY HOUSE:
Frederick Boldero (Fanny)   surgeon
Sarah Berry   cook
Mary Astbury   housemaid
Julia Jeggs   domestic nurse
John Turner   groom

LITTLETON ARMS:
Thomas Robson (Catherine)   innkeeper, farmer
Harry Robson   formerly innkeeper
Emma Robson
Martha Monk   domestic servant, housemaid
Mary Beresford   cook
James Palin   bootboy

CHURCH LANE:

George Powell (Annie)	woodcutter
Frederick Cartwright (Ann)	gardener, coachman
John Emson	gardener
Ann Robins	housekeeper
Thomas Rostance (Elizabeth)	cordwainer

PINFOLD LANE:

Thomas Gregg (Hannah)	retired shepherd
Charles Gregg	herdsman
John Hewitt (Elizabeth)	gas manager, Gas House
William Hall	general labourer
George Griffiths (Sarah)	plumber, employing two men
George Griffiths	plumber
Clement Bromley (Ann)	painter, employing 4 men
John Bromley	painter
William Rutter	retired farm bailiff
Edward Powell (Mary)	agricultural labourer
Thomas Cooper (Sarah)	bricklayer
Samuel Cooper	tailor, unemployed
Charles Cooper	painter
Emma Cooper	dressmaker
Henry Richards (Elizabeth)	gardener

DEANERY:

Isaac Marshall (Alice)	metal merchant
William James (Emma)	commission agent
Jane Rhodes	cook
Jane Biddolphe	nurse

SUNNYSIDE:

Ann Ready	annuitant
Caroline Dunn	annuitant
Sarah Page	servant

GEORGE AND FOX:

Timothy Riley	victualler
Mary Oldbury	servant

BRIDGE COTTAGE:

William Saunders (Hannah)	Inland Revenue Officer

STONE CROSS:

Joseph Husslebee (Mary)	agricultural labourer
William Hough (Emily)	bricklayer
Michael Cope (Ann)	wheelwright

Mary Oakden	
Fanny Oakden	
William Rogers	cooper
William Rogers	clerk
George Clerk	draper's assistant
William Webb (Mary)	butcher, publican, Crown Inn
William Webb	butcher
George Webb	butcher
Sarah Webb	barmaid
Richard Wright (Sarah)	publican, White Hart, commercial Traveller
Maria Whilton	servant
John Cheadle (Elizabeth)	blacksmith
William Ford (Hannah)	grocer
Amelia Gibbs	dressmaker
Thomas Ford	grocer's apprentice
William Cheadle	parish clerk, blacksmith, employing 2 men, 1 boy
Allan Cheadle (Eliza)	blacksmith
Edward Green (Ellen)	grocer
Ellen Green	teacher
George Cliffe (Annie)	master baker, employing 1 man, 1 boy
Mary Stocks	servant
Edward Slater (Anne)	master tailor
Elizabeth Slater	pupil teacher
John Ecclestone	
Marie Ecclestone	
Elizabeth Oakley	lodging-house keeper, and 14 lodgers
Charles Wincer	general labourer
Edmund Gilbert (Fanny)	butcher and farmer
Robert Murphy	clerk
Samuel Evans	butcher's apprentice
Harriet Powell	servant
William Harvey (Ann)	ostler
William Harvey	grocer's apprentice
William Pearson	saddler
George Pearson	pupil teacher
Humphrey Hughes	rural messenger
Ann Hughes	dressmaker
Jane Hughes	dressmaker
William Emery (Mary)	boot machine operator
Alfred Lyons (Elizabeth)	stone mason
Louie Elton	dressmaker
Mary Keeling	
Sarah Belcher	domestic servant
John Thacker (Sarah)	shopman, drapery

POST OFFICE:
Thomas Dukes	plumber, master of 4 men and 3 boys
Catherine Dukes	postmaster
Sarah Dawson	servant

MILL STREET:
Matthews Shutt (Mary)	agricultural machinist
John Shutt (Fanny)	agricultural engineer
William Jones	pit labourer
George Jones	agricultural labourer
George Morris	agricultural labourer
John Davies (Rosetta)	cordwainer
Ann Parker	dressmaker
Michael Cope	carpenter
Elizabeth Cope	dressmaker
Thomas Leese	railway platelayer
Elianour Westwood	
Thomas Westwood	bootmaker
Edmund Westwood	bootmaker
William Hodgetts	bootmaker
Sarah Hodgkiss	lodging-house keeper
Joseph Wall (Sarah)	cowman
Elizabeth Cotton	income from interest of money
Elizabeth Cotton	
Catherine Cotton	
Ann Cotton	
Mary Aston	annuitant
Mary Mills	servant
Thomas Leek (Eliza)	postman and general servant
Matilda Thorley	laundress
David Banham (Emma)	bricklayer's labourer
George Weatherer (Emma)	agricultural labourer
George Jenkinson (Ann)	agricultural labourer
Henry Thrustance	agricultural labourer
William Thrustance	agricultural labourer
Albert Thrustance	farm servant
Elizabeth Emery	
Sarah Emery	servant
George Emery	agricultural labourer
Edwin Thurstance (Emily)	stone quarryman
Thomas Weatherer (Elizabeth)	agricultural labourer
Henry Weatherer	agricultural labourer
William Weatherer	agricultural labourer
Edward Brookes (Frances)	bricklayer
George Shenton	brewer

Louisa Brookes	servant
William Rostance (Emma)	cordwainer
Isaac Stanley	locksmith
William Ives	grocer
Charles Dyke (Sarah)	agricultural labourer
Joseph Dyke	agricultural labourer
James Oakley (Elizabeth)	general labourer
Edwin Oakley	groom
Samuel Jennings (Emma)	stonemason
Mary Webb	
John Webb	railway servant
Alfred Webb	engine driver
Jane Webb	dressmaker
William Webb	agricultural labourer

MILL END:
William Fletcher	agricultural labourer
Caroline Hood	housekeeper
John Rostance (Maria)	carpenter
Joseph Wilcox (Ann)	agricultural labourer
Henry Griffiths (Louisa)	corn miller
Edward Wincer (Mary)	agricultural labourer
George Nagington	miller and farmer
Cecilia Boyden	servant
Maria Griffiths	servant
Richard Wilson	miller's apprentice
Randle Bagnall	woodman
Sarah Bagnall	

BELL BROOK:
William Tooth	gardener
Elizabeth Tooth	laundress
Henry Tooth	stable boy
Joseph Plant (Jane)	coal agent
Joseph Plant	clerk, Goods Depot

RAILWAY STATION HOUSE:
George Walton (Sarah)	station master

WOLGARSTON:
Thomas Cole (Annie)	gardener
George Rogers (Emily)	farmer
Unice Jones	domestic servant
Gertrude Evans	nurse

WOODBANK:
Thomas Wall	general labourer

Sarah Wall	dressmaker
Charles Rostance (Elizabeth)	general labourer
Joseph Wall	general labourer
Fanny Atkins	
Jane Meeson	servant
George Mason (Clara)	bricklayer
Isaac Matthews (Sarah)	farm labourer
Peter Davy (Elizabeth)	drainer
Hannah Davy	dressmaker
John Marshall	waggoner
Edward Marshall	farm labourer
Mary Reynolds	formerly domestic servant
Joseph Reynolds	agricultural labourer
Margaret Reynolds	domestic servant
William Barton	agricultural labourer
William Riley (Martha)	general labourer
Thomas Kent (Hannah)	farm labourer

MARSH:

John Spooner (Eliza)	general labourer
Dinah Berry	shopkeeper
William Nixon (Sophia)	boatman
Charles Nixon	butcher
Benjamin Nixon	boatman
Thomas Davis (Mary)	general labourer
Ann Rutter	needlewoman
Richard Rutter (Lucy)	cowman
Ann Lear	servant
Thomas Skelton (Elizabeth)	general labourer
Mary Skelton	servant
Caleb Skelton	farmer's boy
Mary Butler	
Charles Butler	general labourer
James Emery	saddler apprentice
Richard Green	coachman
Jane Green	laundress
Henry Green	stable boy
Emmanuel Green	stable boy
Mary Woolley	
John Woolley	painter
James Cook (Ann)	farm labourer
William Cook	wheelwright
Alfred Powell (Eliza)	railway platelayer
William Smallwood (Mary)	farm labourer
William Butler	general labourer

Thomas Law (Ann)	railway porter
Edward Law	painter
Elizabeth Timbs	farmer, 15 acres
Margaret Timbs	
Fanny Timbs	assistant agricultural labourer
Mary Lockley	
Henry Powell (Ann)	gardener
John Bradbury	farm labourer
James Lockley (Hannah)	farm labourer
William Payne	ordnance surveyor
Maria Powell	housekeeper
Matilda Capewell	charwoman
Walter Swift	general labourer
John Wall (Elizabeth)	gardener
Hannah Wall	
Robert Williams	platelayer
William Gripton (Harriet)	woodman
James Weatherer (Fanny)	bricklayer's labourer
Thomas Belcher (Lucy)	iron worker
Robert Belcher	garden labourer
Samuel Ball (Elizabeth)	agricultural labourer
Frederick Ball	waggoner's boy
Charles Ball	agricultural labourer
James Rostance (Mary)	railway platelayer
David Barnacle (Mary)	bricklayer
John Thornton (Fanny)	ordnance surveyor
George Bradbury (Sarah)	sawyer
Sarah Bradbury	housemaid
Albert Bradbury	waggoner
William Bradbury	agricultural labourer
Charles Bradbury	apprentice painter
Samuel Meeson (Sarah)	general labourer
Samuel Adams	gate maker
Joseph Bloor (Mary)	shoemaker
Fortune Bloor	labourer
James Cecil (Ann)	carpenter

THE MARSH COMMON

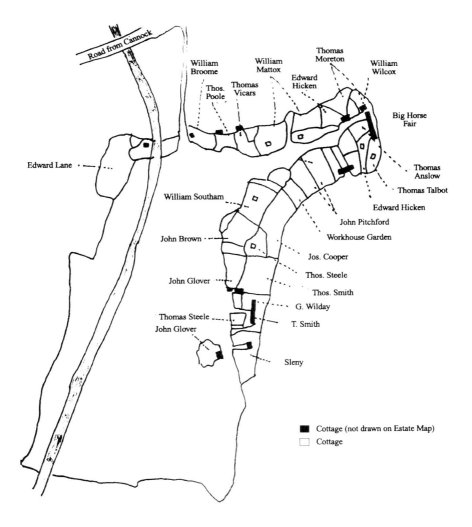

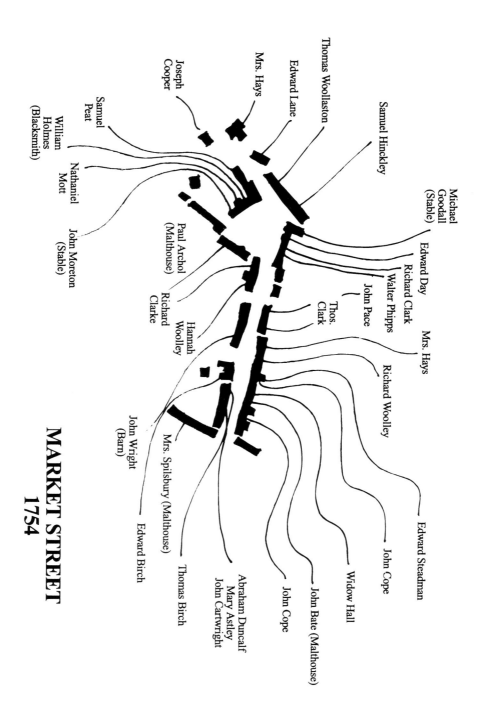

MARKET STREET
1754

Michael
Goodall
(Stable)

Edward Day
Richard Clark
Walter Phipps

John Pace

Thos.
Clark

Mrs. Hays

Richard Woolley

Edward Steadman

John Cope

Widow Hall

John Bate (Malthouse)

Abraham Duncalf
Mary Astley
John Cartwright

John Cope

Thomas Birch

Edward Birch

Mrs. Spilsbury (Malthouse)

John Wright
(Barn)

Hannah
Woolley

Richard
Clarke

Paul Archol
(Malthouse)

Samuel Hinckley

Thomas Woollaston

Edward Lane

Mrs. Hays

Joseph
Cooper

Samuel
Peat

William
Holmes
(Blacksmith)

Nathaniel
Mott

John Moreton
(Stable)

Pte. Edmund Westwood of Mill St. Bell ringer and member of church choir. South Staffs. Regiment. Killed by shell fire, October 1917.

Corporal E. Till of Cannock Rd. Tank Corps. Awarded Military Medal for bravery at Amiens. Mentioned in despatches, battle of Ypres, 1917. Brother Frank killed in 1916.

Pte. Jack Handley, Goods Station, died from gas poisoning and wounds, aged 22, 1918. Worked at Littleton Colliery.

Pte. Felix Burrows, Market Street. Died from gas poisoning, aged 21, 1918. Worked at Mr. Ives' bakery.

Pte. Arthur Plant of Mill End. Killed in action Nov. 4th, 1918, aged 21. Signals Section, South Staffs. Regiment. Worked at Siemans, Stafford.

Pte. Charles Morris. Royal Army Medical Corps. Saved lives of 7 Penkridge "pals" during gas attack. Awarded Military Medal. Penkridge United F.C. and Littleton Colliery.

The Dawson brothers of Lord's Wood, Teddesley. All killed at the Front during the War.

Mr. Joseph Brown,
tenant of Wolgarston Farm,
1914 - 1924. Died 1930, aged 75,
at Reynard Cottage.
(Staffordshire Advertiser)

Bell Brook Cottage, before the brook was culverted. *(Mrs. A. Plant)*

JOHN SPILSBURY,
LITTLETON ARMS INN,
PENKRIDGE.

1840

Neat Post Chaises.

March 19

Horses 14 Miles —	1..1.0
30. Do. 13 Miles —	.19.6
31. to Peddesley & Back	.10.6
April 1. Horses 25 Miles	1.17.6
	£ 4.8.6

Horses to Chillington & Back .18.0

£ 5.6.6

Paid,

John Spilsbury

The Star Inn when the Penkridge Co-op.
Fred and Les Plant under the gas light.   *(Mrs. A. Plant)*

Les Plant's grocery shop (now Billington's) on Crown Bridge. Before 1923.   *(Mrs. A. Plant)*

TO THE PARENTS OF CHILDREN IN THE
NATIONAL SCHOOL AT PENKRIDGE

THE Average Annual cost for the last ten years of Maintaining the Penkridge School, including Salaries, Books, School Apparatus, the Rent and Repairs of the Building, has been £150. 5s. 6d.

This charge has been provided for by

	£.	s.	D.
The Annual Amount of Benefactions constituting the Income of the old Charity School..	36	3	0
Paid by Lord Hatherton, for Salaries and various School expenses	61	0	3
By Lord Hatherton, for Rent and Repairs of Building (last year, £201. 6s. 6½d)	53	2	3
	£150	5	6

In consequence of increased attendance at the School, and the improved system of Instruction about to be introduced, which has rendered necessary an Enlargement of the Building, and the appointment of Assistant Teachers, occasioning a great increase of expense, it has been judged desirable that it should cease to be a *Charity* School: and that the Parents of all the Children (except the limited number provided for by benefactors to the original Charity School) should henceforward contribute towards the Education of their Children, by the payment of a small weekly sum.

Another circumstance which has led Lord Hatherton, the Patron of the National School, to require this payment, is the universal testimony borne throughout England to the great advantages resulting from the system of small payments for Education: the Parents of Children having been almost invariably found to value instruction, to the expense of which they have contributed, more highly than that which has been entirely gratuitous.

The Penkridge School has long been one of the very few of the same class remaining in England in which contributions by the Parents of Children have not been made.

In future, therefore, there will be three rates of payment, namely—2d. a week—4d. a week—and Six Shillings per Quarter:—all payments to be made in advance.

It will be left to the Parent of each Child to determine which payment he will adopt, reserving to the Patron and the Clergyman, (the Rev. J. Fell) the right of refusing to educate any child, who appears to them not a proper object of Charity, except at one of the higher rates of payment.

They are encouraged to take this course by the knowledge that the plan has been adopted elsewhere; and has been cordially approved and acted upon by the Parents of the Children.

In all future admissions, the Parents will have to state which rate of payment they propose to adopt.

When there shall be more than two children from one family paying either 2d. or 4d. a week only, some abatement will be made in the charge.

Some portion of the Elder Girls' time will be employed in needlework, for which they will be paid.

Although Lord Hatherton, as Trustee of the old Charity School, is only required "to provide a Master to instruct eight poor boys in reading, writing, and accounts, and to buy them each a blue bonnet"—it is his intention to admit the twelve Head Boys, and the twelve Head Girls, *entirely free*, and furnish them with Caps and Bonnets. If the Parents of any of this number signify their wish not to avail themselves of this charity for their children, others will be selected in their places

Teddesley, 11th August, 1854.

J. AND W. DREWRY, PRINTERS, EASTGATE-STREET, STAFFORD.

Penkridge schoolchildren sing for Frank James, the "Grand Old Man" of Staffordshire, on the occasion of his 100th birthday. Cuttlestone House, November 1921. *(Staffordshire Advertiser)*

The stocks in the 1920s. Maud Bennett (nee Rudge) and Mrs. B. Plant? *(Mrs. A. Plant)*

A favourite shot of Penkridge photographers. Traffic held up on the main Stafford to Wolverhampton Road for ten minutes by a single, unattended horse and cart. Stone Cross looking South, September 1921. *(Staffordshire Advertiser)*

The Albrighton Hunt meet outside the Littleton Arms, March 1922. *(Staffordshire Advertiser)*

Just part of the cast of "Sleeping Beauty", an open air performance in the Vicarage field, September 1922. *(Staffordshire Advertiser)*

Mr. Joseph Robert Burd, landlord of Boat Inn who died in 1923. A leading member of the community he served in France during World War I, was a member of the Rural District Council and the Board of Guardians and chairman of the Parish Council. Manager of the school and chairman of Penkridge United F.C.

Lord Hatherton about to lay the foundation stone of the Peace Memorial Hall, November 1926.
(Staffordshire Advertiser)

Members of PMH Committee, including the Vicar and Joseph Brown, 1926. *(Staffordshire Advertiser)*

FOX & GEORGE HOTEL AND WHITE HART HOTEL, PENKRIDGE. DATE 1926

Stone Cross, looking North, 1926.

The Plough Team of Deanery Farm, winning prize for best turnout, October 1927.
(Staffordshire Advertiser)

Members of Penkridge Fire
Brigade carry the coffin of
Col. H.M. Whitehead,
October 1935.
The six uniformed pall bearers
were Firemen Morris,
Lyons, Bennett, Lowe, Taylor
and Crutchley.
(Staffordshire Advertiser)

Col. Whitehead, 1875 - 1935.
Engineer and surveyor to Cannock RDC
for 30 years.
Chief Officer of Penkridge Fire Brigade.
(Staffordshire Advertiser)

The Reverend James Kempson leaves Penkridge after 26 ½ years as Vicar, 1937.
Left to Right (seated): Miss Manly, Canon and Mrs. Kempson, Dr. W. Nock. Standing: Messrs, F.
Jones, T.W. Robson, B.C. Robinson (schoolmaster), F.J. Rostance (Vicar's churchwarden) and
J.T. Felthouse (People's churchwarden). *(Staffordshire Advertiser)*

Early photograph of Penkridge taken from church tower. Shows narrowness of Clay Street, the open countryside beyond Mill Street, and Market Street Alms Houses top right on New Road.

Bert Plant's grocery shop (now Ron Keeling's), Market Street c. 1940.
Also Two Steps when it was a public house. *(Mrs. A. Plant)*

Members of Penkridge Cricket Club c. *1950s*. Cyril Felthouse second left and Sidney Barnes fourth left (seated)

Chapter 17

The Penkridge Fire Brigade

For many years one of the greatest sources of pride for Penkridge people was the village fire brigade. The origin of such a small village having its own brigade seems to lie in a particularly fierce battle between two shopkeepers in Market Street in the 1840s. Both Rees Jones, a grocer and draper and Francis Mason, a draper and druggist decided to expand their business as insurance agents. On February 1st 1840 the following advertisement was placed in the Advertiser,

"The Directors of the District Fire Office of Birmingham respectfully inform the nobility, gentry and inhabitants of the neighbourhood surrounding Penkridge that with the view to the immediate protection of their property in case of fire, they forwarded on Monday last, the 27th January, and permanently stationed at Penkridge, under the superintendence of their agent, Mr. Rees Jones, a powerful FIRE ENGINE
and have made such arrangements with Mr. Spilsbury of the Littleton Arms Hotel, Penkridge, as will enable the Engine at very short notice, to be in attendance at any point in the district surrounding Penkridge.

Every further information relating to fire insurance may be obtained on application to the undermentioned Agent of the company,
MR. REES JONES"

Stung into action, the rival of the District Fire Office, the Birmingham Fire Office replied with an advertisement in the very next issue of the paper, praising their own company and fiercely knocking the opposition.

"PENKRIDGE
The very flattering preference shown to the Birmingham Fire Office, and to the great Increase of Insurances lately effected for it by myself, have induced the directors to send on Saturday last, the 8th February, a very powerful, first class

NEW FIRE ENGINE

which they intend shall remain, not for a few weeks only but for a continuancy, for the protection of property without exception or distinction whatever. And I beg to inform the Nobility, Gentry, and Inhabitants in and surrounding Penkridge, that arrangements are now complete, so that the Engine can be sent to any part of the county within a circle of 6 miles at the shortest possible notice. Mr. Thomas Cope jnr. with other able and efficient engineers and firemen are now engaged to undertake its management. I trust these arrangements for the better protection of property from losses by fire, and also from loss of life itself will be duly appreciated by a discerning and liberal public, whose confidence the office I have the honour to represent has enjoyed for the last 35 years and whose exertions will still be continued for the benefit of those who insure with them.

*No charge made for policies transferred from other offices. It may be well to caution the public against the trickery of other institutions; an infant one of lowe chance is acting the fable of "the Daw with borrowed feathers", beware of such.

FRANCIS MASON, PENKRIDGE."

It is quite a common idea that insurance company fire brigades selfishly put out fires only in buildings insured by their company. This is clearly not the case, especially in such small villages as Penkridge. Neither the local drapers nor the long established Cope plumbing family would have been party to such disgraceful behaviour. The fire brigade was a symbol of goodwill and attempted to turn out at all fires speedily and efficiently and so impress possible future customers. Refusing to attend a fire would result in the most damaging publicity. As a result Penkridge benefited from having two fire brigades and two fire engines at a time when Gateshead, a town of 25,000 had no fire brigade at all and Newcastle, with a population of 100,000 had only two insurance company brigades. The two Penkridge brigades were to be put to the test before the end of the year. The Christmas Eve edition of the Staffordshire Advertiser reported that,

"On Wednesday morning last, about one o'clock, the windmill in the occupation of Mr. Philip Taylor, Penkridge, was discovered to be on fire. The two fire engines of the town, one a very powerful engine belonging to the Birmingham Fire Office, and the other to the District, were immediately on the spot but such was the state of the fire when first discovered, that no power on earth could save it."

The reporter went on to state, rather unhelpfully, that the mill and stock had been insured with the Birmingham District Office for £350 only five weeks previously but that "this amount it is said will not cover Mr. Taylor's losses." The cause of the fire was a mystery.

It seems that the Birmingham Fire Office was the better equipped brigade from the start and undoubtedly chose a fine man to be in charge of the force. Thomas Cope junior belonged to one of the oldest Penkridge families and, as a plumber, was well able to deal with the pipes, pumps and valves on a fire engine. He also had a business employing young men who could form the nucleus of the brigade.

Cope, a leading village figure and churchwarden from 1846 to 1849 and 1852 to 1856, created a tradition of service that was to benefit Penkridge for at least 70 years.

By 1848 the District Fire Office engine had been removed from Penkridge. The prediction of Francis Mason had been correct. Despite this, confusion and rivalry in the fire fighting business continued. In June 1848 Sandon Hall burned down. Fire engines from five different organisations attended the blaze. The District Fire Office engine from Stafford arrived an hour and twenty minutes after the alarm was raised. This was considered to be an incredibly short space of time. Second to arrive was the rival Birmingham Fire Office engine followed by the Town engine from Stone. Earl Talbot sent his private engine from Ingestre Hall. Lord Hatherton, who was in Stafford, commanded the Penkridge engine to attend. In the report of the fire the Advertiser confused the two rival insurance companies in Penkridge and was instantly rebuked.

"Sir,
In your paper of Saturday last you have stated that 'the engine of the District Fire Office, from Penkridge was there, under the care of Mr. Thomas Cope' : May I beg you to correct this unintentional mistake of yours as the only engine stationed at Penkridge is from the old Birmingham Fire Office, and is under the care of Mr. Thomas Cope.
    I am Sir, yours truly,
       Francis Mason."

In 1851 Margaret Dukes, a widow living in Pinfold Lane, was reduced to taking in washing to support her six children. In the 1850s this meant that she was only one step above absolute pauperism. Wisely, she apprenticed her fourteen year old son, Thomas, to Thomas Cope who was to train him to be a leading member of the church, a leader of the community and a successful businessman. By 1881 Thomas Dukes was a master plumber employing four men and three boys. His wife was sub-postmistress of Penkridge and he was to be a member of the church choir for fifty years. He followed in his master's footsteps and became Superintendent of the Fire Brigade. In turn Thomas Dukes son, Frank, became Captain of the Brigade in the years before world War One.

Despite the emergence of a trained fire brigade successful fire fighting still often depended on a great community effort. When a spark from a train set fire to a field in 1859 four fire engines attended, two from Teddesley Hall, one from Brewood and the Penkridge engine. All this effort would have been of no avail had not a large crowd of people, in Penkridge for the market, formed a "chain" to pass buckets of water from the River Penk to the engines. Lord Hatherton supervised the men, women and children while Lady Hatherton went into the town to round up more helpers. Obviously the goodwill of the community was crucial when someone suffered a fire. When his barn burned down at Wolgarston Farm in 1865 farmer Henry Wood received help from 70 villagers. He expressed his gratitude by hosting a roast beef and plum pudding supper for them all at the George and Fox.

The Penkridge Fire Brigade was a fine body of men and a source of great pride to the village. The annual dinner for the brigade held in January, a tradition begun in 1896, was always the first great event on the village's social calendar. At one of these celebrations, in 1901, Councillor Cheadle "proposed 'Success to the Fire Brigade' and said it had always been a great pleasure to do what he could for the Fire Brigade. They were a credit to the place and for a county brigade would take some beating for smartness." Neither the annual parish fete nor the celebration of great national events was complete without their presence. To celebrate the Relief of Mafeking in 1900, for example, "the members of the Penkridge Fire Brigade, in full uniform accompanied by the fire engine, paraded the village and then proceeded to Rodbaston."

It was very difficult, however, for a village as small as Penkridge to provide their men with the equipment that they deserved. In 1891 there was a fire at Mr. Cox's grocery and drapery shop in Manchester House. Penkridge's manual engine was used to keep the fire in check while the steam engine came from Stafford. It was reported that "the work of the Penkridge fire engine was sadly hampered by a lack of hose". The council did not supply the fire station in Crown Bridge Street with an alarm bell until 1898. Captain Dukes was not afraid to make the point in 1901 when he replied to Councillor Cheadle at the dinner at the White Hart, saying that "if the brigade could only get up to date appliances they would not fear to compete with other teams that had won honours. They had been in two competitions and though they had not won anything, through want of appliances to drill with, they had not disgraced themselves against some of the best teams in the Midlands."

Penkridge's fire engine was owned by an insurance company as late as 1894. Insurance companies were becoming increasingly reluctant to subsidise these expensive services, however, and after Penkridge Parish Council was formed, in 1894, the Lancashire Fire Insurance Company had a responsible local body to whom to hand over their manual fire engine. Despite local pride in the force, commercial ownership of the brigade had not been very successful. The fire engine was in a poor state and the council called a public meeting in October 1895 to see if the ratepayers would support paying the cost of repairs. The meeting, at the school, was strongly in favour of maintaining the brigade and a volunteer force was formed immediately with Frank Dukes acting as captain. It was soon realised that the old machine would never be good enough and in 1896 a new one was bought together with an extra 500 feet of hose. To celebrate this purchase the first of many Fire Brigade suppers was held at the White Hart in August 1896. To pay for the improvements a scale of charges for the use of the fire engine was introduced, £3 within the rateable area of the parish and £5 outside with "the usual extras for horse hire".

The old fire engine was treated with affection by the people of Penkridge but, dating back to the early years of the reign of Queen Victoria, it was hardly up to the job and the council sold it off. The engine was already virtually a museum piece. In 1897 the vicar took the choir, including perhaps old Mr. Dukes, on a visit to London. In the parish magazine he reported that,

"We had just got to the pay gates at the entrance to the Crystal Palace from the underground railway, when the first thing that met our eyes the other side of the barrier was the old Penkridge Fire Engine which the parish council sold for £5 - the same engine, only very skilfully there had been painted on it to match the name, 1837 - cleverly done - but, of course, we recognised the 'Grand'."

The Parish Council formed the "Joint Fire Extinction Committee" with the brigade but could only find small amounts of money to fund the service.In 1900 they set a rate of ½d for the fire brigade whilst ordering a 1½d precept for the celebrations for the Coronation of Edward VII in 1902. Spending on the brigade was infrequent and small scale. In June 1901 the council allowed them a "special appliance for adjusting the hose" at a cost of £5, and in 1903 they were allowed to buy two new lengths of hose. It is little wonder that concerned individuals, worrying that the men might become disillusioned and give up, made gestures of support. In 1901, Herbert Whitehead, later Chief Officer of the Brigade said "that on several occasions he had seen the smart work that the brigade had done and thought that such a class of men were worth keeping together and he made the offer (of a silver medal) in the hope others would do likewise."

Perhaps the reality of the situation was that in a dispersed rural community like Penkridge and its surrounds there was little that a fire brigade, however efficient, could usefully do. The men would be scattered at their work or at home, there were very few telephones, no water mains to tap into and only horse power to pull the engine. Very few "call outs" are reported in the paper. The one described on December 13th 1902 seems to have been judged to be a great success.

"About 5.30 on Monday evening the Penkridge Fire Brigade received a call to a fire at the Hartley Arms, Wheaton Aston and in less than half an hour the brigade turned out under the command of Lieut. Pearson. They found a large rick of straw well alight. Fortunately a good supply of water was obtained from the canal and the brigade succeeded in preventing the fire from spreading to the adjacent ricks and farm buildings."

In 1905 the council considered the possibility of getting a steam engine to replace the manual one but took no action. Apart from the cost, a disadvantage of a steam fire engine was its weight. A "steamer" could require up to four good horses to pull it. This was a problem for Penkridge since it relied on two horses belonging to Cannock RDC which were used for drawing stones for road repairs.

At the end of 1910 Penkridge at last acquired a steam engine just in time for one of their busiest summers ever. During the last weekend of August 1911 the brigade attended five calls in 48 hours. The Staffordshire Advertiser reported,

"A Series of Fires.

During the weekend the Penkridge Fire Brigade had a very busy time. On the 27th 3 trucks of straw caught fire at the Goods Station and the brigade were promptly on the scene. The outbreak was caused by a spark from a passing engine. About 1.30 on the 28th a field of barley belonging to Mr. Warrington at Dunston was found to be on fire and the brigade turned out with the steamer and manual and a good supply of water being available the outbreak was overcome.

On Saturday about 10.15 an extensive field of barley belonging to Mrs. Ward of Rodbaston was ignited and the brigade, with a willing band of helpers succeeded in subduing the fire and returned to the fire station at 12 o'clock but about 1.15 the field was again set on fire by a spark from a passing engine and the brigade once more turned out. The steamer worked splendidly during this severe test. There was yet another call to a field of wheat belonging to Mr. Dukes (capt. of the brigade) and the manual fire engine was dispatched to attend this."

Despite these successes and the purchase of a "steamer", Penkridge was being left behind as the technology of fire fighting improved. In January 1913 Stafford Corporation bought a new Leyland motor fire engine. It weighed four tons, had six jets, could pump 600 gallons a minute and sped to fires at 50 mph. In 1913 the Penkridge brigade was still using the manual engine for some fires. They were still getting their uniforms from the local draper, Mr. Bellamy. It was, nevertheless, a very experienced force. In 1913 long service awards were given to Captain Dukes, Superintendent Pearson, Third Officer Lees and Firemen Plant, Webb and Morris for up to 15 years service.

In 1920 the truly glamorous days of Penkridge Fire Brigade were ended. Cannock RDC bought three two ton petrol lorries. The light draught horses that had been used to pull the engine were sold off. Henceforth Penkridge's fire engine would be ignominiously towed by a lorry. In 1927 Cannock RDC borrowed £850 so they could buy a 250 gallon motor trailer pump and a motor fire tender with an extension ladder. By 1932 the Penkridge brigade was fully absorbed into the District Fire Brigade run by Cannock RDC. Colonel Whitehead continued to act as chief officer of the brigade until 1935 when he died of a heart attack while attending a car that had burst into flames on the Stafford Road, near Huntington. He was 60 years old and had nearly finished building his new house in Francis Green Lane. At the funeral six uniformed members of the Penkridge brigade, firemen Morris, Lyons, Bennett, Lowe, Taylor and Crutchley carried his coffin upon which rested his helmet and axe. His coffin was followed by 146 mourners including 40 other uniformed firemen.

Chapter 18

Yeoman Farmers

John Goodwin was tenant of Otherton and Mansty Farms in the 1860s and 1870s. With his wife and three children, Joe, Julia and Lucy, he played a vital role in the life of the village. The prosperity of Penkridge depended upon the success of yeoman farmers like John Goodwin. The farmers had to have the intelligence and energy to carry out the agricultural reforms demanded on the Hatherton estate. They needed to farm efficiently and profitably so as to employ and pay the largest section of the village community, the farm labourers. They were the biggest customers for the tradesmen and craftsmen of Penkridge: the saddlers, blacksmiths, painters, plumbers and seed merchants. As well as their economic importance the yeoman families provided the moral backbone or rural life in the mid-nineteenth century. They set, or attempted to set, those standards expected in Victorian England in those areas where the church, the schools and the squire found it difficult to work.

The diaries of Mrs. Goodwin for the years 1866 and 1867 paint a picture of constant hard work. On the land itself the winter was a relatively quiet time when the country pursuits of rabbiting and hare coursing could be followed. Animal husbandry was an all year process, however, and particularly vital in the spring since the first great animal sale of the year was in March and had to raise the £500 necessary to pay debts and the rent. In 1866 John Goodwin had a "tolerable good" sale at Penkridge and received a £500 cheque from the Penkridge auctioneer, Mr. Sollom. Almost immediately the money began to circulate in the local economy. Mrs. Goodwin recorded that,

> April 5th: Rather stormy, windy and very cold. John goes to Stafford to get the cheque cashed. Went to Yew Tree to pay Mr. Keeling about the £100 for manure.
> April 6th: A windy, cold day. John goes to Wheaton Aston to settle with Mr. Shimelt about the £80 we owe him. Joe Adderly and Joe Windows go to Wyrley, they pay the saddler Dyke at Cannock £6..10s..6d and call for Messrs. Hall and Jager's account. I iron. The two Joes make a mistake and

get rather tipsy at Wyrley, are very cold so get some whiskey and water and it overcomes them so that they are sick, sleepy and almost unconscious for some hours.

During the cold spring John Goodwin took the opportunity to get on with threshing. The farm did not employ men unnecessarily during the winter so contracted men and their machine to do the work. This could be risky since threshing could not continue if it started to rain. Milking continued during the year and by early May there was enough surplus milk for Mrs. Goodwin to start butter making. On May 17th she churned her first batch of 17lbs. The welfare of the cattle was a continual worry, especially in 1866 when foot and mouth disease was present in the area. On Sunday, March 7th, 1866 a collection was taken in Penkridge Church, "the money given to sufferers from the plague". Two weeks later the Goodwins had a scare.

March 20th: A stirk at Otherton dies from eating Barley and another ill, puts John about very much just now before the sale.
March 21st: Joe Windows goes to Stafford to get Mr. Carless to come to look at the stirks to see that it is not the plague. He sends some medicine and says he will come in the morning.
March 22nd: John goes down after breakfast to meet Mr. Carless, he says the second stirk will get well again. The maids take a walk to Penkridge.

On the first dry days of spring, preparations for the coming growing season were started. On April 23rd the scrub on the common was burned. On May 10th the farm took delivery of 12,000 cabbage plants from Uttoxeter. Farming practices were changing, and in early summer Mrs. Goodwin noted,

June 2nd: Mr. Wootton and Mr. Bradney come to the common to see if Lord Hatherton's cultivator can work the common. Lord Hatherton came to John up there yesterday and said he should have it if it could work there.
June 4th: Lord Hatherton sends the steamer to work the common, our men up there as well.
June 12th: Lord Hatherton's scuffle on the common at work all this week and nine of our men draining it.

By July a very good, hot summer for Penkridge was well under way. The next great tasks for the farm were the hay harvest and the sowing of turnips. At crucial times like hay-making friends, neighbours and servants were expected to lend a hand. Mrs. Goodwin described the scene.

July 4th: Showery and cool. Thomas's team here yesterday and today helping to get the large field ready for turnips. Mr. Barnes' team also helping. John poorly. Mr. Barnes had tea with us. Says that the Middletons have got the cattle plague.
July 9th: Very busy with clover and turnip field.

136

July 10th: Very hot again, busy carrying the clover, also sowing turnips etc. The maids go in the hay field and help.
July 14th: Very hot again, very busy with hay at both places. Young Smith of Whiston murdered by a poacher.

The hay harvest was completed in a week. The farm then turned to the harvesting of rye, oats and barley. The tradition of supplying workers drink for their long, hot days in the field was so strong that it survived even the 1887 Truck Act which made it illegal for employers to pay their workers in any form of alcohol, but the practice was not without its drawbacks. On September 13th Mrs. Goodwin wrote in her diary,

Very busy carrying, the gardeners here helping. I fill the bottles of beer for the men, some of them tipsy. Makes John very cross.
The maids go out after dinner.

In the following year the diary records,

Sept 9th: A lovely day. Carrying at both farms by day and by moon-light. I think it must be the Harvest Moon. J. Allsop tipsy, fell and hurt his eye.

The end of the harvest was a relief to all concerned. A successful harvest secured the future wages of the labourers. At Penkridge the tradition of singing "Harvest Home" at the end of the last day was observed. On September 18th 1867 Mrs. Goodwin wrote, "A fine cool day. We finish corn harvest. The men shout well over the finishing bottle".

Another tradition that was viewed with mixed feelings was the Harvest Supper. The ancient celebration of safely getting the harvest in had in many eyes become associated with general disorder and the custom of "largesse" whereby farm workers went from house to house after the supper begging from the friends and connections of their employer. The Goodwins did not attend a Harvest Supper every year but on August 22nd 1867 Mrs. Goodwin reported,

A fine day and moonlit night. Carrying at Otherton. The men, women and children assemble to supper in the Granary to the number of about 70 and about 18 Irishmen. It passed off very well. We all went down, returned about 1 o'clock. No one broke into our house in our absence.

It was at the end of August that some of the Irish workers began to return home, to their own smallholdings. Others stayed on until December. Several different sources indicate that they were highly thought of in Penkridge and regarded with genuine affection. In 1866 the diary records,

December 8th: John goes to Stafford. He settles with the Irishmen, they are going back to Ireland.

Dec. 9th: One of the best calves was dead at Otherton this morning. John, Joe and myself went to bid the Irishmen good-bye.
Dec. 10th: A fine day. A cow John bought off Thos. Shemilt for £10 was dead this morning. The Irishmen went early this morning and are on the sea now, if all be well.

In April 1867 Mrs. Goodwin wrote, "Go to see Patrick at the Irishmen's house. They take the badly Irishman into the house at Otherton till he is better." In September she recorded, "We bid Murphy good-bye. Give him a pair of trousers and some ale and two that go with him".

After the harvest, work in the fields declined. Some of the men were involved in threshing but they were not really busy until lambing started in the following spring. At Christmas the farm workers got their Christmas Ale from Mrs. Goodwin and had a holiday. The farm at Otherton received many visitors including the village's choir, drum and fife band and the bell ringers. The postman, the beadle and others also called for their Christmas boxes. The male members of the family would go to the great coursing meeting and lunch at the Old Hall at Pillaton on Boxing Day.

A more detailed account of the sort of work done by labourers during the 1860s can be found in the account book of the Deanery Farm. The regular, full time workers on Deanery Farm were, at various times Fred and John Wincer, Samuel Till, Ben Lowe and James Taylor. Most regular workers earned 2s..2d a day in the 1860s. Lads earned 6d a day and women 10d a day. Other workers were brought in for particular jobs. In May 1861 the Deanery employed William Richards for ridging, John Adison as shepherd, Joseph Horton for subsoiling, J. Parkes for thatching and riddling guano. Two women were taken on to pick squitch from the fields. J. Baker, James Adams and J. Warrender were sowing manure and clover. Like Otherton Farm the Deanery employed twelve Irishmen during the summer. Two jobs that needed to be done all year were picking stones and squitch grass from the fields. Stone picking was piece work. It paid 1 shilling a load and the work was probably done by the farm's employees at the end of their regular day's work.

Although many Penkridge farms were kept going with temporary, part time seasonal and piece workers, the traditional farm labourer, the old retainer working on the same farm for years, also existed and was treated with a certain respect. The Bagnall family was one of the oldest in Penkridge. They could trace their ancestors in the parish register back to the seventeenth century. Randle Bagnall was born in 1805, the year of Trafalgar. In 1841 he was living on the Cannock Road and working as an agricultural labourer. He had relatives living on Clay Street, High Street, the Cannock Road and the Great Marsh. Towards the end of his life he lived with his sister, Sarah, at Mill End. When they died, on the same day in January 1891, they were accorded an obituary in the Advertiser, an unusual honour for a woodcutter and a servant. The description of this industrious working class family provides a contrast to the contemporary complaints about feckless servants and drunken labourers. The paper reported that,

> Sarah Bagnall was one of the most regular attendants at all church services; even on the last Sunday of the old year she, in spite of the inclement weather and the dangerous state of the roads, was at the night service. Randle worked on the Teddesley estate nearly the whole of his life as a woodcutter. His last spell was 45 years without a break. Those who have travelled from Bednall Head to Huntington will have noticed the woods and what is called The Belt, and also that picturesque part around Pottal Pool like a miniature Wales; all these he is understood to have planted. He attended work most regularly all weathers to some eight years ago. He was as honest in his time at work as he was in his payments - a property, I am afraid few men now possess. He was an early riser, usually to be heard about by 4 o'clock in the morning, and after his long weary day's work he cultivated his large plot of land. I may add that Lord Hatherton allowed Randle a pension from the time he ceased work up to the last.

Life in the farm house, under the supervision of Mrs. Goodwin remained busy throughout the year. The regular work included brewing beer from the barley, using up to twenty bushels at a time, churning butter, looking after the chickens and the ducks, cleaning the house, and making some of the family's clothes. Mrs. Goodwin not only starched and ironed the linen but made her own starch to begin with. During the early part of the year, pig killing created much work for the household. Once Thomas Lowe had dispatched the animals Mrs. Goodwin had them cut up, cooked "pig puddings", salted the bacon, made the lard and hung the flitches of bacon and ham in the dairy. She made the bags in which the hams hung and regularly washed and replaced them. The diary entries for one week in February 1867 reflect the amount of work involved.

> Feb. 5th: Showery. Kill two pigs, one for Mrs. Lister.
> Feb. 6th: Busy. Have pigs cut up, salt bacon, cut lard and pork for pies.
> Feb. 7th: A fine day, bake bread, then an oven full of pies.
> Feb. 8th: Very windy and a little showery. Roast a fowl and a piece of spare rib, mashed potatoes for supper. I send Mrs. Barnes three pork pies and a piece of spare rib, Mr. Fell a hare and a couple of rabbits.
> We must send him a brace of pheasants some time. He was very good signing certificates of our sale.
> Feb. 11th: Busy. Prepare for washing, turn the bacon. Some people coursing here.

Mrs. Goodwin had two maids to help with her work. Tabetha Powell and Ann Keeling. About sixty girls in Penkridge worked as domestic servants. The nineteenth century mistress-servant relationship was a very difficult one. Very young girls from the village were isolated in their employer's house. Losing their job could be an economic disaster for their family. They would find it very difficult to get another position if their employer did not give them a reference or "character". Their masters and mistresses took it upon themselves to be their educators and moral guardians. Mrs. Goodwin did her best to look after the moral welfare of her servants. Every Sunday she read with them from improving books like Wesley's Journals. She made sure that they had the time off to go to church to prepare for their confirmation. Nevertheless Mrs. Goodwin was to have a good deal of trouble with the servants at both of the farms.

The trouble began with a few small incidents in 1866:

> August 9th: Tabetha irons. Breaks a pane in the kitchen while I am away.
> Aug. 10th: Charlotte leaves Otherton, is very naughty.
> Aug. 11th: Charlotte's mother brings her back to Otherton.
> Sept. 1st: Showery. Ann lets Rover in the Dairy and he eats 5¼lb out of a leg of mutton.

On October 28th events took a more serious turn. Mrs. Goodwin's diary reveals a tense and rather unhappy household.

> I perceive that the maids have been up to mischief while I was away, making strawberry preserve pastys. Tabetha had stole my preserves twice they acknowledged but I expect more times. I threatened to send for a policeman if they did not confess.

This crisis blew over but the end of the year was a bad time to misbehave since a servants "contract" came to an end on Boxing Day and both sides could decide whether they wanted it to continue. John Goodwin asked the maids whether they wanted to stay and they replied that they did. The servants had little time off. Their Christmas holiday began on December 26th and ended on January 2nd. They were allowed home on Penkridge Wakes Sunday and on special occasions such as to see a "wild beast show" at Penkridge. Servants could also have permission to visit relatives. It was the abuse of this "privilege" that caused the next row.

> February 17th: We go to church. After dinner at Otherton we came up to Mansty. The girls behaved shamefully. Ann asked to go with her mother on a visit to her aunt at Preston. She went to Leeses at Huntington instead, told that falsehood to Tabetha knowing I had allowed her to go out. Went to Cannock and staid till after 10 o'clock leaving the dinner things about. I gave them both notice.

Both Ann's and Tabetha's mothers came to sort out the problem. Mrs. Goodwin told them that she did not wish either of them to leave, "but stay and be good". At the end of the year Mrs. Keeling came to take Ann Keeling away but Mrs. Powell negotiated a new contract for her daughter who was "to have £6 to £10 a year, a little more if good". Mrs. Goodwin did not have much success with Ann's replacement, Mary Owen. In October 1868 she noted in her diary,

> I think Mary Owen is in the family way. She is very self willed and queer.
> Blacksmith, gardener and wheelwright here, a drunken trio.

At the end of 1868 Mary was let go, apparently without a "character". Tabetha decided to look for work in Wolverhampton.

The life of female servants in nineteenth century Penkridge could be precarious and lonely. They had little job security with their "contract" ending every year just after Christmas. Their lives were ruled by their employer and their own family. When Sarah Ann Bennett sued her employer, Mrs. Foxall, for the balance of her wages in 1881, it became clear in court that she did not know how much she was being paid as her mother had made the hiring for her and was receiving the wages. The vicar felt that the servants made up an "unseen" class of people, cut off from the rest of respectable society. In 1895 he appealed for more contact.

> "I very much wish that more servants would come to the class on Sunday afternoons at 4 o'clock. It only lasts half an hour; and may I draw attention to what I have often spoken of before. It is one of the only opportunities I have of getting to know those whose work lies in private houses."

The status and working conditions of servants improved if their employer was higher up the social scale. Lady Shakerley of Haling Grove could be very particular when hiring servants and demanded a peculiar mixture of sacred and profane qualities when advertising in 1887.

> Wanted, a thorough House - Parlour Maid, tall and good appearance;
> must understand waiting, plate and lamp cleaning; age, about 30;
> Church of England.

The Goodwins attended Penkridge Church or the Wesleyan Chapel at Cannock every Sunday. Religion was a very important part of their lives. Mrs. Goodwin noted down the theme of the sermons that she heard and often gave a critique of the preacher's performance. In March 1866 she wrote that, "Mr. Fell preached from these words, 'Blessed is the womb that bare thee and the paps that thou hast sucked'." In July she met a new preacher. "I don't know if he is come to stay or on trial," she wrote. "A fresh one last Sunday as well, with a great beard and we did not like him nearly as well". Going to church was also the social highlight of the week. It was the chance to meet and shake hands with Lord and Lady Hatherton and wear one's finest clothes. Mrs. Goodwin, a serious church goer, would stay at home if her best bonnet was still at the milliners. A family wedding at Penkridge Church was the opportunity for a great display. When Lucy Goodwin married in December 1867 the family arrived in three carriages with postillions dressed in scarlet and two groomsmen in black coats.

The Goodwins were aware of their responsibility to look after the poor.

Begging was common. If a local family was involved, the requests for charity were often granted. In August 1866 Mrs. Goodwin wrote, "Mrs. Smith calls begging. I have no silver. Gave her some ale and bread and butter". The Otherton farm was close to the cottages of the poorest people of Penkridge, living on Boscomoor. John Goodwin would visit the poor people and often accompanied clergymen on their missions of charity. He did his best to keep his neighbours out of the workhouse. In January 1870 Mrs. Goodwin wrote,

> Mr. Fell calls this afternoon. John rode with him to Boscomoor. Had been to Biddles Bank to take a recommendation for Elizabeth Stokes to remain in the infirmary.

Mrs. Goodwin recorded many events that disturbed the slow, seasonal turn of the farming year. In the seven years between 1866 and 1873 she noted two local murders and the suicide of old Mrs. Dukes who drowned herself in her own soft water tub. The farm was hit by two foot and mouth epidemics. She describes the great storm of June 1872 which caught John and Joe at the cattle auction and tells how she went to Wolverhampton in 1866 to see Queen Victoria unveil the statue of Prince Albert. Her main concern was her family. Her niece, Bella Shipley, who married Edward Chell who farmed at Pillaton, was the grandmother of Cyril Felthouse whose recollections are recorded in a later chapter.

Chapter 19

Diphtheria and Drains
Penkridge in the 1870s

Despite the scare of 1832 Penkridge survived the great cholera epidemics of the mid-nineteenth century unscathed. Fear of cholera, which struck England in 1832, 1854, 1866 and 1871, brought about the great Public Health Movement which attempted to clean up the filthy cities of the Industrial Revolution. Important laws were passed to achieve this end like the first Public Health Act of 1848, the Sanitary Act of 1866 and the 1875 Public Health Act. The results of this legislation were often disappointing. It took many years for the death rate from epidemic and endemic disease to fall in the cities. Even where the reforms were most needed, apathy and even direct opposition held up progress. It is not surprising that a small rural village like Penkridge became utterly complacent. Spending on public health had been avoided and by the 1870s the people of Penkridge were due for a great shock.

Why should the rate payers of Penkridge spend money on improving public health? The village, after all, had a reputation in the county for its salubriousness. Sir Edwin Chadwick himself, the founder and greatest leader of the Public Health Movement, had chosen healthy Penkridge to provide the contrast with disease ridden Wolverhampton in his 1842 Report on the "Sanitary Conditions of the Labouring Population". He discovered that a baby born in Penkridge would, on average, live for 12 years and 10 months longer than a baby born in Wolverhampton. An adult in Penkridge, over the age of twenty, could expect to live 4 years and 2 months longer than a citizen of Wolverhampton.

On the surface it seemed that Penkridge had very little to worry about. The 1871 census showed that the village with a population of 2,435 had lost 200 inhabitants since 1851. The real public health problems should come in places like Cannock where the population had trebled to 6,650 during the same period. Penkridge seemed a very attractive place in the 1870s. The first impression many visitors received of the village was of the railway station. A traveller in 1877 claimed that,

"The station at Penkridge presents a marked contrast to the dreary appearance of most others and may claim the distinction of being the prettiest rural station in Staffordshire. On either side of the railway, bordering the platform are rows of the mountain ash, and at the present season of the year when the fruit of this, one of the prettiest trees of the wood has attained to ripeness, the effect produced by the masses of red berries is so beautiful."

Penkridge had a reputation for clean water and good fishing. When the Chief Constable wanted to raid the pubs of the village in a crack down on illegal gambling in 1874, he disguised his policemen as visiting fishermen to avoid suspicion. Local people felt privileged to live there. Old Thomas Croyden of Market Street told of how, less than 60 feet from his garden fence, he could catch good trout in the brook which had the reputation of being "one of the finest trout streams in this part of the county." The water for the village came from wells and it was usually cool and bright and good to drink.

Despite appearances things were going badly wrong in Penkridge. In July 1875 the village suffered two weeks of heavy rain followed by a great storm. The description of the resulting floods, in the Staffordshire Advertiser, hinted at a poor state of public cleanliness.

"Towards nine o'clock not only the Penk but the Boscomoor and Mansty brooks, which enter the town from the south west began perceptibly to rise and a good deal of alarm was manifested by the inhabitants whose dwellings adjoin the river or the two brook courses.

So rapid was the rising of these streams, flooding cellars and the lower rooms of houses that the gravest apprehensions were entertained and as the night advanced the inmates of piggeries and cowsheds adjoining the river were driven for safety to high parts of the town and house furniture and other valuables were removed to the upper chambers.

A great volume of water swept over the meadows through which the Boscomoor brook winds its way, the arch at the Crown Bridge being insufficient to carry it away, and two old thatched cottages along side the bridge narrowly escaped destruction, the water forcing its way through the lower rooms in a stream 2 or 3 feet deep. The stream also inundated the lower rooms of the Horse and Jockey Inn, the shops of Mr. Laurence, chemist, Mr. Pearson, saddler, Mr. Evans, butcher, and Mr. Green, grocer; while the flooding of cellars in that part of town was almost general. The Mansty Brook which flows through the grounds of Haling Grove (Mr. Haden Corser) and Wyre Hall (Mr.Wm. Cox) assumed large proportions."

The people of Penkridge were living in a low lying and badly drained area, cheek by jowl with their pigs and cattle. The village was, in fact, a dirty place and a public health disaster was just around the corner to knock the ratepayers out of their complacency.

In February 1876 Dr. Boldero was called to a house on the Marsh. For the first time in Penkridge he came face to face with a case of diphtheria. It was the start of an epidemic that was to cause several deaths, decline and then reappear in June. The doctor reported that the necessary steps were being taken to stop the spread of the disease but diphtheria was too serious for the parish vestry to deal with on their own.Thirty years of public health legislation had left a confusing picture of vague responsibilities and overlapping powers. The problem of diphtheria in Penkridge was considered by the Vestry, the Poor Law Guardians, the Cannock Rural Sanitary Authority and the Local Government Board in London. Most of the vigour and pressure for action and reform came from the Medical Officer of Health of the Rural Sanitary Authority supported by the Local Government Board. A LGB doctor was sent for and he conducted a searching inquiry into the health of the village.

The report of Dr. Airey was a damning document. He noted that the diphtheria outbreak had shocked people because it was a new disease in what had been considered a healthy area. When he had analysed the statistics, however, he found that the people of Penkridge had no right to be surprised. Penkridge had been suffering constantly from epidemic and infectious diseases and had managed to ignore the situation. Even before he tackled the question of the diphtheria outbreak he stated that,

"The deaths from zymotic (infectious) disease during the 6 years showed an average rate of 3 per annum for every thousand persons living. The diarrhoea death rate alone (confined almost entirely to children) furnished an average of more than one per thousand living, which exceeded that for the country at large, and pointed to something decidedly unwholesome in the condition of infantile life in Penkridge."

Dr. Airey reported that the first case of diphtheria had struck one of the poorest families of the town, who occupied "a ruinous house in the Marsh", but despite "the unwholesome condition of their dwelling" he doubted whether the disease had started there. A study of the first cases pointed to the school as being the centre of the infection. When he visited the National Schools in Market Square he found that the sanitary arrangements were "defective". Once a disease had broken out in the village the poor people were at risk. He found that the houses of the poor were "generally deficient in ventilation and protection against damp is not sufficiently thought of ".

The doctor's harshest words were reserved for the town's water supply. Dealing a savage blow to the village's reputation for "salubrity" he reported that,

"The water of the town, which is obtained from wells, is naturally soft and wholesome, but from the position of the wells in relation to the privies it is impossible to doubt that much of the water is contaminated. The privy accommodation and the drainage are also defective. The large brook which runs through the town is in itself an open sewer, and its bed is choked with accumulated refuse of all kinds in various stages of decay. A smaller brook is also in a foul condition and nuisances from pigsties are a frequent occurrence in the town."

The Local Government Board report ended with a list of expensive recommendations. Penkridge should either get a completely new and purer supply of water or take steps to guard the existing supply from all risks of impurity by adopting "some form of closet in which dry earth or ashes would be used as a deodorizer". This would stop liquid waste leaking into the water supply. The old drains had to be repaired and new drains had to be laid so that the waste of the village passed into the main sewer and not into the two brooks. The beds of the brooks had to be thoroughly cleaned and then kept clean. The village also ought to provide some sort of fever hospital so that cases of infectious disease could be isolated.

The Poor Law Guardians discussed the report. Being representatives of the main ratepayers, the Guardians' first step was to take action that was cheap and easy. They instructed the Inspector of Nuisances to visit the houses in Penkridge and force the owners or occupiers to clean up their nuisances, such as piles of pig manure. He also was given the unpleasant task of inspecting all the cess pits and privies and reporting those that were leaking into the brooks and water supply. Perhaps hoping for a more favourable report, they also commissioned a new investigation into the village's water supply.

Such tentative action was not good enough for the Medical Officer of Health, Dr. M'Culley. He felt that all the obvious and easy action had already been taken and yet he was still reporting fresh cases of diphtheria and deaths. He asked the Guardians and the Sanitary Authority to give prompt and serious consideration to Dr. Airey's recommendations and warned them that "it is just possible that all minor efforts may be of no avail in stamping out the epidemic."

The analyst, Dr. Hill Hassell, took samples from three wells in different parts of the village and he reported to the Rural Sanitary Authority at the end of November. His findings were more specific and even more shocking than those of Dr. Airey. The first well he examined belonged to a house next to the bank on the corner of Bellbrook and the Cannock Road. He found that the water contained "73.64 parts solids in 100,000, to be very highly contaminated with surface water or sewage, to be quite unfit for drinking and of the most dangerous character."

A second sample was taken from a well in Clay Street which was considered to be the best part of the village. This water "contained 86.48 parts solid per 100,000, besides decaying vegetable matter, not necessarily dangerous to health in its present condition but of so doubtful a character that its use should be discontinued."

The third sample was expected to be the worst since it was taken from a well near the river in the lowest part of the village and was likely to be polluted by surface and sub-soil water. Even so the leaders of Penkridge society could hardly have been prepared for the severe comments of the analyst. He found that the water had "102.16 parts solid per 100,000, to contain decaying vegetable matter, to be contaminated to a very great extent with sewage or surface matter, and must be considered as a liquid poison, the use of which for drinking purposes could not be fast enough abandoned."

The doctor concluded by saying that "these waters are all of a very bad quality - no better than slightly diluted sewage. Sewage in fact, may be purer than these so-called waters. A better supply must needs be obtained, difficult though it may be to get it." Such uncompromising words, coming more than three months after the first Local Government Board investigation should have led to immediate and dramatic action. Penkridge had been told in the clearest possible terms that its wells were deadly and that a piped water supply pumped from a local reservoir was the only answer. A solution to the problem was at hand since the South Staffordshire Water Company could have supplied pure water from its Huntington reservoir.

Instead of taking action Penkridge set up another committee, consisting of Lord Hatherton, Keeling, Aston, Rogers, Foden, Cox, Jeavons, Henry Anderson, R. and T. Croydon, C.D. Day, Richard Doughty and H. Robson. The committee met twice and then decided that things could not be as bad as Dr. Hill Hassell had said and that they might get a more favourable report from the Wolverhampton Borough Analyst. Whilst more wells were being tested they would dig up the main sewer in Market Street and make repairs. The Inspector of Nuisances would once again check leaking privies, especially those near to wells.

The Parochial Sanitary Committee met again at the end of December, ten months after the first outbreak of diphtheria. This time Mr. Lister read out the results of the analysis. He said that the only good water came from a well by the police station. A well in Clay Street was of "questionable wholesomeness" and contained excessive amounts of nitrates and chlorides which were "very unfavourable and suspicious features". A well near Mr. Doughty's was "better avoided for drinking" and wells near the Tanyard and Bull Bridge "gave unmistakeable evidence of sewage or animal pollution to such an extent as to render it totally unfit for drinking, and probably highly dangerous".

The situation called for a complete overhaul of Penkridge's water and sanitary system. The village needed piped water, a reservoir, proper closets and drains. Penkridge mill needed to be converted to steam power so that the mill weir could be lowered thus improving the drainage and therefore the sanitation of the area. Instead, the Parochial Sanitary Committee embarked on a desultory and piecemeal campaign of action. Very slowly a few drains and privies were moved and a few wells were drained, examined and cleaned.

The lack of significant action through most of 1878 was typical of many rural communities in Staffordshire. Such apathy provoked an angry editorial in the Staffordshire Advertiser which could have been aimed directly at Penkridge.

"The water supply in country places has been wholly uncared for as a rule, both owners and tenants paying little attention to the state of the water itself or of its surroundings. As often as not the country cottager's well is within a few feet of his pigsty, and the close proximity of a privy or two, to say nothing of slop drainage and other usual uncleanness is to him a matter of indifference. The unfortunate results are generally confined to his children and occasionally include his wife, he himself but being rarely affected. Perhaps this may be accounted for in some measure by his greater strength and matured health, but no doubt his very slight acquaintance with the raw material has something to do with his exemption from the effects of drinking bad water.

From time to time on the appearance of the epidemic which such a state of things usually entails, the local authorities have been led to inquire into the degree of unwholesomeness...; but owing to the uncertainty of the powers of the Rural Sanitary Authorities, or to the laxity which is characteristic of rural representatives in such matters generally, the whole question has rarely advanced beyond an "inquiry" by an official of the Local Government Board, followed by suggestions by that Board, which, on account of the heavy expenses they would involve were they adopted, are disregarded.

We could mention more than one instance in this neighbourhood which would bear us out in the foregoing statements."

By the end of 1878 Penkridge was still going through the motions of discovering how foul its wells were. This time the work was entrusted to the village plumber and leader of the fire brigade, Mr. Dukes. Unfortunately for the Parochial Sanitary Committee every report they received seemed to be worse than the one before. Mr. Dukes told them,

"I have completed the work recommended by the Parochial Sanitary Committee. The depth of the well at Tanyard Cottage was only 9 feet: with difficulty, it being in moving sand, by means of barrel kerbs I sank it 4 ft 6 ins deeper, puddled it with clay from bottom, and secured it from surface water. The well in this case was not dirty but the earth excavated from around was most offensive, not unlikely caused by the tanpits not having been cleaned before filling up, as cows horns, legs, bones etc were found, also much sewage matter.

The well in Clay Street was in a most filthy state; sewage evidently found its way through the soil, and a drain ran directly over and leaked into it. The well is 21 feet deep, but by means of boring into the rock 14 feet below the bottom a copious spring of clear water was obtained. It was then bricked and puddled from bottom and well secured at top."

The report was approved and the committee, hoping against hope, decided to have the water analysed again, after time had elapsed, to test the efficiency of Mr. Dukes' repairs. The Medical Officer of Health regarded this action as utterly futile. Reporting to the Cannock Rural Sanitary Authority in 1879 he said,

"In regards to the drainage of Penkridge, nothing had been done. The difficulties which were pointed out in the report for the last quarter of 1877 still exist. A very sturdy lesson has been learned as to the impossibility of making surface wells absolutely safe from outside pollution."

He predicted that epidemic diseases would continue to flourish in Penkridge and warned the inhabitants to boil their water to avoid dysentery, diarrhoea and enteric fever. To those people who refused to believe that their delicious water was dangerous, he explained that,

"Contaminated well waters do not reveal their dangerous qualities to the common observer; they are frequently clear, bright, sparkling and cool; and so far seem to compare favourably with a purer supply. But these qualities are actually conveyed by the products of sewage contamination, the bright sparkling character being due to carbonic acid gas and the coolness in some degree to the large quantities of nitrates they contain. These ingredients, harmless in themselves, are the products of decomposition of surface filth of the most abominable kind, and are evidence of the constant risk being accompanied by deadly germs of disease which a passage through a layer of earth has not sufficed to render harmless."

Penkridge's Sanitary Committee had neglected to use the powers at their disposal. They could have forced house owners to spend up to £8 to make sure that they were properly connected to the drains. They could have paid for a pure water supply by accepting a loan from the Local Government Board as did many small villages in Staffordshire. They could have sunk an artesian well at a relatively low cost to supply the whole of the village with pure water. They did not and the people of Penkridge were condemned to another twenty years of disease, epidemics and high infantile mortality.

Chapter 20

Education

In 1876 old Thomas Croyden was asked by Lady Hatherton to write down his memories of the church in the early days of the century. Although he was 74 years old and had served about 50 years as a churchwarden he had not forgotten his school days. Recalling the year 1805 he remembered that,

"A schoolhouse stood at the North West corner of the old church yard, which I attended. The school master was named Starkey, and the hours of teaching was from 8 till 12, and from 1 till 5 o'clock. The average attendance was about 70." Penkridge's first school was beyond even his experience but he recalled that, " the room over the south porch was I believe formerly occupied as a school by a Mr. Bowman, and as long as I can remember it has been known as 'Bowman's Chamber'."

The school in the churchyard which Thomas Croyden attended had been planned in 1693 when Edward Littleton and John Eggington took over the land from the vicar and the churchwarden. As always with schools, finance was the major concern. The school was built in 1695 but needed regular injections of money to keep it going. In 1719 a major effort was made to put the school on a sound financial footing. In the eighteenth century education for its own sake was a rare idea and the motivating force behind the school was undoubtedly the fear of a turbulent and heathen working class. The Trustees and Subscribers to the Charity School unequivocally stated their aims in April, 1719.

"Whereas Prophaness and Debauchery are ensuing to a gross ignorance of the Christian religion, especially among the poorer sort, and whereas nothing is more likely to promote the growth of Christianity and Virtue than an early and pious education of youth, and whereas many poor people are desirous of having their children taught but are not able to afford them a Christian and useful education all those whose names are underwritten do hereby agree to pay yearly at four equal payments (during psalms) the several sums of money against our names for the setting up of a Charity School in the Parish of Penkridge for teaching poor boys and girls to Read and instructing them in the knowledge and practice of the Christian religion as professed in the Church of England and such other things as are suitable to their condition and capacity."

It is clear that the educational aims of the school were limited and that the subscribers did not harbour any sentimental ideas about educating the pupils above their allotted role in life. Nevertheless the school still ran into money trouble and after about ten years foundered for a second time as the original subscribers grew too old to contribute or died. When the Charity School was re-founded in 1730 the prospectus maintained the blood curdling view of the working class and its potential for trouble, stating that,

"Whereas it is found by experience that the Decay of Charity is always attended with the increase of Ignorance, Wickedness, & Debauchery, & many other infamous and dangerous vices; (especially amongst the Poorer sort) to the dishonour of Almighty God & the discouragement of the Christian Religion We whose names are underwritten, being willing and desirous to promote the practice of Christianity and Virtue, by keeping up and re-establishing that early and pious education of poor children do hereby agree to continue and promote it."

Although Thomas Croyden tells us that the average attendance was about 70, only twenty Penkridge children were offered free clothing and free places. The Trustees laid down that,

"We agree that 12 Poor Boys shall be clothed and instructed in reading, writing and accompts and likewise 8 Girls in the same, and in knitting and sewing besides. Which Boys and Girls shall be elected and approved of by the Trustees herein after named, or by the majority of them."

It is clear that the children were being offered a very basic curriculum that would make them more useful farm workers, clerks and, in the case of the girls, servants and wives. The school had two teachers, a master and a mistress, who were paid eight pounds a year. If Thomas Croyden's account of the average attendance is correct this would mean a class size of about 35. The tradesmen of Penkridge who were expected to support the school not unnaturally expected in return that they should benefit by supplying the school's needs. The Trustees agreed, therefore that,

"All the cloth both linnen, and woollen and all other necessaries for the clothing and education of these poor children shall be bought only of such Tradesmen within the Parish of Penkridge provided they will sell us good Goods, and as cheap as others."

Money for the school came from several sources. There were twenty six subscribers from Penkridge when the school opened in 1719, headed by Edward Littleton who contributed two guineas, which was the value of twelve Bibles and one pound in cash. The list is notable in containing many of the old established family names in Penkridge - Byrch, Haddersich, Baxter, Hinkley and Woolley. There were seven subscribers from Wolgarston, including three members of the Goodall family, and eight from Pillaton. The subscriptions were augmented by more irregular payments including collections at sermons and sacraments and contributions from the churchwardens when they had money to spare. Francis Sherratt was the treasurer to the Trustees in 1719 and survived to head the list of subscribers in 1730. He clearly was a strong supporter of the school and made a permanent provision for it in his will in 1734. He left two fields in Penkridge, called Clayfield Piece and Kinvaston Leasow, to Sir Edward Littleton and his heirs on the understanding that he would,

"Find and provide a Schoolmaster in Penkridge to teach and instruct eight poor boys in reading the Bible and writing, four of which boys should be from time to time appointed by his wife Ann Sherratt during her life and after her decease by the Churchwardens of the Parish and the other four boys by the said Sir Edward Littleton and his heirs".

Francis Sherratt stipulated that the boys should stay at the school for four years and wear blue bonnets, provided by the school.

The Charity School in the churchyard remained Penkridge's main school for the rest of the century. The Trustees met at the Kings Arms from time to time to elect pupils to be admitted to the school. All the pupils appear to be aged 7, 8 or 9. Of the names recorded from 1779 onwards only two can be identified with certainty as having survived to be recorded on the 1841 census. Both, John Oakley, who was elected in 1780 and William Gibbons, 1798, grew up to be agricultural labourers.

The full list of children for 1798 was

George Wilcox	Wm.Gibbons
Thomas Gilbert	Thomas Bates
Thomas Cooper	Thomas Bird
James Pool	Henry Powell
Thomas Winders	Jonathan Smith
James Cheatham	Thomas Bullock
Mary Bourne	Sarah Bannister
Jane Glover	Elizabeth Lockley
Ann Barns	Elizabeth Talbot
Ann Woolley	Ann Bannister
Mary Ellis.	

The affairs and the running of the school were very much a local matter. When important issues arose an announcement was made in the church on a Sunday. The Trustees, local land owners and farmers, gathered at the Littleton Arms to make their decisions. Thus the management of the school was swift and direct. At one meeting in 1800" it was unanimously resolved that Thomas Maiden be dismissed from the mastership of the school at Michaelmas next and that Mr. William Brew be appointed." John Starkey, the master that Thomas Croyden remembered, was appointed in 1806. Mr. Starkey resigned in 1831. By this time the days of the church yard school were numbered. In 1831 the Trustees ordered that the building be pulled down and the pupils be transferred to the school building in the Market Place.

By the early nineteenth century it had become clear that charity schools could not cope with the growing demand for elementary education. A far more efficient and organised method was needed. As a result the British and Foreign Schools Society was set up by Joseph Lancaster to organise a network of schools using the Monitorial System. This method, which broke lessons down into many small and simple parts which could be passed on by older pupils or monitors allowed huge numbers of children to be taught by a single master. The British and Foreign Schools Society claimed to be non - sectarian but was perceived to be a non - conformist threat to the virtual Church of England monopoly of education.

Not surprisingly Sir Edward Littleton reacted by building a new school in Penkridge which adopted the monitorial system but which came under the auspices of the National Society for Promoting the Education of the Poor, a Church of England organisation founded by Andrew Bell in 1811. The opening of the school was announced in February 1820. It was built to cater for three hundred children and so was a much more ambitious project than the school in the churchyard. The building itself quickly became an important social centre for the village, providing a venue for large events which could not be suitably held at an inn. On July 21st, 1821, to celebrate the Coronation of George IV, the Reverend Richard Slaney "treated the boys and girls of the National School (about 240) with roast beef, plum pudding and ale, and distributed a medal to each".

Obviously, a school of this size needed a lot of fund raising. By 1827 an Annual Charity Ball, held at the National School, became one of the social highlights of the village's year. Tickets cost five shillings for ladies and seven and sixpence for gentlemen. The profits from the occasion were used to buy a suit of clothes each for poor children on their leaving the National School "to go to service". The wealthy inhabitants of Penkridge were enjoying themselves and ensuring a steady supply of servants in the future.

The National School in the Market Place was a very large enterprise for a village of Penkridge's size. After 1831 it benefited from the income that had belonged to the church charity school. As well as rent from the Clay Field the school began to earn royalties on the clay dug out to make bricks. In 1858 £5..16s..8d was earned from the royalties on 77,824 bricks. The school could not have existed, however, without the large sums donated by Lord Hatherton which were invested in government stocks. By 1854 the charity income of the school amounted to about £36 a year whilst Lord Hatherton was contributing about £114 a year. This state of affairs could not continue. As education became more expensive it was clear that the status of the school would have to change.

The late 1840s and 1850s were a time of educational expansion both nationally and in Penkridge. Since 1833 the government had been giving small grants to the National Schools and a system of teacher training, pupil-teachers and government inspection had developed. In Penkridge school attendance was rising, buildings were enlarged and Assistant Teachers were appointed. Charity could no longer support these ambitious plans and Lord Hatherton wrote to the parents of the children asking them to pay a small weekly sum towards the costs.

Lord Hatherton explained that the Penkridge school was one of the few left in England that was entirely free. He was sure that parents and children would value the education provided much more, if they paid something towards it. The children were, therefore, divided into three categories; those to pay 2d a week, those to pay 4d a week and those who would pay six shillings a quarter. Whilst the parents decided into which group their child would fall, the vicar and Lord Hatherton would exclude any child who, they thought, was paying too little. Parents who had more than one child in the 2d and 4d bands could get a reduction in charges. The elder girls could offset some of the charges by being employed in needlework during school hours. The old school charities did not die away, however. Twelve deserving boys and twelve girls were still admitted free and given their blue caps and bonnets and were called Head Boys and Head Girls.

Having taken so much trouble to provide Penkridge children with an elementary education, Lord Hatherton tried to ensure that the lessons were not forgotten once they started work. He employed 25 boys between the ages of 12 and 14 on his farm at Teddesley and in 1853 started a Farm School. The boys were placed under the supervision of a "superintendent labourer" who instructed them in agricultural work. The boys were expected to have a reasonable standard of education. They were not given a job unless they brought a certificate from their clergyman saying that they could repeat the church catechism and could read and write. The boys had to attend a class every day in the farm yard from 6 to 8 am before the day's work. They were instructed in reading, writing and arithmetic so that they retained and increased the information they had gained at previous schools. The farm school was visited by an inspector who said he was "struck by the marked improvement in manners, conduct and knowledge of the boys since he had seen them shortly before the opening of the school on Lady Day."

In 1862 the Government, concerned that the tax payers' money given to education was being wasted, introduced a "Revised Code" of regulations on education grants, popularly known as "Payment by Results". This new scheme which cut the government grant to education had a disastrous effect on many schools as the wages of teachers had to be reduced when the children failed to pass tests in the basic subjects. Penkridge was saved from the worst effects of Payment by Results by having a rich, local benefactor who was clearly more interested in the good of the village than educational theory. Lord Hatherton appointed a new Headmaster in 1862 in order to meet the challenge of the Revised Code. He decided to pay him £80 a year plus half of the Government grant to the school. If half of the grant did not amount to £25 because of Payment by Results, Lord Hatherton agreed to make the sum up.

The new headmaster, Edward Chambers, did not find Lord Hatherton to be a "soft" employer, however. He had to work hard for his money. He was appointed at first for only three months and so was very much on trial. He had to teach for up to thirty hours a week and supervise the children when they were at the Sunday School. He had to "maintain good order and discipline among the scholars and to train them in good habits and manners." Edward Chambers survived his three month probation but by 1870 had had enough, preferring the rigours of 19th century Canada to teaching children in Penkridge. He said the school work was too much for his strength and his health was failing. Having given up teaching he became a leading educational expert in the New World.

In 1867 Penkridge school was clearly a large and flourishing concern. In the nineteenth century local people usually referred to the school in the plural as they saw it as three schools, for boys, girls and infants. Lord Hatherton was generous financially to the school and in many ways it was enlightened self interest since so many of the pupils had direct links with his estate. In October 1867 the school book recorded the number of pupils and their connection with the Hatherton estate.

Number of boys	114
Parents who work for Lord Hatherton and live in his house	17
Parents who do not work for Lord Hatherton but live in his house	36
Parents who work for Lord Hatherton but do not live in his house	2
Parents with no connection	59
Girls	92
Parents who work for Lord Hatherton and live in his house	12
Parents who do not work for Lord Hatherton but live in his house	35
Parents who work for Lord Hatherton but do not live in his house	2
Parents with no connection	43
Infants	100
Parents who work for Lord Hatherton and live in his house	12
Parents who do not work for Lord Hatherton but live in his house	25
Parents who work for Lord Hatherton but do not live in his house	2
Parents with no connection	61

The 306 children who attended Penkridge National School had only three teachers, Edward Chambers, Catherine Barber and Sarah Ann Cooke. The classes would have been very large, even with the use of Pupil Teachers. By 1871 the number of pupils had fallen to a more manageable 239. The headmaster recorded the names of the "Free boys" in receipt of the ancient Penkridge charity as being,

Thomas Davies	Mill Street
James Turner	Crown Bridge
Edward Rutter	Stone Cross
Charles Rushton	Police Station
Edward Haler	Crown Bridge
Joseph Smith	Preston
Charles Jones	Market Place
William Wincer	Market Place
Robert Belcher	Marsh
John Wilcox	Mill Street
William Cook	Pillaton

Penkridge seems to have had a thriving National School when the 1870 Education Act came into force. The act was designed to fill the gaps left by Voluntary religious schools, with Board Schools. These new schools were to be financed from the rates and government grants and run by democratically elected School Boards. A Board School in Penkridge would have been anathema to the Church and Lord Hatherton. It would have meant an increase in the rates and highly charged political elections setting Liberal against Conservative and Nonconformist against Anglican. As the religious teaching of any particular denomination was banned in Board Schools the Church of England regarded them as "godless" and to be avoided at all costs.

There was little threat of the imposition of a Board School in 1870. By 1888, however, the situation had changed. The Penkridge National Schools had entered a period of decline. The original school building, opened in 1823, needed extensive enlargements and repairs. It was reported that the schools were "inadequate in size and still more inadequate in their sanitary and general condition to satisfy the requirements of the Board of Education and it is quite evident that nothing short of a speedy and courageous effort on the part of the people of Penkridge will save the parish the great cost of maintaining a board school." A printed letter to the inhabitants of Penkridge declared that,

"The Managers of the above Schools are placed in a somewhat serious difficulty by the necessity which is imposed upon them by Renewing and Enlarging the school buildings.

Her Majesty's Inspector on the occasion of his last visit to Penkridge reported that 'he ranked the School Buildings in Penkridge as amongst the worst in the district' and he further said that unless some steps were promptly taken to improve their condition 'the Government Grant would be endangered' ."

The inhabitants and ratepayers of the widely extensive parish of Penkridge are thus brought within measurable distance of a costly and objectionable School Board superseding the present voluntary system of Education, to meet local requirements.

The school managers regard it as very fortunate and opportune that the projected Memorial to the Late Lord Hatherton is to take the form of a Girls or Infants school."

The people of Penkridge rallied round and enough money was raised to make the necessary improvements. It was a significant triumph for the Church and the re-opening of the school was attended by the Bishop.

Being a Voluntary Religious School meant that Penkridge National School underwent two forms of inspection, Government and Diocesan. The report on Religious Instruction by Church inspectors reveals that the problems of teaching are fairly constant.

"Much very good work has been done with Division 1 and in many instances the answering was very intelligent. But on the other hand I am sorry to say, some of the girls showed rather a want of brightness and interest in the work and appeared to be almost indifferent as to whether they answered the questions or not. On the whole excellent. The order is perhaps a little lax and it is somewhat difficult to keep the attention of the children".

In the years following 1870 a series of educational reforms gradually brought a state system of education into being. In 1880 attendance at school was made compulsory up to the age of 13 and Richard Wedge, Penkridge's School Attendance Officer, became busy bringing parents before the local Police Court for their children's non-attendance. Remarking upon the changes, The Staffordshire Advertiser said,

"Education is now so abundant everywhere, the smallest child of the poorest person is so hurried, worried and hunted into school, that one is apt to forget how short a time ago it is that popular education was the exception, rather than the rule."

The 1902 Education Act further reduced the independence of the voluntary religious schools like Penkridge's by bringing them under the auspices of newly created Local Education Authorities. Henceforth the L.E.A. would pay for the running costs of the school and the teachers' wages.

Whilst the state was gradually encroaching upon the local educational preserve of the Church the Vicar came to realise that all was not well with his Sunday School either. In 1897 he admitted that the Church was seemingly losing its grip on the people of Penkridge. In a cry from the heart in the Parish Magazine he said that,

"We are doing our best to make our Sunday Schools as perfect as possible, but it is very disheartening when we find that it is possible for parents calling themselves church people, because their children do not get a prize, to send them to the chapel school.

Every person has a right to do and to be what he or she likes, within certain limits, but a churchman who, if he comes to church must pray Sunday after Sunday 'from all false doctrine, heresy and schism, Good Lord deliver us' and praying thus, allows his children to attend a schismatic school is false to his faith."

Whilst the nineteenth century saw increasing regulation, uniformity and state interference in elementary education for the poor, middle class education remained relatively untouched. A small village like Penkridge with good communications was well placed for the establishment of private schools for the middle class. In the early nineteenth century a long lasting school in Penkridge was run by Mrs. Perrin. She advertised regularly in the Staffordshire Advertiser, soliciting new customers and advising parents of the dates of the new term. On July 4th 1818 she announced that,

> "PREPARATORY SCHOOL PENKRIDGE
> Will re-open on Monday 20 July
> Terms
> Board and Instruction including plain sewing, English Grammar, Writing and Arithmetic, 14 Guineas per Annum. Washing 10s 6d per quarter, for young ladies under 10yrs, and young gentlemen under 8yrs of age.
>
> Each border to bring a pair of sheets, napkin, spoon, knife and fork, which will be returned.
>
> Mrs. Perrin cannot permit the present opportunity to pass over without expressing her most grateful thanks for the favours conferred upon her since she first opened the above school and assures those who favour her with the care of their children that no exertion on her part will be wanting to render it advantageous to the pupils and satisfactory to their friends."

Mrs. Perrin charged fourteen guineas a year with French and Music lessons extra. Local parents could also send their children to Mr. Taylor's Dancing Academy which, instead of an open day, held an annual ball at Penkridge in the 1820s. School teaching was considered to be a suitable career for clergymen. In the 1820s Penkridge had a Classical School run by the Reverend E. Price who announced that he had "removed to the house formerly occupied by the late Mr. Bennet and continues to receive a limited number of Pupils (not exceeding 10) to Board and Educate."

In the late 1830s Mrs. Perrin was succeeded by Miss Mary Ford as Penkridge's leading independent school teacher. In May, 1831, at the age of 27 she advertised in the Staffordshire Advertiser announcing that she had taken over Ivy House.

> "LADIES SEMINARY, PENKRIDGE
> Miss Ford grateful for the encouragement she has received since her commencement in Penkridge and humbly soliciting an extension of the

favours and support of her friends and the public, begs to inform them she has taken the airy and commodious house pleasantly situated near the church, and formerly the residence of the late Rev. Richard Slaney, where she purposes conducting her Establishment with the aid of talented and Accomplished Mistresses; and that by combining the comforts of home with the duties of school, united with unremitting attention to the moral and intellectual improvement of the young ladies committed to her care, to merit a continuation of their patronage.

Terms, including writing, arithmetic, grammar, geography, history, plain and ornamental needlework etc. 20 gs. per annum, under 10 years of age 18gs. Dancing, drawing, French, Italian and music each one g. per quarter. Each young lady is required to bring her own chamber linen, knife and fork, and dressed spoon, which will be returned on leaving school."

A private boys' school was run by a Mr. Holt at Bridge Cottage in the 1830s and 1840s. It was also a boarding school and charged sixteen guineas a year for pupils under ten and twenty guineas for those over that age. Penkridge continued to be the location of private schools in the late nineteenth century. In 1871 the curate of Penkridge, Henry Lovatt, retired from his church post and opened a school on Clay Street. By 1881, with his Swiss wife Rosa, he had built up a school with nine boarders seemingly catering mainly for the children of officers of the British Empire. The 1881 census shows that the nine boarders were born in Cape Town, Bombay, Greece and Wolverhampton.

Chapter 21

Politics and Progress
1850 - 1887

On Midsummer Day, 1872, Penkridge suffered the storm of the century. It was a Monday and the fortnightly cattle market had just finished. As the buyers and sellers queued to pay the clerk in the auctioneer's box the storm hit the Smithfield with "unexampled fury". The box, with the clerk still in it, was lifted into the air and carried into the next field, down to the banks of the Penk, where the clerk emerged shaken and bleeding. Other sheds on the market were destroyed with parts of them being found half a mile away. A waggon belonging to Lord Hatherton was blown over two hedges into a nearby garden. The vicarage was struck by lightning and three pinnacles were blown from the church. A barn on the turnpike road was blown down and the debris wounded men sowing turnips in the fields. Haystacks were blown up to a mile away. Just outside the station a train was halted where the driver had been knocked out by a ball of lightning.

The events of June 24th 1872 were memorable, if not historically significant. The lightning flashes of that day illuminate a picture of an agricultural community going about its business. The village was obviously much closer to farming and country pursuits then than now. Another anecdote, now part of Penkridge folklore, supports this. On Friday 21st December 1866, Thomas Adcock, a builder, was sitting in his kitchen at home on the Cannock Road when a fox slipped in through the door. "Reynard", the fox, had broken cover at Somerford and run all the way from Brewood, being chased by the hounds and three hundred members of the Albrighton Hunt. Tradition has it that the fox escaped the dogs by jumping out of a window. Unfortunately "Reynard's" fate was rather more predictable. The pack poured in through the door and killed its quarry on the kitchen floor. Thomas Adcock, a man used to the ways of the country and not unduly concerned by this surprising turn of events, had a knife to hand and cut off the brush of the fox. The Advertiser reported that,

> "The cottage (which by the bye, is in future to be known as Reynard Cottage) was almost immediately surrounded by members of the hunt, one of whom asked for a loan of the brush for a few minutes, and at once presented it to Miss Hellier, who was amongst the first in at the death; and

it must be added that Mr. Adcock gallantly waived his claim to the brush as soon as he saw it in the hands of that lady."

It is not surprising that even as late as the 1920s it was considered an appropriate task for Penkridge schoolboys to learn the rhyme,

"The fox was strong,
And full of running,
He could run for an hour,
And still be cunning."

In the 1850s and 1860s Penkridge was still predominantly an agricultural village, its fortunes closely linked to the weather, the prosperity of the tenant farmers and the management of the Littleton estate. Despite fears that the repeal of the Corn Laws in 1846 would destroy British farming by allowing the importing of cheap foreign food the period was one of relative progress and prosperity. This encouraging state of affairs was reflected in the number of paupers in the workhouse which reached an all time low in 1852. A farmer who had been in favour of protection grudgingly admitted that "it is certainly an evidence that farming is not quite ruined in this district."

Penkridge farmers and labourers were among the most fortunate in Staffordshire. While the rest of the county suffered from high rents and emigration, the Teddesley estate had been cutting its rents since the Napoleonic war. By 1850 rents were 35% lower than they had been in 1813. A farm labourer in the Penkridge area was earning about 9 or 10 shillings a week while the rent of a cottage with a good sized garden was about £3..10s a year. The rent of a larger house in Market Square was 5s..4d a week. With the close proximity of work available in industry Penkridge was in the happy position of having no able bodied paupers.

All the Penkridge farmers were benefiting from a disciplined workforce trained at Lord Hatherton's home farm at Teddesley. So many efficient labourers were produced that the area almost eliminated the employment of women in the fields outside of harvest time. Lord Hatherton's farm school was described by a reporter in 1850.

"About 30 boys, between the ages of 10 and 14 were busily at work, collecting and throwing into a cart all the stones lying on the surface of a piece of ploughed land. A labourer, rather advanced in years, moved among them and watched how they worked. It was his duty to show them the quickest, easiest and best way of doing whatever they were required to do, to make them work systematically and to punish them if they quarrelled or otherwise misconducted themselves. Master and scholar worked together at all light operations, such as picking couch grass and stones, hand weeding, hoeing turnips, carrots or mangold wurzels or making hay. They have implements suited to their age and do their work excellently taking a great interest in what requires skill and showing a strong spirit of emulation. They work the same number of hours as the men but are said not to be fatigued thereby 'as they play about and are full of cheerfulness on their way home at night' ".

The boys were paid 6d a day. Women at that time were being paid 9d or 10d a day for work in the fields. The 3 shillings a week that their children brought home meant that it was far more profitable for them to stay at home and "attend to the important economies of the labourer's cottage".

By 1850 the benefits of the enclosure were being reaped on the Teddesley estate. Lord Hatherton farmed about 1,700 acres himself, land which was described as being, in 1827, "in a most neglected state, great parts of it a worthless waste without roads, undrained and open and exposed to the wintry blasts which sweep over the elevated ground of the midland counties". In 1850 the same land was rich and fertile with luxuriant crops of wheat and barley. Woods sheltered healthy flocks of Southdown sheep. The old bogs and swamps now drained into a reservoir which supplied the farm buildings and turned a 38 foot diameter mill wheel which powered a mill, a chaff cutter and a threshing machine. When waste land was reclaimed Lord Hatherton allowed his labourers three or four years free use of the land, after drainage, to grow potatoes. This softened part of the blow of enclosure and benefited the land, which was being dug over.

Having established a basic prosperity through enclosure, efficient drainage and a four course rotation, Lord Hatherton went on to make Teddesley a centre for agricultural progress. The newest farm machinery was used and demonstrated to local farmers. In 1857 a steam plough was introduced at Teddesley. It was a fantastic machine which attracted many visitors. The steam engine was placed in the middle of large fields and pulled a plough, which made furrows nine inches deep, by means of wires one inch in diameter and three quarters of a mile long. The machine, built by a Mr. Massey of Shropshire, was deemed a great success as it saved on time and horse labour. It was doubly welcomed since it needed six men and three boys to operate it and so didn't cause unemployment. In the same season Bell's reaping machine was demonstrated on Charles Keeling's farm at Congreve in front of a hundred people.

The advance of scientific farming meant that many jobs were created on the fringes of agriculture. A thriving business was sustained at Wolgarston because of the demand for artificial fertilizers. Mr. Wood combined his farming activities with the manufacture of superphosphate of lime. He bought the raw material, bones, from collectors in Wolverhampton and Lichfield and boiled them in a huge pot of water. The fat from the bones was skimmed off the surface of the water, placed in barrels and sent to soap boilers. The bones yielded one twentieth of their weight in fat which sold at £20 a ton.

After the bones were dried the process continued, as described by the

Advertiser in 1850.

"After being boiled the bones are easily ground by the crushing mill. When crushed, they are carried to a large wooden trough into which 10 bushels at a time are thrown. Upon these, previously moistened by water, a carboy of sulphuric acid is emptied, the mass is then well stirred about, and in 15 to 20 minutes removed from the trough and thrown into a heap where the dissolving process slowly goes on. After a day or two the mixture is passed through a set of crushing rollers by which it is reduced to powder and is then ready for sale. For the convenience of farmers, mixtures of guano and superphosphate are made up here in such proportions as may be desired: 2 cwt of guano and 2 cwt of superphosphates, mixed together are found an excellent application for the turnip crop."

Despite the progress being made in agriculture the village of Penkridge was stagnating in the 1850s and early 1860s. It did not have a clean water supply, an efficient post office or gas lighting. The centre of the village was a dark and dismal place at night. A frustrated businessman described the scene in February 1846.

"The Post Office is in one of the darkest situations in the town. We have to ascend to it by steps, and I have known people sometimes tumble up, and sometimes down them. When I have letters of consequence to post, I take them myself, not daring to trust them with anyone else, fearing they might not be deposited where they ought, there not being the least light either from without or within the office, the shutters being closed over the window in which the box is fixed. As the generality of letters are posted in the evening, at this time of year it is a difficult matter to find the house, and much more so the window and box; and people living near the office are continually annoyed by strangers from the country who have letters to post enquiring where the office is, or by borrowing a lantern and candle to find it."

The problem of house and street lighting in Penkridge was not tackled until 1869, long after many villages of comparable size and situation. A group of leading citizens, virtually the vestry under another name, called a meeting at the Littleton Arms to promote the Penkridge Gas Co. Ltd. They proposed to raise £2,000 in shares with contributions limited to £5 "to enable every householder to share in the profits which each light he uses will assist in making". Once the Gas Company had been set up it offered a system of street lighting to the ratepayers of Penkridge. There was a great deal of opposition to this new expenditure and the plan was accepted by only a small majority.

By the winter of 1870 "this formerly very dull and dark place [was] nightly illuminated". The Advertiser reported that "still the gloom has not all been dispelled owing to the deficient number of lamps in some parts which has caused no little dissatisfaction and complaint". These were the first of many complaints against the Gas Company. It soon discovered that it could never supply the village with gas at a low enough price and complaints continued until the company was wound up in 1912.

By the late 1860s Penkridge was beginning to make progress. In 1866 the first commercial bank came to the village when Lloyds opened a branch after having taken over the Stafford Old Bank. In July 1870 Penkridge became linked to the outside world by the electric telegraph to be found at the post office, "the want of such a convenience being felt for a very long time". Also in 1870 the Oddfellows opened a hall behind the George and Fox thus adding entertainment to their list of social services which included sick pay and care of widows and orphans.

In 1877 a forerunner of the village hall, church hall and library was opened. It was felt that Penkridge was not doing enough to keep the labouring men out of the public houses in the evenings. A house in the Market Place was rented and converted into a Reading Room. It was open between 6pm and 10pm in the summer and 4pm and 10pm in the winter. Its first annual report described the great efforts that were made to make the room as warm and convivial as a pub.

"The kitchen is set apart for the playing of games; the present stock consisting of draughts, Fox and Geese, Go-Bang and Dominoes, all of which are in great request, and in this room the refreshments are supplied. Tea, coffee and cocoa at one penny per cup, a plate of two slices of bread and butter for one penny, and ginger beer at three-half-pence a bottle. In the kitchen only is smoking allowed.

In the sitting or newspaper room the following papers and periodicals have been taken in: The Standard, The Daily News, The Birmingham Daily Gazette, The Staffordshire Advertiser, The Graphic, The Illustrated London News, The Penny Illustrated Paper, The Day of Rest, The Cottager and Artisan and The British Workman."

One hundred and ninety men used the Reading Room during its first year, women and boys under 16 being excluded. It was progress of a sort but the real solution to keeping men out of the pubs was to pay them wages high enough to afford warm and welcoming houses of their own. This became more difficult from the mid 1870s onwards as agricultural depression exerted a downward pressure on wages. In 1872 Joseph Arch formed the Agricultural Labourer's Union in Warwickshire, lighting a beacon "which would prove a rallying point for the agricultural labourers throughout the country". As Joseph Arch's fame spread, local combinations of labourers in neighbouring counties were emboldened to join together to demand a better deal. In Penkridge a meeting was held in February 1872 at the George and Fox where it was "Resolved that the waggoners, cowmen and shepherds require 18 shillings and the labourers 17 shillings per week, with existing privileges, double wages in harvest time, to leave off work on Saturdays at 5 o'clock in summer and 4 in winter, and with six months notice of dismissal; also that the thatchers demand 1 shilling per day extra"

The concerns of the farm labourer did not play a significant part in politics in the 1870s since the rural worker did not have the vote. Perhaps because of this elections in Penkridge were rather quiet before 1884. The Western Division of Staffordshire, of which Penkridge was a part, was formed in 1868 but the constituency was uncontested until 1880 when two Liberals stood against two Conservatives for the two seats. The Conservatives held a meeting at the Littleton Arms but not even their leading local supporter, Mr. Keeling, could raise much enthusiasm for the cause. "Whether Liberals or Conservatives were in power very little was done for the agricultural interest", he complained. The result of the election revealed an evenly divided constituency. 8,279 men voted and there were only 400 votes between the second placed Conservative and the leading Liberal candidate.

After the rural working class was enfranchised in 1884, elections in Penkridge became much more vigorous, with both the Conservative and Liberal parties fighting for the working class vote. The general election of 1885 proved to be particularly rowdy. The tone of the campaign was set at Brewood where the Liberal candidate, Mr. Hamer Bass, was shouted down at his own meeting, with the Conservative candidate, Mr. Monckton, looking on from the front row. The Liberals held their first big meeting in Penkridge at the Oddfellows Hall on Wednesday October 14th. The atmosphere was extremely tense as the room was very crowded and there were a large number of Conservative supporters present. When Bass claimed that "the working class of the country had nothing to thank the Conservatives for in the last forty years" disturbances broke out in the hall. The rowdyism was just about kept in check by the respected presence of J.C. Tildesley in the chair and a reproving cry of "We are not at Brewood" from the hall. Bass' claim that the Liberals stood for free trade which gave the workers cheap food, beer and clothes was met by a shout from the audience, "And no money to buy them with."

On the following Monday the Conservatives held their meeting at the Littleton Arms. It coincided with the Penkridge Wakes so, although everybody was reported to be in "a well disposed and happy frame of mind", drink undoubtedly fuelled many of the disturbances. When Monckton claimed that reform of land ownership would lead to a ruinous revolution the labourers in the audience cried, "No". Monckton was asked to explain why he had voted against giving the vote to the working class. His evasive answer caused uproar and when the chairman called for order he was met with the jeer, "What about Brewood?". Monckton said that he was opposed to free education since it was unfair on bachelors and childless couples. He dismissed the idea of land reform as being impracticable. A Penkridge labourer might dream of being given an allotment, near his cottage, from the Littleton estate, "But it must be remembered that all Wolverhampton and Cannock would need to be considered and they would have to have their share of land somewhere".

As election day approached behaviour in Penkridge deteriorated. The Liberals held their last meeting on December 3rd at the Oddfellows Hall. The Staffordshire Advertiser reported that,

> "It was the most disorderly meeting which has yet been held in connection with the election contest in West Staffs. The room was crowded to the door and throughout the proceedings the speakers were subjected to continual interruption. At times the meeting was a scene of the greatest confusion and anything like sober argument was made impossible by the misconduct of the audience."

Because of the constant uproar, howls, groans, cheers and "boos" the resolution to support Hamer Bass had to be performed in mime. An Irishman in the audience, predicting the result of the election shouted, "They will be quiet enough on Tuesday."

On election day itself there were many problems caused by the increased electorate, many of whom were illiterate. The only disturbances in the whole of the West Staffordshire constituency were at Penkridge and the chief constable had to send extra police to the village. Despite all the excitement the votes of an evenly divided community like Penkridge probably counted for little. Hamer Bass was returned with a comfortable majority, buttressed by the massive support of the Cannock Chase miners.

The defeat was a bitter blow to local Conservatives and they set about re-organising themselves to avoid a repetition of the disaster. A Penkridge branch of the Primrose League was started by Mr. Keeling, Haden Corser and Dr. Boldero and it soon had a hundred members. Politics in the 1880s were very volatile, however, and in the general election of 1886, one year after the most divisive election in living memory, Hamer Bass was returned unopposed. The Conservatives of West Staffordshire supported their former Liberal enemy because he had opposed and voted against Gladstone's Bill granting Home Rule for Ireland. By 1892 Hamer Bass had become a fully fledged Unionist or Conservative and stood against a Liberal Candidate in the election. Penkridge showed that it had developed a taste for unpleasant politics when, in a mock funeral, a "body" of the Liberal Candidate was buried on the day before voting.

Chapter 22

"Days and Moments Quickly Flying"
1887 - 1897

On Sunday December 3rd, 1887, a service of dedication was held for the church clock, Penkridge's permanent memorial of Queen Victoria's Golden Jubilee. The words of the hymn, "Days and Moments Quickly Flying" sung by the church choir under the porch must have struck Thomas Croyden as being particularly apt. A retired farmer, living in Market Street with his two unmarried daughters, Betsy and Harriet, Thomas had been born in Penkridge and could distinctly remember the celebrations he had enjoyed as a seven year old that marked the jubilee of George III in 1809.

Despite his advanced years Thomas Croyden had taken an active part in the village festivities, organised by Dr. Boldero and held in June to celebrate the Queen's fifty years on the throne. Flags, flowers and evergreens had been hung across the main streets and all the village's Sunday School children had been assembled in the school square to be given commemorative medals. Afterwards they marched behind a band to the packed church for a service. Before a second service in the afternoon the parishioners divided for more secular nourishment. The children took tea and cakes at the National School and 350 adults had roast beef and plum pudding at the Littleton and the George and Fox. After the afternoon service there was a sports day held on Stone Pits field, with twenty events organised by the curate, the Rev. R. Rigden which included races and pole climbing. The day was rounded off with a fireworks display.

Thomas Croyden was a prominent citizen of Penkridge and had served the village as churchwarden for twenty years between 1856 and 1876. Longevity and years of public service must have made him sensitive to history and the passage of time. Fanny, his daughter, was married to J.C. Tildesley, the lock manufacturer from Willenhall, who, the previous year, had published his History of Penkridge. Who better to appreciate the great ceremony attached to the funeral of Lord Hatherton in 1888 than a man who in 1812 had attended the funeral of the eighth Sir Edward Littleton, thus being a human link in an historical chain that stretched back to 1742 when Sir Edward had come into his Penkridge inheritance?

The funeral of Lord Hatherton took place on April 10 1888. Born in the year of Waterloo, his funeral was to be the occasion of almost feudal public respect and deference which recalled even earlier days. The inhabitants of Penkridge were informed that,

"The funeral of the Late Lord Hatherton will take place on Tuesday next April 10 at 2.30 in Penkridge Church. The Labourers on the estate will assemble at the church yard East Gate and line the road on either side up to the south porch.

The Tenants attending the funeral are requested to assemble at the West entrance of the church yard at the same hour, lining the road on either side to the church porch. The procession will start from the south porch, the Tenants falling in two and two behind Mr. Foden and the Labourers in the same manner behind Mr. Jones."

The bearers were Isaac Matthews, James Hayes, George Hucker, William Hucker, Martin Callaghan and James Holford, the oldest labourers on the estate. The oldest tenants, Thomas Croyden, C.R. Keeling, J. Aston, G.B. Keeling, T.J. Griffin, C.C. Cope, J. Lees, T. Atkins, J.R. Briggs and E.T. Chell were pall bearers.

More than anyone else present at the funeral Thomas Croyden would have felt at home in the church. He clearly remembered its less happy days in the 1820s when "the effigies in the church were for many years in a dilapidated condition and part of them, including that now within the communion rails, were enclosed with folding doors against the north side of the chancel". As an ex-churchwarden he was an expert on the history of the church and described for Lady Hatherton how "the church was restored in later years by a fund from property owners and a grant from the Incorporated Society, the latter being conditional on 500 free seats being provided for the poor forever. The tower contained 5 bells (of which 2 were cracked) until replaced by the present peal of 8, one of which bears the name of the late John Brewster in recognition of a handsome donation."

Penkridge had changed so much during Croyden's lifetime. By 1876, when he wrote his memoir, the payment of cash for sparrows' heads by the churchwardens was an historical curiosity, yet he had done just that himself. He recalled from his early days as churchwarden that wills were "then proved at Penkridge and for many years after; I having proved some myself as recently as 1843, the Proctors attending being the late Mr. John Mott, Mr. Fell and others." Despite all these changes one gathers the impression that Thomas Croyden's favourite story from the past concerned a strike by the church choir. He remembered that,

"In 1805 and for many years following there was a good choir, led by reed instruments, but owing to a misunderstanding between them and the churchwarden as to payments they declined to sing and for a long time the clerk (Wm. Brookes) an elderly man and another patriarch named Day (commonly called "Old Dicky

Day") used to sing from the clerk's desk the 100th Psalm (Old Version) as a duet! The late Lord Hatherton, then the Right Hon. E.J. Littleton, being at this time virtually sole MP for the whole county, and consequently much engrossed by public affairs did not for some time learn how matters stood. On doing so he asked the late William Cope of Park Gates, who was a good musician and leader of Penkridge band, to get up a choir, which was accordingly done. The choir as nearly as I can remember being as follows

Choirmaster, 1st clarinet	Mr. J. Cope, Park Gate
Second clarinet	J. Southern, Mill End
German flute	C. Wotton, Kinvaston
German flute	J. Croyden, Drayton
1st Bassoon	Jno. Hart
2nd Bassoon	Wm. Hodgetts
Bass voice	Jesse Seabridge
Tenor	Jno. Bennett (solicitor)
Tenor	Wm. Price
Counter	Geo. Poole

and others. This choir lasted until the introduction of the organ."

Thomas Croyden himself died in 1896 at the age of 94. Almost as old as the century he had seen the growth of great national prosperity and many public celebrations. He had also witnessed, however, the depths of poverty in the 1830s and 1840s. He embodied many of the elements which characterized the important aspects of the history of Penkridge during these years. He had known personally six generations of the Littleton family and his family had been resident on the Littleton estate for nearly three hundred years. As we have seen he had followed the proud and ancient tradition of public service. His obituary recalled the "quiet, unostentatious way, Mr. Croyden in the course of his prolonged life rendered active and useful service in various ways to his native parish. For nearly 30 years he filled the office of churchwarden; he was for a long time a Poor Law Guardian, and in other public offices he did much useful work."

By the time that he died in 1896 the police were well established as the guardians of law and order. Thomas Croyden could remember the difficult days before the police force and as a young man, sixty years previously, he had personally helped to quell the miners' riots in Bilston as a member of the Staffordshire Yeomanry. He embodied the ideal of stewardship. With the ownership of property went the duty of public service and private charity. His obituary noted that he "was a generous supporter of the church, the schools, and the charities of the Parish and his private gifts to the deserving poor, although never made public, were constant and liberal to a degree."

The passing of Mr. Croyden must have been seen by many as the end of an era. It was one of the last times when the whole village indulged in an act of public mourning for one of their leading figures. The Staffordshire Advertiser reported that,

> "The tradesmen in the village closed their shops at the time of the funeral and nearly every house had drawn blinds, the demonstration of respect to the memory of the deceased being general through the parish."

Although life for most had improved by the end of the century Croyden and Penkridge's other inhabitants must have realised that they were living in a village and a society with many remaining problems. In the late 1800's in Penkridge there was undoubtedly a deep concern over deteriorating standards of public behaviour. The problem surfaced, at least in the parish magazine and in the Vestry minutes when, in 1893, Mr. Littleton was replaced as vicar by Ticehurst Corfield. It is not clear whether Mr. Corfield was acting as a new broom, tackling an old problem with vigour or that the departure of an authoritative Littleton vicar loosened the bonds of social restraint. The Bishop stated, enigmatically, that the Rev. Littleton "filled a somewhat difficult position with fidelity and success". However, in the parish magazine of April 1896 Ticehurst Corfield mentioned the fact that "complaints had been made of the behaviour of a few young men and women at the Sunday evening service. It was decided to take such steps as it is hoped will put a stop to them." At a vestry meeting the churchwardens were asked to sit at the extreme west of the nave at Sunday Evening Services to control the conduct of "certain persons" and to take action against those misconducting themselves. From remarks in the parish magazine concerning a confirmation service in the following year, it seems that the problem was not rapidly solved.

> "The behaviour of the candidates was very reverent, a fact remarked on by the Bishop. They set an example which it would have been well if some members of the congregation followed."

Even the law-abiding majority of the congregation was falling short of the Vicar's expectations. In 1896 he complained that,

> "The offertory taken at the evening service on Sunday is, we are sorry to say, a disgrace to the congregation, many more than half the congregation giving nothing at all. Large congregations on Sunday evenings as an average do not contribute a ½d a person."

The problem of anti-social behaviour was not confined to the parish church. One of the main aims of the Parish Council in 1895 was "to put a stop to the bad language so often heard in the streets which is a disgrace to the village, and also to put an end to another black spot in our social life which shall be nameless. Now I am speaking of matters urgently needing alteration. What so perplexes one in dealing with such things is to find that bad behaviour in Church, or bad behaviour in the village, comes from quarters that one would least suspect it, and in many cases from the sons and daughters of those who must be very grieved if they know about it".

It would be most unjust, however, to leave an impresion of Ticehurst Corfield as a querulous priest trying vainly to control his flock. The Vicar showed a true Christian concern for the real problems of the village. He would visit without question during the night if called to the home of a sick parishioner. "First he would pray, and then his practical side would predominate. He would make the poultice and apply it, and would sit all night if necessary by the bedside of the sufferer." He was a very familiar figure in the village, in his cassock and mortar board, driving from house to house in a dog cart pulled by his white pony, "Taffy". During the winter of 1895 he noted

"The soup kitchen has, I believe, been a great help during the severe weather. The soup has always been very good, and much appreciated, and I am sure the bread was wanted as much as the soup. The Sick Fund is overdrawn, the Relief Fund is all gone and half the expense of the Soup Kitchen has yet to be met."

The Penkridge soup kitchens created lasting memories. One parishioner, interviewed in 1961 at the age of 80 recalled that,
"there was the time of the hard frost that lasted months and hit the farmers badly. A soup kitchen was opened at the back of Miss Carol Anne Bastone's place."

It says much for the spirit of our ancestors and the community spirit of small villages like Penkridge that, in the midst of such adversity, they celebrated with vigour and enthusiasm local seasonal and great patriotic events like the celebrations to mark the Diamond Jubilee of Queen Victoria in June 1897. Enjoying what had become known as the splendid "Queen's Weather" the inhabitants assembled in the Market Square and then proceeded through the decorated streets to the vicarage field for a service of thanksgiving, the church being too small for the congregation. After three verses of the National Anthem, led by the church choir and the Stafford Borough Band, the villagers dispersed for lunch. Eight hundred and thirty people dined at the inns and schools of Penkridge.

After dinner the people reformed on Crown Bridge and went to Stone Pits field which had been lent by Mr. Tomlinson for village sports.

The list of races and the winning competitors convey a sense of fun undiminished over a hundred years later.

Egg and Spoon Race	S. Emberton, F. Cheadle
100 yds Leap Frog Race	E. Leeke, W. Keates, H. Lyons
Throwing the Cricket Ball	John Jones
120 yds Flat	J. Davies
Long Jump	James Price
Potato Race	Jno. Jones
Wheelbarrow Race	F. Perry
Hurdle Race	F. Plant

Bicycle Slow Race	E. Brooks, W. Stubbs
Sack Race	F. Leach
Obstacle Race	?
Needle and Thread Race for Women	?
Fireman's Race, in uniform	A. Weatherer
Old Men and Women's Race over 60	?

Five hundred and fifty children were also given tea and there was a demonstration by the fire brigade who later went on, unsurprisingly, to win the ten-a-side tug of war. There was a "delightful parade of beautifully decorated bicycles" and the day finished with the grand illumination of the church with acetylene gas and two tiers of fairy lights around the battlements.

Despite its problems Penkridge was not an inward looking village. The parish magazine listed the schoolchildren of the village who had donated their Lent savings for the relief of an Indian famine. These were some of the children who were to face the perils of the twentieth century:

Charles Snape, Arthur Morgan, Rose Griffiths, Gerty Jones, Alice Simcox, Frank Stubbs, Joseph Plant, the Cliffes, Martha Robins, Ellen Kenderdine, Harold Sprenger, Maria Hollis, Ida Parsons, Kate Russel, Florrie Cheadle, Hon. H.F. Littleton, Albert Bagnall, Jessie Grey, Ethel Heath, Wm. Burns, Willie Steele, Arthur Dean, Louie Ecclestone, Ada Davies, Connie Burns, Annie Smith, Jessie Oakley, Albert Talbot, Daisy Thurstance, Edith Davies, Charles Rodwell, Rose Rodwell, Jane Faulkner, Margaret Robbins, Ethel Morris, Jessie Robins, Lily Richards and Thomas Tooth.

Chapter 23

The Parish Council

The Parish Council began its first full year of work in 1895. Before it addressed the serious business of the health and safety of the people of Penkridge it had to tidy up some of the loose ends of three hundred years of less organised local government. One of the councillors' first tasks was to review the village's charitable "doles". They found that there were 49 of them, of which only 25 related to the poor. Some of the money had disappeared due to the neglect of trustees in olden time. Sir Stephen Slaney's bequest of £40, made in 1622 for the use of the poor and the marrying of poor maidens had dried up in 1741.

Having dealt with the past, the Council looked to the future. They decided that one of their top priorities was to "provide a suitable bathing place, with the necessary accommodation for the youths of the village .... in the best part of the river". That bathing in the Penk could be contemplated at all marked something of an improvement since only eight years earlier it had been reported that "the pollution of the River Penk by sewage or other offensive matter has for some years been a matter of notoriety ... The colour of the stream is now a deep yellow ochre and a wholesale destruction of fish is inevitable. The malaria emanating from so foul a water course must soon render what has so long been the charm of the Penk valley little less than a public nuisance". The Council acted rapidly and built a bathing hut but soon found that public service and democratic accountability were an uneasy combination when they were flooded by complaints that the bathers could be seen from the road.

The Council also started on their most serious work, protecting the health and safety of the villagers. They inherited the dilemma of the Select Vestry of how to balance the welfare of the people against the financial worries of the ratepayers. An added difficulty was that it was not entirely clear who was responsible for dealing with the major problems, the Parish, the District or the County Council. Penkridge Parish Council was often to find itself at the centre of a bureaucratic tangle, receiving complaints from the village and putting pressure on the District and County for action. In the summer of 1895 the inadequacy of Penkridge's sewers again became obvious during the hot weather. The Parish Clerk was ordered to write to the County Council's Inspector of Nuisances and to the District Council. The new Parish Council also had to deal with complaints about the cleanliness and lighting of Pinfold Lane, New Road and Goods Station Lane. They asked the County Council to take over the road to the station and the short road leading from Stone Cross to the Post Office.

Sitting on the Parish Council was clearly going to be a difficult and not particularly rewarding occupation. To boost their morale they accepted from Mr. Williams of the Uplands a design for a village seal showing the Bull Bridge, the Church, the river and cattle grazing in the meadow. J.C. Tildesley had the seal embossed. On the whole it seemed to have been a satisfactory first year's work. When the Council invited criticisms at the first Parish Meeting a Mr. Cooper, who had opposed their election, said that he had pleasure in bearing high testimony to their work and that he did not think a more efficient Parish Council could be found anywhere.

The Parish Council may have been efficient but the problems were immense. There was no room at all for complacency when poverty and illness were so common. In 1896 the schools were closed down for three weeks because of an epidemic of measles. In the winter of 1896 the Vicar commented that, "there has been much illness in the parish lately and not a few have been called hence. May they rest in peace." Ticehurst Corfield worked hard, organising a Sick and Poor Fund which, amongst its other work, bought coal for the poor. The general standard of hygiene was very low and the Vicar devoted space in the parish magazine to inform his parishioners that,

> "The best insect destroyer known is hot alum water.
> Put alum into hot water and boil until dissolved, then
> apply with a brush to all cracks, cupboards, bedsteads
> and other places where insects may be found. Ants,
> cockroaches, fleas and other creeping things are killed."

The winters were hard but it was during the summers that Penkridge's real problem was most noticeable. In August 1897 Ticehurst Corfield wrote that "there has for the time of the year been much sickness in the parish. Oh, that Penkridge might have a regular supply of water. I never knew a place so sorely in need of it". Poverty, epidemics and a poor water supply inevitably made their mark on the death rate. The parish burial register for December 1896, for example, makes dismal reading with its high proportion of infant deaths.

Keziah Hollingshead	3
Winifred Bagnall	5 months
Ethel Holt	17 months
Forrester Hollingshead	10 months
Samuel Wall	56
Caroline Belcher	59
Jane Yeomans	63

From 1896 the Parish Council inspected and repaired the wells and pumps in the village although, as the Vestry had found before them, this was an endless and fruitless task. They spent £148 on new sewerage works and dug new, deep self flushing sewers. From 1898 they were prepared to take property owners to court if they did not join their drains to the deep sewers. A great many houses did not have flush toilets and each household had to dispose of the contents of their privy as they saw fit. In 1898 and 1899 the Council agreed that they should organise the removal of "night soil" and ashes, but the task was still in the hands of individuals after the turn of the century.

In 1901 the Parish Council despaired of making any progress and turned the whole matter over to the Rural District Council, together with the associated problem of street cleaning and rubbish removal, or "scavenging" as it was called. This became one of the most controversial decisions ever taken by the Council. The following Parish Meeting in April 1901 was packed when the issue was discussed. Most people agreed that the removal of refuse, when left to individuals, was badly done and that, as a result, Penkridge was suffering insanitary conditions and poor public health. The difficulty arose in deciding who should pay for the improvements. Those who lived in the village itself, the area that was lit by the gas lamps, were willing to pay a rate to cover the costs. Unfortunately the Local Government Board would not allow this and insisted that the rate be levied upon the whole parish. The "outsiders" objected to this and attended the meeting in large numbers. As a result no progress could be made and J.C. Tildesley remarked bitterly that "only official red tape obstructed a very necessary public work." Eventually, in 1903, the County Medical Officer of Health insisted that the adverse vote at the Parish Meeting should not be allowed to stand in the way of reform.

Opposition to this relatively cheap reform had been so strong that it is little wonder that the much more expensive introduction of piped water was so long in coming. H.M. Whitehead, the Rural District Council's Engineer, first produced plans for a water supply in 1909 but the parish balked at a rate increase of 3d in the pound. The 1910 Parish Meeting appointed F. Jones and G. Brown to attend a public enquiry and protest at the expense of the scheme. In 1911 a proposed sewerage and water scheme provoked a bitter argument on the Parish Council. Many speakers claimed that the proposal would increase the rates by 10d in the pound and denied that there was any immediate necessity for such a scheme. The Council voted to oppose the introduction of a clean water supply "to the utmost extent".

Poverty, ignorance and a poor water supply was a dangerous combination. Many households were found to be in distressing states when H.M. Whitehead of the District Council, Sergeant Campbell and the NSPCC began to enforce the law rigorously at the turn of the century. In 1897 a Penkridge woman was jailed for seven days for child neglect. The NSPCC applied for an order to detain the child in the workhouse because when "they had returned with the mother to the old hovel where they lived, a doctor certified that they must be removed at once as the place was uninhabitable". General overcrowding was common, especially in Clay Street where Campbell and Whitehead enforced sanitary regulations. In 1900 Sergeant Campbell was called to Mill Street when a boy was attacked by his step-mother with a mop. He discovered a very dirty house and that the boy had to feed himself from the neighbours' pig bins. A charge of ill-treatment was dismissed because it emerged that the father was crippled and the family of eight were living on three shillings of groceries a week from the parish. In 1914 a case of child neglect at Biddles Bank, Penkridge, led to the discovery of a house in a disgusting condition. Six people lived in two rooms. The bedding was "saturated and rotten rags" and the mattress was described as being "more like a manure heap than anything else".

One of the main pre-occupations of the Parish Council was the state of the roads and footpaths. In 1898 they repaired the footpath between Bull Bridge and the White Hart, replacing the "unsightly" cobbles with blue bricks. With the District Council they assumed responsibility at a time of increasing road traffic. The long years of neglect since the coming of the railway meant there was much to do. In 1901 the condition of the Cannock Road by the canal bridge was a public scandal. It carried much traffic since it was part of the main route from Stafford to Walsall yet locals insisted that it had not been repaired in living memory and certainly not within the previous fifty three years. The Parish Council heard that the County Council ought to have been in charge but that the last work carried out on the road had been done by the Vestry's old Surveyor of Highways.

Traffic, and the speed of traffic, were increasing all the time but road work was done with the complete lack of urgency suitable to the previous, more leisurely, age. Dangerous road conditions were left uncorrected for years. In 1894 a traveller complained that,

> "Between Penkridge and Acton Trussell there is a long stretch of canal separated from the main road by the towing path only. On a dark or foggy night it is quite as easy to walk or drive into the canal as to keep on the road."

Heavy snowfall in the winter of 1902 blocked the village streets but clearing work was not carried out, even on the main roads, for a fortnight. Complaints about this and the state of the footpaths along the main road, to the County Council, proved to be "fruitless". By 1907 the speed of motor vehicles through the narrow streets was becoming a problem. The Parish Council had a long discussion over imposing a speed limit and decided to erect large warning signs at the outskirts of the village. The quality of the road surfaces was poor and in dry weather during the summer huge clouds of dust were caused by traffic and the wind. In 1909 the Parish Council decided it would be too expensive for them to buy a watering cart and asked the District Council to do something about it.

Penkridge had always been a busy commercial centre but rising expectations of public order and tidiness meant that the Council had to deal with the problems caused by this success. Villagers were annoyed by the state of Market Street on Saturday afternoons and Sunday mornings. The weekend's busy shopping left the road strewn with paper. The Council explained that they did not have the power to employ a man to clean up on Sunday mornings. Equally exasperating was the condition of Crown Bridge. This area enjoyed a freedom from bye-laws, a survival from the days of manorial common rights. As a result the road was often congested with hawkers and stall holders who erected booths, ran sideshows after dark, stayed on at night in their caravans and left large amounts of litter behind. In 1900 the Parish Council made them pay a small charge for the privilege, but the problem was not solved until 1902 when Lord Hatherton delegated his power as Lord of the Manor to the Council and they banned the erection of stalls and booths at that spot. A similar problem afflicted the Horsefair. This land was used by villagers as a recreation ground and was particularly popular with footballers. Unfortunately it also attracted large numbers of hawkers and travelling showmen. In 1913 Lord Hatherton gave the land to the Parish Council and they immediately fenced it off and banned gypsies from camping there. The fence was erected by H. Cheadle for a cost of £51 and the money was recovered by charging hawkers for using the site. The loss of this facility had been probable since 1908 when much of the land had been earmarked for the County Education Department's proposed new public elementary school for 150 pupils.

Probably the most beneficial decision taken by the Council was that to wind up the Penkridge Gas Company and hand over the enterprise to Stafford Corporation. Relations between the old company and the village had always been unhappy with over priced gas producing a grudging and penny pinching response. The Streets were only lit from September to April and in 1912, the last year of the company's operation, the village was actually cutting the number of its street lights. The capital for investment and the economy of scale brought by Stafford Corporation ushered in a bright new era for the village. Gas consumption increased so rapidly that in 1913 Stafford built a huge new gasholder for the village. The steel tank held 60,000 cubic feet of gas and two million gallons of water. It delivered gas at a pressure high enough to reach Brewood. At the opening ceremony it was predicted that "future generations would look upon that day's ceremony as one of the bright spots in the history of Penkridge". In the twelve months that they had been the supplier, Stafford Corporation had doubled the output of gas from two to four million cubic feet. They were supplying an extra 99 gas cookers and fires and had recruited an extra 54 pre-payment customers. In all, 150 Penkridge households received gas. The price of gas had fallen from 4/6d to 3/6d a thousand cubic feet.

The role of the Parish Council was not easy. Increasingly real power lay elsewhere, with the District and the County. Penkridge Parish Council, like its predecessor, the Vestry, showed short sightedness in resisting much needed schemes for sewage disposal and water supply. Nevertheless it had many successes, due in great part to its close relationship with Lord Hatherton and H.M. Whitehead, an invaluable link with the Rural District Council. It reflects well upon the Council that during the year of this country's most bitter party politics, 1910, the Penkridge parish elections passed without incident and almost without notice. Sixty villagers attended the public meeting and elected the Council by show of hands. Only two of those present demanded a poll and they could not find the necessary five supporters.

Chapter 24

Policing Penkridge
1842 - 1914

When the County Police Force was being set up in Staffordshire in the 1840s most people accepted that the more modern methods of law enforcement were needed in the Mining and Pottery districts. The establishment of a Rural Police Force, however, created a bitter and long lasting controversy. For years on end the Quarter Sessions at Stafford began with prolonged arguments amongst the magistrates as to whether the new arrangements were necessary or cost effective.

The Rural Police Force certainly seemed costly to people used to paying only the expenses of the manorial village constables. In 1843 Staffordshire Rural Police Force had 12 inspectors being paid £70 a year, 30 sub-inspectors paid £54 and 133 constables who earned up to 18 shillings a week. Men of property, living in small villages, could not see the justification for such expenditure. They were content to rely on the protection of their neighbours, tenants, labourers and servants. They knew all of these people and preferred them to a police constable, earning 18 shillings a week, doing nothing and perhaps visiting the village once a week. Penkridge had survived quite happily with a High Constable from the Hundred court and a village constable whose entire expenses were less than his rate bill. It must have come as a shock in 1843 when the estimates came in for a lock up, a police station and the police wages. In 1848 the cost of policing the whole Penkridge Union was £111,000. Many villagers must have agreed with the magistrates who called the force "entirely useless" and "no better than old women" when they realised that Penkridge benefited from this to the tune of seven arrests and £2..11s..9d in recovered money for the first six months of that year.

All arguments about the Rural Police Force ended in 1856 when an Act of Parliament made county forces compulsory. By then, however, Penkridge had become used to having a police presence in the village. The first constable to be described in action was Reuben Billet. In 1852 he had been called to the Boat Inn where Thomas Dobson was being abusive to the landlady. Billet threw Dobson out of the inn. Policing even a small village could be difficult and Billet's authority did not go untested. Dobson went home, got his fire poker and waited behind a garden wall until Billet passed by on his beat. He leaped over the wall and tried to stab the constable who was saved by his heavy greatcoat. With the help of villagers, Billet subdued his assailant and took him to the lock up where he remained until the magistrates court was in session. Dobson was given two months hard labour.

Throughout most of the nineteenth century the forces of law and order in Penkridge consisted of a resident sergeant in the police house in Bell Brook Lane and a constable who was usually his lodger. By the 1880s the sergeant could call on up to four constables for help though they were not all resident in the village. Up until 1881 the lock up was regularly in use. The village stocks were already an historical curiosity but were actually used later than might be supposed. In April 1871 a well respected sergeant, George Barratt, waded into the Penk and saved chimney sweep, James Smith, from drowning. When the magistrates heard that Smith had been drunk they asked whether the village had a set of stocks. Barratt replied that Penkridge did but that they were never used. The bench sentenced the sweep to a fine of 10s..6d or six hours in the stocks.

Once a fortnight Penkridge magistrates court sat at the Littleton Arms. After the police force was established they were called the Police Court and sat every week, alternating with Cannock. In 1881 the County took over the old bank building on the corner of Bell Brook and the Cannock Road and converted it into a police station with quarters for a sergeant, a constable and two cells. The magistrates court also switched to the new premises. The new court was clearly "home ground" for the police and up to 1889 they acted there as solicitors, prosecuting their own cases and cross examining witnesses. In Penkridge it was felt that they were taking advantage of this situation, using their supposed ignorance of the rules of evidence to press home their prosecutions. The court became the focus of national attention, briefly in September 1903, when George Ernest Thompson Edalji was remanded to the quarter sessions on suspicion of committing the Great Wyrley Outrages, the cattle maiming case, which later attracted the interest of Sir Arthur Conan Doyle. Lord Hatherton disqualified himself from hearing the case as he had known Edalji for seven years.

Despite predictions that the rural force would have little to do, policing Penkridge proved to be far from easy. On Christmas Day 1874 Sergeant Barratt was called to the George and Fox where a customer was having a fierce argument with the ostler. Barratt decided that the man was drunk and, taking hold of his arm, advised him to go home. The man responded by hitting him in the mouth and running up Goods Station Lane. The sergeant chased him and with four other men held him in a cart which took him to the lock up. The violence of the episode was underlined when the case came to court. The defendant claimed that he had been hit eight times with a police truncheon. The magistrate discounted this as being "wholly unworthy of belief" yet said, when sentencing,

"Taking into consideration the punishment which has been received by the defendant, whose caput, obdurate as it has shown itself in some respects, bears 'striking' evidence that it was no match for a policeman's staff, we fine him only 5 shillings."

The magistrates clearly took a robust attitude to law enforcement, saying that they "were quite satisfied that Sergeant Barratt had acted perfectly in accordance with his duty." The task of policing Penkridge could be tough and demanding. Penkridge's officers were often assaulted, though not always in the village itself. In March 1900 P.C.s Knight and Dean were arresting a violent man in Penkridge when they suffered violent blows to the backs of their necks as they slipped on the handcuffs. They turned to see a member of the public attempting to rescue their prisoner. In 1902 Sergeant Campbell and P.C. Knight ejected a local man from the White Hart. He refused to go home and had to be carried, struggling and kicking violently to the station by the police and three civilians. These cases show that while some villagers were likely to react violently towards the police others were prepared to come to their aid in a dangerous fight.

The life of a police officer in Penkridge was not always as exciting. More usually they courted unpopularity through the routine enforcement of petty regulations and traffic laws. Showing a sturdy independence they prosecuted the vicar for putting on a stage play without a licence in 1897 and local dog owners for allowing their pets to be at large without muzzles, under the Muzzling Order of 1892. One of the commonest offences committed in Penkridge was that of leaving a horse and cart unattended on the highway. This, obviously, could be quite dangerous but there was also a moral side to the prosecutions since almost invariably the horses and carts were left outside pubs. A sharp eyed constable could always find work to do. In 1876 the police prosecuted Penkridge coal dealer, William Bond, for not having his name painted on the side of his cart and Edward Trow for riding his horse without reins.

In the nineteenth century traffic offences happened at a slower speed but still could be very dangerous. In 1891 the police stopped Alfred Sturgess as he was driving into Penkridge because he had fallen asleep on top of his cart. He claimed to be delivering salt but when they searched the waggon they found 16 cwt of gelignite. Not surprisingly Sturgess received 21 days hard labour for so foolishly risking a collision and an explosion. A more common misdemeanour in Penkridge was "furious riding". In May 1891, for example, Joseph Holt of the Cross Keys beer house was charged with the crime, having "galloped at a furious pace across the Market Square at a late hour of the evening and turned the corner by the police station in a way which endangered the safety of a little boy".

When motor cars arrived in Penkridge at the turn of the century great confusion sometimes arose, in the courts as well as on the roads. In July 1900 a Birmingham man was charged with "furiously driving" his car on the Stafford Road in Penkridge. The landlord of the Crown Inn, William Crockford, said that the car was travelling at 25mph. On cross examination he admitted that he had only been in a car once and that he had estimated the speed by comparing it with that of a horse. Crockford's two sons, who were overtaking a cart on their bicycles, met the car coming the other way. After much "zig-zagging" both bikes and car ended in a ditch. Joseph Bird of the White Hart said that the car had been doing 20mph but local car expert, William Dunn said that the model could only reach 15mph and not even that with a passenger. The case was dismissed.

The police in the 19th century Penkridge did very little detecting. They usually knew who had committed the crime. This was particularly true of poaching. In October 1852 John Choyce of Dunston was prosecuted for breaking down a fence belonging to a tenant of Lord Hatherton and trespassing on his land, using a private farm road. Choyce claimed that it was a public road, until the enclosure award was brought in to court to show that the commissioners had "stopped up" the road. Choyce refused to pay his fine and was sentenced to 14 days hard labour. Bearing a grudge springing from the unfairness of the 1827 enclosure of the waste and commons, it appears that Choyce went on to found a dynasty of disgruntled poachers.

In 1886 Albert Choyce and George Lakin, described as "members of the Dunston Heath Poaching Gang", were caught by Sergeant Price who was on duty at 3.30 am at Park Gates. Albert Choyce, who had been convicted many times for poaching that year, had his gun confiscated and was fined £5. Choyce was completely unrepentant. When he and Lakin were caught rabbiting later in the year he told the magistrate, "The more you fine me, the more rabbits and hares I have to catch to pay." George Lakin, who had 34 convictions for poaching between 1877 and 1888 lived with Choyce on 1½ acres at Dunston. When caught on a farm he would run away or threaten the farmer with his gun but he was well known and the police would arrest him later, at home.

Not surprisingly, over the years the police and the poachers developed an antagonistic relationship. The police knew who the poachers were but persistent close surveillance was still needed because it was quite difficult to prove guilt in court. In June 1891 under the headline, "THE CHOYCE FAMILY AGAIN", the Staffordshire Advertiser told how Herbert Choyce and Zillah Choyce, alias Wright, of Dunston Heath, were charged with poaching and obstructing the police. PC Shaffery had met them on the road to Coppenhall, driving to Stafford. He stopped them and tried to search their cart. Choyce hit the policeman with his crutch and tried to drive away. Shaffery found 20 rabbits in the cart. He told the court that the police had watched Choyce's 1½ acres for 3 years and had seen no game of any kind on it. He admitted that he would always search Choyce if he saw him in the area. Choyce's lawyer said that having game was not an offence and that men had to be seen coming from the land where the game was poached. He claimed that it was disreputable of the police to summon Zillah as "alias Wright", which had been done merely from private spleen. The magistrates dismissed the charge of poaching but fined Choyce for the obstruction of the police.

Other poachers were on friendlier terms with the gamekeepers and the police. When they were caught "red handed" it was always worth trying to talk their way out of the situation. In March 1903 Penkridge miner, John Follows, was caught by Lord Hatherton's gamekeeper, William Pilsbury. Follows proposed the compromise, "I will shoot the dog, Will, if you won't summons me." Postman, Edward Brookes, was a well known Penkridge character. When Sergeant Harris met him at the Spread Eagle with bulging pockets he suspected that he was carrying more than letters. When asked to turn out his pockets he said, "Don't be so simple, Sergeant; you know I am a postman and you must be careful what you are doing with me. If you search me I shall report you." When Harris found two pheasants and eighteen cartridges he pleaded, "For God's sake, Sergeant, don't make a case of this." Brookes was fined £3.

Although much time and effort went into catching poachers, the most characteristic work of the Penkridge police in the nineteenth and early twentieth century was combating the sort of anti-social behaviour more usually associated with large towns and cities. They kept a strict watch on the many Penkridge pubs in their campaign against drunkenness and gambling. When cases in the magistrates court began to be reported in the Advertiser in the 1860s hardly a month went by without named villagers being fined for drunkenness, Pub landlords had to be very careful.

In 1861 William Dyke, of the George and Fox, was found guilty of keeping his house in a "disorderly condition" when the police found a man drunk and asleep in the tap room. In 1877 Sergeant Buckley dropped in at the White Hart and found a man lying on his back under the kitchen table, bleeding from the back of his head. He claimed that he had been sitting on the end of a bench and had only drunk one pint when all his companions got up at once and he had been tipped onto the floor. He was fined 2/6d and the landlord, Moore, was fined a pound and had his licence endorsed. In 1901 Anna Frape was fined for allowing drunkenness at the Cross Keys. Sergeant Campbell went in when he saw two very drunk men fighting outside. On entering he found the house had been turned upside down by eight men, with beer splashed around in all directions.

With so many pubs in Penkridge it is not surprising that drunkenness figured so largely in the court reports. What is really startling is the campaign of the Penkridge police against bad language in the village. Prosecutions for bad language began to be reported in the 1890s and continued up to the First World War. In many cases the use of bad language involved groups of disorderly youths whom many villagers clearly found menacing. In 1898 there were many complaints to the council about the foul language used by young men playing football on the Horsefair on Sunday afternoons. In July 1900 three young girls were charged with disorderly conduct in Clay Street. Sergeant Campbell said it was a very common occurrence in that neighbourhood and was becoming a public nuisance. The Church of England's St. Margaret's Home for Waifs and Strays was close by and the magistrates commented that, "it was a very bad example for them to hear filthy language used." Long summer evenings in the village could be spoiled by such behaviour. In August 1904 the residents of Stone Cross sent a note to the council complaining of "the continuous disorderly conduct of a gang of youths" and the police were asked to act. This was easier said than done. In 1902 PC Flavell saw same lads obstructing the footpath at the corner of Market Street and Mill Street. When asked to move on they refused. In court Lord Hatherton said he quite believed the officer but that it would be quite unsafe to convict on the police evidence alone.

The most remarkable aspect of the police campaign against bad language was that it extended into people's own homes. Although the dividing line between home and street was not so clearly marked in the nineteenth century, with large families crowded into small houses packed onto the main streets of the village, this extension of police action was deeply resented. In July 1902 a local man was charged with using bad language in his own house in Market Street. The defendant, alleged to be drunk in court by the Advertiser, said that he thought that a man should be allowed to say "what h'ad a mind" in his own home. He was fined 20 shillings or fourteen days hard labour. In the same year five villager were charged with using bad language in a house in Clay Street. Sergeant Campbell, revealing the relentless nature of the police operation, claimed he had heard the most filthy language from 11pm to midnight. The intrusive police campaign was still going strong in 1909. In court a Penkridge man denied using bad language at home and complained that his house was watched by the police day and night. Lord Hatherton remarked, unsympathetically, that he supposed that the defendant used bad language so often that he didn't know when he used it.

It is difficult to tell at this distance how far police action in Penkridge erred towards harassment. Noisy and unruly neighbours were a greater nuisance in the nineteenth century, when houses were more closely packed together, than they are today. However, it was clearly an unhappy situation in which a resident police force in a small village regularly and persistently arrested the same small group of people. Between 1860 and 1914 it is evident that police attention centred on just seven related Penkridge families. They were mainly agricultural labourers living on Market Street, Mill Street and Clay Street. Almost every prosecution for bad language, disorderly behaviour, drunkenness and obstructing the police involved one of them. Interestingly, they were involved in no other types of crime and after the First World War this type of misbehaviour seems to have disappeared almost entirely.

One looks in vain in the records of the magistrates court for evidence of a "golden age" of rural policing, amongst the reports of attacks on the police, drunkenness and alienated youths gathering on the streets of the village. In only a few cases does one recognise an attitude born of a different age. In 1901 a nine year old boy was charged with throwing a stone at the Stafford and Birmingham express and shattering the window of a second class compartment. As the incident happened near to the home of one of his "target" families Sergeant Campbell soon discovered the culprit. He questioned the boy who admitted throwing the stone but denied intending to actually hit the train. This timeless story concludes in a way that places it firmly in a previous age. The Advertiser reported that, "in lieu of a fine the boy's father consented to administer six strokes of the birch in the presence of Sergeant Campbell."

Chapter 25

The Good Old Grit
1900 - 1914

Saturday, May 26th, 1900 was a day of relief and great celebration for the people of Penkridge. The village was draped in flags and bunting, and the bells of St. Michael's rang throughout the day. In the afternoon the school children were dressed up as soldiers and sailors and paraded around the village singing patriotic songs. On the Sunday the Rev. Ticehurst Corfield and his curate preached joyful sermons and the National Anthem was sung at each service. On Tuesday evening the members of the Penkridge Fire Brigade, in full uniform, paraded around the village and Rodbaston with the fire engine. Someone dressed up as Baden Powell and was carried on a cart together with an effigy of Paul Kruger. As darkness fell the scene was lit by Chinese lanterns and the effigy of the Boer leader was burned on the Horsefair surrounded by a noisy demonstration with the blowing of horns.

The four days of jubilation were to celebrate the Relief of Mafeking. It was the second such outburst of patriotism, coming three weeks after the news of the Relief of Ladysmith, and marked the end of an uneasy period in the Boer War when the greatest empire the world had seen was having undue difficulty in defeating the irregular forces of a few South African farmers. It was a small war but touched many of the villagers closely. On Wednesday, four days before the great weekend festivities, a much more sombre event had taken place. The parents and friends of Private George Harvey of the 6th Dragoon Guards had packed the church for a memorial service for the local boy who had died of enteric fever a month earlier at Bloemfontein. After the Vicar's "touching and appropriate address" the "Dead March from Saul" was played and the church bells rang a muffled peal.

It would not be long, however, before live heroes returned from the war to the village. In July 1901 a special dinner was held at the Littleton Arms to honour Corporal W.H. Keeling of the Imperial Yeomanry. The great pride that the villagers felt in his achievements was unmistakable, with one of the speakers at the dinner stating that,

"The little town of Penkridge has always responded to the country's call by sending out volunteers to the front but when the names of Boycott, Keeling, Rogers, Masfen and others are amongst those who volunteered it showed us that the good old grit of our forefathers is still in our veins".

As is often the way with returning heroes, Corporal Keeling made a modest reply, saying that "I little thought whilst with my colleagues on the veldt, that on my return home my friends would have rallied round in the splendid manner they have tonight to welcome me back to the old country." Mr. Cyril Felthouse, whose grandfather served in the Staffordshire Yeomanry in the 1870s, says that if you were a tenant farmer on one of the large estates it was "understood" that one of your sons would serve in the Yeomanry.

The Conservative government did not hesitate to exploit the country's surge of patriotism and called the "Khaki" election in 1900 which they won well. The Liberals had an ambivalent attitude to the war, with their radical "star", Lloyd George, complaining about the ruthless methods employed by the British and promising that, "If I have the courage, I shall protest with the vehemence at my command against the outrage which is perpetuated in the name of freedom." Penkridge was a Conservative village and its Conservative Association was glad to associate itself with the war effort. At the Annual Conservative Dinner of 1900 at the Littleton Arms, 130 people welcomed back Trooper Masfen of the Rhodesia Horse, who had been invalided home. The main speaker of the evening was the local Conservative or Unionist M.P. for West Staffordshire, Mr. Henderson, who declared that,

"At any rate the English have something to be proud of, and if we boast it is only natural. We have today the greatest empire in the world, with a population loyal and devoted to our Queen."

Henderson was one of the beneficiaries of the country's patriotic fervour, having been returned unopposed in the "Khaki" election.

By the time of the Conservative Association Dinner of 1903, held at the George and Fox, events had moved on. The old Queen had died in 1901 when it was reported that, in Penkridge, "general sorrow is evinced among all the classes at the irreparable loss which has befallen the Empire". The Boer War had ended with the Peace of Vereenigeng in 1902. Disquiet had grown about the conduct of the war which had not augured well for any future conflict with a great military and industrial power, like Germany for instance. The guest of honour at the Conservative Dinner, Colonel Wight-Boycott dealt with some of the criticisms in a bluff and hearty speech which contained ominous words for those of his countrymen who would be found on the Somme, thirteen years later. To great applause from Penkridge Conservatives he said,

"You have seen criticisms of officers in the papers but you have never seen any criticism of Tommy Atkins. I have a great admiration for the British infantry soldier. It was a magnificent sight to see those men go into action, line after line, facing almost certain death, and never wavering for a moment although their comrades fell on all sides. It made me proud to feel I was an Englishman."

Time, however, was running out for the complacent Conservatives of Penkridge and West Staffordshire. Their government seemed to be tiring in office and it was making political mistakes. In 1906 the unthinkable happened and West Staffordshire was swept away in the election landslide which produced a Liberal government with a majority of 220 over the Unionists. A chastened Sir Alexander Henderson returned to the George and Fox in 1907 and explained that he had suffered the "bitter blow" of losing a seat that should always be Unionist, because the government had upset and aroused the opposition of non-conformists with their 1902 Education Act, and offended the working class with a Trade Disputes Bill, and by allowing the use of Chinese indentured, or "coolie", labour in South Africa.

At the dinner, organised by Frank Dukes, the Secretary of the Conservative Association, attended by the leading citizens of Penkridge, including Lord Hatherton, Dr. Boldero, Mr. A.R. Keeling, Mr. Heath, Mr. T.J. Rostance, Mr. W.W. Stubbs, Mr. E. Lees, Mr. A. Cheadle, Mr. F. Sprenger and Mr. C. Creswell, the counter attack on the Liberal government was vigorous. The local Conservatives played their strongest cards: patriotism and defence. Mr. R.E. Murphy, member of the Parish Vestry and sidesman in the church, gave the toast of "The Imperial Forces" and in referring to the Navy said that,

"Some who commanded the great leviathan battleships of England would do well to emulate the bravery of Drake and the immortal Nelson. From what I can read the Navy is now to be made more efficient by a reduction of its size. [laughter] Penkridge has provided men to fight in the old wars, and some who have gone out have lost their lives in the more recent campaign in South Africa and I think that the village, which has provided judges for the courts, will be able to find soldiers for the King should the necessity arise. [applause]."

H.M. Whitehead, surveyor to the Rural District Council and Captain of the Penkridge Fire Brigade, responded by saying that "he thought it was a false economy for the government to reduce the strength of the army and navy and also to dispose of so many employees from Woolwich Arsenal. It meant that where the present government saved one thousand pounds, it would cause the next to spend two thousand to replace what had been lost."

The years after 1906 were awkward ones for places like Penkridge. Society was founded on respect for and deference to authority, yet years of what has been called "relentless political warfare" strained these foundations to breaking point. It almost seemed that, following the death of the old Queen, Victorian Society itself was decomposing. The Conservatives felt that they were fighting a deliberate assault on their property and privileges and more or less refused to accept the result of the 1906 election. Their leader, Arthur Balfour declared that,

"The great Unionist Party should still control, whether in power or opposition, the destinies of this great Empire."

Mr. Balfour ruthlessly used the permanent Conservative majority in the House of Lords to thwart the democratically elected Commons, eventually forcing the Government to call an election in 1910 when the Budget was rejected in the Upper House. The Conservatives of West Staffordshire were determined to win back their seat and it seems quite clear that the viciousness of party politics in London descended to the local level and helped to poison the atmosphere in Penkridge.

On election day, according to the secretary of the West Staffordshire Liberal Association,

"The respectable residents of Penkridge, including ladies, were allowed to assemble in front of the residencies of Liberal voters and encourage rowdy youths to throw rotten tomatoes at the windows and doors, and a crowd of men and youths were permitted to remain outside the Liberal Committee room in Market Square all day and insult those who came near to the place. The windows of the Committee Room were broken and this took place in full view of the officers in charge at the polling station close to, but not a single effort was made to put a stop to it. We are forced to the conclusion that political bias was at the bottom of the whole affair and that someone behind the scenes has prompted the action of the police".

All this was in marked contrast to the actions of the police in Cheslyn Hay. There, according to the Liberals, they had diligently identified, tracked down and prosecuted 70 miners who had taken part in a peaceful parade in support of the Government on polling day.

When the count at the Shire Hall in Stafford revealed that the Conservative candidate, Mr. George Lloyd had won the seat for the Unionists, the Conservatives of Penkridge were jubilant. The Staffordshire Advertiser reported that,

"At Penkridge, the fire bell was rung when news of Mr. Lloyd's victory came to hand. It was intimated that the new member would pass through Penkridge about 2 o'clock, and steps were taken to give him a rousing reception. Banners and flags were quickly displayed. A band of workers prepared to meet Mr. Lloyd's car on the Bull Bridge. Here the Member was taken out of his car and carried shoulder high to the square accompanied by numerous supporters. The fire engine was taken out and Mr. Lloyd utilized this as a platform from which he thanked the Penkridge supporters."

Lloyd later proclaimed that,

"West Staffs had sent a message to the whole Empire."

The Conservatives regained West Staffordshire but, to their great surprise, failed to dislodge the Liberal Government which, having now the same number of MPs as the Conservatives, retained power with the support of the Irish Nationalists and the small Labour party. Party politics continued on its downward spiral. A second election in 1910 with an almost identical result led to a reduction in the powers of the House of Lords and, in theory, opened the gates to greater social reform and Home Rule for Ireland. Instead it seemed to lead to four years of festering discontent which threatened to bring social upheaval from the suffragettes, civil war over Ireland and class warfare from the trade unions. Ripples from some of these mighty events were felt in Penkridge in the years before 1914.

Some of the Liberal social reforms were so beneficial that they were accepted by the Conservatives without too much dissent. The Old Age Pensions Act was one of these and it profoundly improved the lives of working people who no longer had to fear the workhouse in old age or work until they dropped. Pensions were distributed at the post office and it is appropriate that the first recorded example in Penkridge of retirement being a joyful occasion should be that of a postman. Thomas Leek of Mill Street had just turned 70, and, under the terms of the Act was entitled to his pension of 5 shillings a week. In May 1911 the Advertiser reported that,

"One by one the old links with Penkridge are becoming severed. On Tuesday afternoon the local Postmistress, Miss Dukes, entertained the postal staff to tea, and afterwards on behalf of the staff, she made a presentation to Thomas Leek of an easy chair on his retirement as postman after 39 years of service."

Auld Lang Syne was sung and Thomas was carried home shoulder high in his chair. He supplemented his pension with work as a jobbing gardener and survived until 1919 when he fractured his skull in a fall while working at Mill House.

The Liberals also introduced a Children's Charter, part of which brought in juvenile courts. The local police court, usually presided over by Lord Hatherton, no longer dealt with children and adults together and young offenders were granted anonymity in the papers. An example of this is reported in 1911 when an unnamed Penkridge child, aged seven years, was accused of stealing. His father had whipped him and fastened him in the cellar to no good effect. The court remanded the boy for 14 days and then sent him to an industrial school until he was 16.

The failure of the Liberals and the Labour party to reverse Conservative anti-trade union legislation quickly enough, convinced many union leaders that the answer to the problems of the working class lay not in Parliament but in syndicalism, which envisaged the use of the general strike as a political weapon to gain control of the state. The idea led in 1911 to the first ever national railway strike. This put the 21 men and boys employed by the LNWR and stationed at Penkridge and Gailey in a very difficult position, being industrial workers isolated in the middle of a rural and Conservative area. It seems very probable that great pressure was put on the railway men of Penkridge to stay at work during the strike. In October 1911 a public meeting was held at the Penkridge schools. The Advertiser reported that,

"The Rev. Kempson explained that they were met together to dispense a fund which had been raised publicly for the benefit of the railway servants stationed at Penkridge and Gailey as a mark of appreciation of the loyal work done by them during the trying time of the late strike."

Many meetings were organised in Penkridge to oppose the government policy of disestablishing the Church of England in Wales. The highest levels of Penkridge society were involved in this protest movement. At a meeting in the church room Lord Hatherton himself described the bill as "the meanest he had ever known to be considered by the British Parliament." Despite this, the government reform which aroused the most hostility from the most people in Penkridge was, surprisingly, the National Insurance Act of 1911 which introduced a scheme of unemployment and sickness benefits.

In June 1912 opponents of the National Insurance Act organised a meeting at the Littleton Arms. So many people came that the Littleton could not hold them all and the crowd gathered in the street and the steps leading to the Inn were used as the platform. The Act proposed using existing Friendly Societies and Insurance Companies as agents for the National Insurance scheme. A great many people in Penkridge had been members of the Oddfellows Friendly Society for years and were outraged by what they saw as the unfairness of the Act. It was pointed out that a man who joined a Friendly Society then would get the same benefits as someone who had been paying in all his working life. There was, however, an even greater injustice. The visiting speaker told the crowd that,

"I know that in Penkridge you have one of the most wealthy lodges in connection with the Manchester Unity of Oddfellows in the whole district. You have been able to build up enormous funds but there are other societies which are insolvent. You, the members of the Penkridge lodge, will have to help out of your funds, to make these other societies solvent. Why has your lodge of Oddfellows been able to build up this money? It is simply because the members are members of an agricultural community, who are, as is well known, the most healthy people in the country."

It seemed quite unfair that the Penkridge lodge which had built up reserves of £13,500 should have to support, say, Hednesford lodge which only had £887. The Penkridge farm workers, with their low agricultural wages, would be paying in all their healthy working lives and gaining nothing since at the age of 70 they would get their Old Age Pension. Factory workers and Hednesford miners had much higher wages but would pay the same contribution of 4d as farm workers and were much more likely to be ill and collect benefits.

The National Insurance Scheme was inferior to their own Oddfellows one. For a 6½d weekly contribution their lodge at Penkridge had been able to pay members who joined between the ages of 21 and 50, 10 shillings a week for 52 weeks and 5 shillings a week afterwards. The Insurance Act would pay only 10 shillings a week for 26 weeks and 5 shillings a week afterwards. It appeared that the farm worker was to be "filched" for the benefit of towns.

At the end of the meeting Mr. James Heath proposed the resolution, "That this meeting of employers and employees pledges itself to refuse to carry out the demands of the National Insurance Act until it is amended in such a manner as to give fair treatment to the rural districts." In a remarkable example of how much the old fabric of society had disintegrated this respectable farmer, a leading light of the Penkridge Branch of the Midland Farmers Association and sometime member of the Parish Council, went on to declare that,

"For my part I won't pay the contribution; I won't collect it. I will face the police court and will do a week or two in gaol before I will pay, until such time as the Act is amended to give the agricultural labourer and the inhabitants of rural districts fair play."

When the National Insurance Act became law it came as an unpleasant surprise to some despite all the publicity. Mr. Cyril Felthouse remembers being in his father's farm kitchen at Pillaton on the first pay day that contributions were due. One old labourer looked at his money and said, "This ain't right, Gaffer." Mr. Felthouse explained it was due to Lloyd George's Scheme. The labourer said "I'm not paying it" and threw his wages across the kitchen floor. He picked them up later!

Despite the troubles of the pre-war years, however, Penkridge maintained an outward and visible show of patriotism and almost military discipline. Almost any occasion, ranging from a coronation to the meeting of the Oddfellows, was used as an excuse for parading on the Market Square, marching round the village or following a band down to the church. The village had much closer links with the army than is possible today. In May 1912, for example, a company of the West Yorkshire Regiment marched into the village on a Friday and was billeted there for the weekend. On the Sunday morning they paraded at Stone Cross together with the Yeomanry and cycle divisions and then marched out with baggage waggons and water carts to take part in night manoeuvres on the Chase. The West Yorkshires had been previously billeted in Cannock to deter trouble during the recent coal strike but this had not prevented good relations developing with them in both areas.

Patriotism, love of Empire and military values were drilled into the young. In 1913 the Penkridge Troop of Boy Scouts together with three troops from Stafford and one from Brereton assembled at Penkridge and then marched to Mitton to receive their colours. They were given a Union Jack and told that it was "a flag that was most honoured in the world". It was dedicated in St. Michael's Church "To the Glory of God and for the use of St. Michael's Penkridge Troop for ever". There was a Penkridge branch of the Junior Imperial League with one hundred members. Early in 1914 they received a lantern lecture on the British Empire. Lord Hatherton presented them with a Union Jack and told them that, "So long as our Kingdom remained united it would remain the greatest empire the world had ever known."

Chapter 26

The Great War
1914 - 1918

Of all the meetings held during the winter months of early 1914 the most interesting for Charles Morris was probably the smoking concert at the Boat Inn. It was being held to raise money for Penkridge United FC and Charles was a prominent member of the team. He had been keen on football since he was a boy and it had sometimes got him into trouble. He was a tough lad and once, in 1907 he had been playing football with his brother George, Charles Till and Joseph and Albert Weatherer when an opponent from Dunston stepped out of line and had to be taught a lesson. He was knocked down and the Penkridge boys took him to the bridge and dangled him over for about half an hour, threatening to deposit him in the Penk. Charles now worked at the Littleton Colliery and would attend the concert if he could because Penkridge were half way through one of their best seasons and would eventually come second in the Stafford and District League. Before the year was out a more awesome distinction would be thrust upon this collection of men and boys.

The 1907 example of football violence eventually found its way into the police court. In 1914 Lord Hatherton was still regularly working his way through a dreary catalogue of petty crime in Penkridge Police Court. He was 75 and took his duties as magistrate, Poor Law Guardian, Chairman of Staffordshire County Council and landowner very seriously indeed. It was said he knew every villager personally and it must have been dispiriting for him to see the same faces brought before him for justice year after year.

The 1914 legal year began in Penkridge with the continuing campaign against bad language. Joseph Handley, a miner living at the Goods Station, was summoned for using indecent language at his mother-in-law's house on Christmas Eve. Lord Hatherton commented that, "It is perfectly disgraceful that people in the street should have to hear such language". In February the court dealt with cases of poor school attendance. In May it dealt with two cases of indecent language, two cases of violent conduct and clamped down on the riding of bikes without lights at Quarry Heath. In July Lord Hatherton tried to stem the considerable crime and vandalism associated with the churchyard by fining a woman for stealing geraniums from a grave. After many years on the magistrates' bench it is perhaps little wonder that Lord Hatherton began to lose confidence in the character of his neighbours and was moved to comment that,

"I think that there was more enthusiasm and more patriotism and more desire to defend the country in the past than there appears to be now."

A more obvious source of patriotic leadership could be found at a January meeting at the George and Fox. Here about eighty villagers enjoyed the eighteenth annual dinner of the Penkridge Fire Brigade. The brigade had seen their usefulness eroded by competition from the greatly improved Stafford brigade but embodied military virtues and had been used to celebrate many patriotic occasions. The chief officer of the brigade and chairman of the dinner was Captain Whitehead. He lived at Congreve Manor and was a very prominent member of Penkridge society being the surveyor of the Rural District Council and a leading member of the Conservative Association.

The Church, of course, was expected to provide leadership in the village and many of the meetings and events of early 1914 were organised by it. In February the Rev. Kempson carried out the traditional distribution of the Candlemass doles in the Church room. He handed out the Littleton Dole of £2 to forty poor people, Miss Pott's Dole of £2..3s..8d to thirty four poor people and Miss Price's Dole £2..8s..4d to twelve widows. There were soon to be many more candidates for the last piece of charity. Kempson was assisted by his curate E.L. Frossard who had been in Penkridge for three years. There were many regular church meetings. Two hundred people attended the Sunday School prize-giving in February and the choir and bellringers, including Edmund Westwood of Mill Street, met every week. The Church of England's Men's Society had a concert and whist drive in January. Lady Stamer, of Haling Dene, helped to organise the Girls' Friendly Society annual tea and social gathering in the Hatherton Memorial School.

When the war came in August 1914 the worst of fears of Lord Hatherton were not realised and the men of Penkridge joined the rush to volunteer. By 1915, a year before full conscription was introduced, the Church Vestry reported that 140 parishioners had joined the armed forces. Lord Hatherton estimated that 10% of the village were serving King and Country in some capacity. Both the vicar Kempson and his curate E.L. Frossard joined the army. Captain Whitehead joined the Sherwood Foresters. The great majority of the volunteers were not these leaders of society, of course, but ordinary working men: the farm workers, miners and shop assistants. Many of the young men Lord Hatherton had seen in court in the previous ten years went to do their duty. Looking back, the last meeting of Penkridge Football Club seemed a poignant affair. The secretary of the club, J.R. Burd reported in 1915 that every single member of the team who had received a runners-up medal for the 1913 - 14 season had enlisted, plus eighteen other reserves and club members.

The patriotic urge was undoubtedly strong in Penkridge but the moral pressure to volunteer should not be overlooked. Penkridge was a small community and Lord Hatherton dominated the lives of many: he was their landlord, employer and magistrate. Just as the casualty lists from the first battle of Ypres were being published, in November 1914, Lord Hatherton addressed a recruiting meeting at Cannock. He said that,

"I am glad to see that there are some ladies present, and I trust that you will communicate with all your sisters in order that they may be the very best of recruiting mediums. If all the ladies present in this hall will only see to it that unless your brothers or sweethearts and your male relatives go to the Front, you would put a white feather in the back of their collars. Many of the men will then enlist."

By the end of 1914 ninety young men had already left Penkridge to join the armed forces. As the first Christmas of the war approached Miss Stamer of Haling Dene organised a village collection and sent each one a parcel containing warm clothing and a pocket Testament from the vicar and cigarettes from the boys of Penkridge School.

Much of the enthusiasm for volunteering was founded on the optimistic belief that the war would be short, glorious and victorious. While the early recruits were being trained, the fate of the regulars and reservists of the British Expeditionary Force put paid to this notion. Old hands, like Sidney Thursfield who had rejoined the Coldstream Guards just before the war started, faced the enemy at the battle of Mons in 1914 and won the Military Medal in 1915. Finding the British Expeditionary Force dwarfed by the armies of France and Germany, he would have understood that the war was going to be long and bloody and that his friends and neighbours back home really were going to be needed.

As the seriousness of the war sank in, a large open air service of intercession was held in Penkridge. All denominations were invited in July 1915 to the Market Place to attend a service led by the Rev. Kempson before he too left to do his duty. In August 1915, the Government, desperate for recruits but unwilling to introduce conscription, instituted a National Registration Day. Penkridge responded with a big recruiting rally on the Crown Bridge. Soldiers and leading gentlemen of the area spoke but even Lord Hatherton had to admit that there was little more Penkridge could do since so many had already volunteered.

As the manpower situation worsened, the Government dithered. Instead of full conscription it introduced the Derby Scheme under which men were expected to "attest", making themselves available for the call up on the understanding that single men would go first. The scheme was not compulsory and relied on moral blackmail. In Penkridge James Heath held a recruiting meeting at the School in November 1915 to implement the scheme. Since so many had already volunteered it is not surprising that a willing band of helpers arrived to hunt out the backsliders and the area was divided up into districts so that pressure could be more effectively applied.

Universal conscription was finally introduced in May 1916. From then on anyone hoping to avoid the call-up had to apply to the Cannock Rural Tribunal. Not many Penkridge people seem to have applied for exemption but Lord Hatherton, who was a tribunal member, had a rather embarrassing moment when one of his gardeners appeared before him. Lord Hatherton explained to his colleagues that this was his last gardener and that he was not growing flowers but two tons of desperately needed potatoes for the war effort. Farmers could claim exemption on the condition that they cultivated their land to the utmost extent.

Penkridge responded quickly to the demands of the war. It seemed a well integrated village with a large supply of people with experience of leadership in local government and voluntary groups. There was an alternative network of organisations like the schools, the church and the fire brigade which had their own lines of communication which could adapt to new situations rapidly. A good example of this was the War Savings Campaign of 1916. The government introduced a democratic method of financing the war which would benefit the working classes by selling War Savings Certificates which could be purchased for a few shillings up to a limit of 500 certificates. The county set up a pyramid of War Savings Committees. "Onlooker" in the Staffordshire Advertiser noted that, "The result has been that with the single exception of Penkridge and a few adjacent villages, the whole county has been covered by local committees".
Penkridge, in the shape of Caroline Stamer of Haling Dene did not take this slur lying down. She informed "Onlooker" that Penkridge was the first place in the county to get involved and that the work had been done by the Girls' Friendly Society. They had already raised £3,350. She dismissed the journalist, saying,

"Penkridge and the adjoining villages are fully alive to the importance of helping the nation to run the war."

Penkridge had a long and honourable history of self help and voluntary effort. The massive and rapid response to the call for volunteers in 1914 was perhaps the high point of this tradition. Such was the patriotism of the village and its desire for an efficient war effort that it came to accept state compulsion and hold feeble government action in contempt. When, late in the war, the government created the Ministry of National Service to make "the best voluntary use of all persons, whether men or women, able to work in any industry, occupation or service" Penkridge acted immediately but, led by Frank Dukes, passed the following resolution,

"That this meeting, while willing to carry out the work asked for under the voluntary system, desire to record their opinion that a compulsory scheme would be more effectual and just."

Penkridge people were well used to arranging events to raise money. In war time the tradition continued. In 1915 Lady Stamer opened the grounds of Haling Dene for an "American Tea" in aid of the Red Cross. There were many stalls and tea was taken on the terrace. A popular side show was "Throwing at the Kaiser". The Railway Smithfield organised a Fresh Fruit and Vegetable Fund for the Fleet. In January 1916 they sold and resold a bottle of Bass beer brewed by Edward VII in 1902 for £5. The last of 110 buyers was Jesse Olarenshaw who survived to become the "Grand Old Man" of Penkridge, living at Trees, Francis Green Lane in 1961.

Apart from the casualty lists the impact of the war on Penkridge was far from calamitous. Descriptions of Zeppelin raids on the Midlands in the newspapers were unsettling, the more so because the censors did not allow the exact locations to be revealed. Penkridge was not really worried, however, and when the question of air raid alarms was discussed by the Parish Council in April 1916 they just decided to leave the matter in the hands of the Parish Clerk and the police. The easiest way to fall foul of the Defence of the Realm Act was to leave a light shining at night. The police enforced a blackout and the Penkridge Police Court imposed stiff fines on Martha Worsey of Boscomoor, James Heath at the Littleton Arms and Gertrude Handley at the Goods Station.

Some of the effects of the war were directly beneficial to the people of Penkridge. High prices and rationing were irksome but Frank Dukes, Chairman of the Penkridge Food Control Committee, made sure there was a positive side to his work. Food economy lectures were given, a communal kitchen for school children was set up and each house in the village was visited to make sure the best use of the food was being made. Real poverty with its devastating effect on children was reduced during the war. Child care came to be seen as an important issue and in 1918 the Rural District Council set up its first Maternity and Child Welfare Clinic.

Many families in Penkridge were better off than ever before as a result of the war. The labour shortage meant that jobs and wages were plentiful. The availability of money combined with the absence of male heads of households could, however, lead to a certain demoralisation. In October 1915 there was a pitched battle in Mill Street involving six women. Lord Hatherton commented from the bench "that there was either too much money flying about or the women did not know what to do with it. Money seemed to be improperly spent."

Penkridge's main contribution to the war effort on the Home Front was the production of food. Before the war started, Penkridge farmers were anticipating a good harvest. The River Penk had just been belatedly cleansed and the low lying meadows were producing excellent grass. Rain in July had greatly improved the pastures elsewhere. The wheat and mangolds were looking good and a top quality harvest of potatoes was expected. Although British agriculture had not prospered in the previous few decades many people still felt that the farming life embodied the English virtues for which they were fighting. When describing local agriculture in 1917, the Staffordshire Advertiser was moved to say,

"Wolgarston is a very ancient farm. It was such I believe in 1066 when William the Norman cast his avaricious eyes on the fair heritage of England and William the German would no doubt like to follow the Norman's example and include it in a Doomsday Book for 1917."

The tenant of Wolgarston was Mr. Joseph Brown. The farm consisted of about 338 acres, of which 210 were arable. The land was level and all the ploughing was done with a two horse team. In 1917 Joseph Brown was growing 45 acres of wheat, 20 acres of oats, 12 acres of a mixture of oats, barley and peas mainly to feed the stock and 26 acres of barley - Bass's Best Malting. There were also 6 acres of potatoes, 46 acres of swedes, turnips and mangolds and a small acreage of rape and vetch on which sheep would be folded. A few dairy cows were kept for milk and butter for his household and 40 cattle were fed up during the year for the local butchers. The main business of the farm was, however, a herd of 450 Shropshire sheep.

Brown was an excellent farmer and had won many prizes for his sheep. The war had convinced him, however, that he had to act like a business man engaged on the wholesale production of food. He felt that the old system of judging animals in shows had to be abandoned if it did not lead to the production of the greatest quantity of food in the easiest and cheapest ways. He maintained that the war had made farmers more practical in many ways.

Like most farmers, Brown was irritated by the war time regulations. He suspected the government were being devious when they said farmers could not sell a horse without a licence. He felt that if he were to apply for a licence the Army would be alerted that he had a horse surplus to requirements and that it would only be a matter of time before an army buyer arrived with a cheque the size of which could not be negotiated. He took a dim view of the campaign to plough up more land. If the country's land was farmed better, with better buildings and better equipment he thought there would be no need to bother about it.

Brown's biggest grievance was the fixing of farm prices. He believed that high wheat prices would have acted as an incentive to farmers to grow more, and more land would have been brought naturally under cultivation. Then the prices would have righted themselves. He put much of the blame for high prices during the war down to middlemen rather than farmers. Brown was supported by other Penkridge farmers. The summary of Penkridge farming opinion in 1917 was that the Food Controller was giving the farmer no encouragement. Lord Hatherton also supported his tenants. He said, "The farmers have done well. They have done their best but they have been hampered by the government who don't seem to realise that the cost of feeding stuff and the scarcity of labour all militate against the farmers who cannot produce food as cheaply as they used to."

Although the last hay harvest of the war in Penkridge was damaged by a combination of wet weather and an unexpected government call-up of men, the area did not suffer too much from a general labour shortage. Joseph Brown maintained that you could hang on to good workers if you provided them with good cottages, of which he had six. Penkridge farms employed Land Army girls and unskilled workers were fairly plentiful since the farmers could get prisoners of war and soldiers from the local camps. Tractors also made their appearance on the fields under a scheme organised by the County War Agricultural Committee which was chaired by Lord Hatherton.

The real price of the war was being paid, of course, by the young men of the village. One of the first casualties occurred, tragically, not at the Front, but near the village itself. Private John Brookes of the South Staffordshire Regiment fell asleep on the train when returning to Penkridge on leave. He missed the station, attempted to get off the moving train and was killed on the track.

By 1916 news of fighting involving local people was being published. John Adderley who worked on his father's farms at Otherton and Mansty was reported as being killed in action, having been hit several times in the leg. Luckily John survived and his story provided a graphic account of conditions at the Front. He was stuck in No Man's Land from a Sunday morning to Friday night without food or water.
He said,

"I lay in shell holes in the day time and crawled about by night. Several times when it got dark I started to crawl to our lines, only to find the next morning I had turned about and gone towards the German lines, when I had to lie quiet another day. At last on Friday night I landed on our wire and I was then 20 yards off our lines, so I went to sleep. They spotted me from our lines and thought I was a German. When I awoke there were six around me with a rifle apiece. They soon recognised who I was, however, when I spoke and a sergeant carried me on his back and gave me water."

News from the war gave new meaning to traditional celebrations. Trafalgar Day in October 1916 became a much more important event with the news that local man Allan Rostance had taken part in the battle of Jutland. It was reported that,

"Children paraded in Market Square under the Union Jack. A laurel wreath hung at the side of the flag pole and was inscribed as follows 'Nelson and Trafalgar, Allan Rostance and J. Banks, Jellicoe and Jutland'. Mr. Frank James brought forcibly home to them the splendid lesson of duty and discipline, showing what their line of duty should be to their teachers, and the lesson of obedience."

As the war progressed the news from the Front inevitably got worse. In November 1917 Edmund Westwood, a leading member of the choir and the bellringers was reported killed by shellfire. Edmund lived in Mill Street. In the same month more bad news came concerning Victor Caine of Market Street. Aged twenty he had been shot in the head and killed. He had died before he could be presented with the Military Medal awarded to him for exceptional bravery on the 9th August.

By 1918 telegrams and letters of condolence were arriving regularly in Penkridge. Ernest Haywood, a farm labourer who worked for James Bassett of Longridge, had been in France for 3½ years, serving with the South Wales Borderers. He had been married for only four months when his wife received a letter from the matron of the hospital where he had died from his wounds. She wrote,

"I cannot pretend to realise for one minute all that this sad news will mean to you, but all my sympathy is yours, and when you are feeling your most acute sorrow you will always have the proud feeling that your poor husband made the supreme sacrifice for his country in its greatest hour of need, and was one of the great war's heroes whose name will always be sacred."

The Haywoods were a patriotic family. Ernest had volunteered a month after the war had broken out. His brother Arthur had been killed in France four months before Ernest. Following the news of their deaths the youngest son of the family, Frederick, joined up. Thomas Till of Cannock Road had three sons who all volunteered at the start of the war. Corporal E. Till was in the Tank Corps and won the Military Medal for his bravery at the Battle of Amiens and was mentioned in despatches for the Battle of Ypres in 1917. His brother Frank had been killed in 1916.

At least nine Penkridge soldiers won the Military Medal. Charles Morris, the footballer, served for four years in the Royal Army Medical Corps. He was attached to a section which included about nine other men from Penkridge. A section comprised about 14 men so the possibility of complete disaster hitting the village was great. This nearly happened in May 1918 when they were gassed. Two of the Penkridge men were killed but Charles helped to save the rest and was awarded his medal. When these casualties were reported the headline was "Death of Two Penkridge Pals". The story continued,

"Mrs. Burrows, Market Street, has received official information that her son Pte. Felix Burrows, aged 21 years, had died from gas poisoning while on active service in France. Before joining up he was in the employ of Mr. W.R. Ives, baker. Another son, Pte. Eric Burrows, Durham Light Infantry, was wounded in the right arm and back on the 21st March.

Another Penkridge lad, Pte. Jack Handley, aged 22, died from gas poisoning and of wounds received while on active service in France. He was a son of Mr. and Mrs. J. Handley, Goods Station, Penkridge. He and Pte. Felix Burrows were school 'pals', enlisted together and died about the same time. He had served 3½ years and worked at the Littleton Colliery."

Two of the other Military Medals were won by the sons of E. Haycock of Francis Green Lane who was a gardener at Haling Dene. Another Military Medal was won by a near neighbour of the Handleys' John Rotchell. He lived near the Goods Station, worked at the Gas Works and won the medal for conspicuous bravery and gallantry.

During the war Captain Whitehead was promoted to Colonel and worked as aid-de-camp to his general in the Sherwood Foresters. The highest award to a fighting soldier reported in the Advertiser was the Distinguished Conduct Medal won by Sidney Thursfield for conspicuous gallantry and devotion to duty. His citation in the London Gazette read,

"When commanding a platoon he handled it with great ability, and by his efficient fire control inflicted considerable casualties upon the hostile infantry. He led his platoon onto the final objective with the greatest dash, and on reaching it began the work of consolidation with great energy. At this point, on the enemy opening up an intense machine-gun fire, he got his machine-gun into action and succeeded in silencing the hostile gun. By his courage and coolness under harassing fire he set a fine example to his men."

There are three Talbots on the War Memorial. One of them, Pte. Albert Talbot, of Quarry Heath, died on 28th June 1918 at Basra. In 1916 he had caught a fever while fighting on the Somme. When he had recovered he was sent to Mesopotamia where he died of the fever. He had worked at Home Farm, Teddesley. Three brothers who came from Lord's Wood, Teddesley, the Dawsons, were killed in the war although they are not all on the memorial.

After the war ended two Penkridge families heard that they had lost their sons. In December 1918 Mr. and Mrs. A. Plant received the news that only son Sidney Arthur had been killed in action on November 4th, only seven days before the Armistice. In June 1919 official confirmation came of the death of Lieutenant George Webb, R.A.F. who had been reported missing in June 1918. He had begun in a North Midland Field Ambulance section and rose to become sergeant. He had been recruited into the R.A.F. but suffered engine failure on the way back from a bombing mission and had been attacked by a "Hun machine". He was an electrician at the Littleton Colliery and was an active member of Penkridge FC.

Penkridge celebrated the end of the war officially in July 1919. There was a traditional parade around the village organised by Colonel Whitehead. School children carrying coloured cards formed a living Union Jack on the sports field. Lord Hatherton presented Military Medals to Sgt. Major Bastone, Sgt. Till, Sgt. H. Brough, Sgt. E. Eccleshall, the mother of the late Victor Caine, Corporal John Rochell, Lance Corporal Haycock, Pte. Haycock and Charles Morris.

Rotchell, Lance Corporal Haycock, Pte. Haycock and Charles Morris.

The War Memorial was unveiled and dedicated on Easter Sunday 1921. Over a thousand people attended the ceremony. The relatives of the dead soldiers symbolically stood beside seventy Penkridge school children. The service began with the hymn, "O God our help in Ages Past". Lord Hatherton unveiled the memorial and gave thanks to God for having given them victory. "From henceforth", he said, "they should show their gratitude by living new and better lives - lives of more kindness, gentleness and brotherly feeling to all, especially to their friends and neighbours". He thought their hearts must go out with deep feelings of sympathy with the bereaved, the widows, orphans, mothers, fathers and relations of these gallant men to whom they in Penkridge owed a debt. By their love of country, self sacrifice and bravery they had saved the country from the horrors that were permitted in Northern France and Belgium.

"They died for England, to save her from the external enemy. Let us each one of us live for England, that we may save her from her internal foes."

The memorial was then dedicated and placed under the care of the People's Churchwarden and the Parish Council who were solemnly charged with preserving it forever. The congregation then sang "For All the Saints" and two trumpeters played the Last Post and Reveille. After the National Anthem the school children and the bereaved filed past the memorial and placed before it tokens of remembrance and wreaths.

Chapter 27

Anxious Times
1919 - 1939

When the war ended Penkridge entered into a period of modernisation and change. The Rural District Council quickly reduced the number of horses it used when Colonel Whitehead bought three army surplus Foden steam waggons in 1919. The era of dirty and dusty roads came to an end when Whitehead replaced the horse-drawn watering cart, and introduced the much cheaper and efficient practice of tar spraying, in the same year. By January 1920 the Council had bought 10,000 tons of tarmacadam and owned £7,000 worth of highway machinery. This equipment was often employed to break up the military roads that served the army camps on Cannock Chase, in order to use the rubble in local roads. In 1920 the Council bought three petrol lorries and decided that it now had so much expensive machinery that a new depot was needed to house it in Mill Street.

In the early 1920s the village seemed on the edge of an exciting new era in transport and communication. At a meeting of the R.D.C. at the Littleton Arms in July 1923 an engineer presented a plan for a motorway from Liverpool to London which would pass by Penkridge. He described a road that would be fifty feet wide, running within fences one hundred and twenty feet apart. The road would take all the heavy traffic from the local roads and horses and pedestrians would be banned. It was proposed that work would begin in October 1924. The District Council approved the plan unanimously and the Parish Council wrote to Penkridge's M.P. asking him to support the bill for the road in Parliament.

After the war a serious attempt was made to remedy the overcrowding caused by Penkridge's housing shortage. The first action taken by the R.D.C. was to dismantle the army huts at Brocton camp and re-erect them at Huntington and Great Wyrley. Each hut used was converted into two houses. This was expected to ease the pressure on housing in Penkridge but a more ambitious scheme was needed. In November 1919 the Housing of the Working Classes Committee met at the Littleton Arms and heard of plans for 507 new houses of which 20 were to be in Penkridge and 200 in Huntington. The Huntington houses were especially welcomed as they would liberate up to 80 cottages in Penkridge which were then occupied by mining families. It was expected that miners would move in order to be nearer their work. H.M.Whitehead inspected three sites in Penkridge and recommended that the 20 new homes be built on 2½ acres by the Wolverhampton Road where gas and water mains already existed.

Subsidised houses were built in Penkridge, on and off, for the rest of the inter-war period. In 1924 the R.D.C. applied to the Ministry of Health for a loan to purchase more land for assisted houses. The local builder J. Brookes, won the contract to build sixteen semi-detached non-parlour houses at £485..10s each. In 1931 the Rural District and County Councils combined to build nine new houses, three parlour types and two blocks of three non-parlour houses in the Cannock Road. In 1938 the R.D.C. bought land from the Teddesley estate at the corner of Marsh Lane and Teddesley Road, to a depth of 60 yards, for subsidised housing. As the Second World War started 18 houses and 2 bungalows were under construction.

It was during this period that the perennial problems of Penkridge's drainage, sewerage and water supply were tackled at last. In 1922 the R.D.C. received £850 from the Public Works Loan Board to make a start on building new sewers. As late as 1925, however, the council heard that Penkridge was in a "serious state of affairs" due to the bad state of the drains and a lack of a local sewage works. The council ordered a report on the main drainage system but little progress had been made by 1927 when the sanitary inspector reported that Penkridge was not sewered to any extent and that it was vital that the village should have a proper system of sewers and sewage disposal.

In the late 1920s it seemed as if the problem of pollution was actually getting worse. In 1929 the R.D.C. was rapped over the knuckles by the Board of Conservators of the Trent Fishery District who had taken a sample of water from the Bellbrook and found that it contained considerable amounts of untreated sewage. The Council was held responsible for this state of affairs under the Salmon and Freshwater Fishery Act of 1923 and the Conservators demanded to know what they proposed to do about it. The Council had no option but to dust down H.M. Whitehead's longstanding scheme for the drainage and water supply of Penkridge and they sent his plan to the Ministry of Health with a request for £23,000. In 1930 Penkridge received a grant of £24,000 which meant that the work of providing a proper sewerage, drainage and water supply system could begin. The programme was still continuing in 1939.

Better housing and purer water were not the only advances made in Penkridge between the wars. In 1927 work started on bringing electricity into the village from Cannock via a system of poles and wires. Some farmers protested about having poles in their fields and the Parish Council was alarmed at the prospect of overhead wires in the very narrow streets of the village but the electricity came. In 1921 the Rodbaston Institute opened, filling the educational gap between elementary school and the Harper Adams College. In 1934 the work of the Rural District Council had increased so much that it bought the Haling Dene from

Sidney Thomas for its headquarters. Council expenditure on the roads alone had increased from £700 in 1897 to £26,000 in 1930. Plans for the introduction of an automatic telephone exchange were approved in 1936.

There were many signs that the village was becoming a better place in which to live. In June 1921 Lord Hatherton was presented with a pair of white gloves to celebrate the historic fact that for the first time in 30 years Penkridge Magistrates Court had no crimes to deal with. Even the old enemy of drunk and disorderly behaviour was being brought under control. A general decline in drunkenness was noticed by 1931. When, on Christmas Eve, 1933, six youths from Mill Street and the Tanyard left a pub and started "bawling" carols outside the houses of Mrs. Bridgewater and Dr. Nock there was a real sense of disappointment since it had been a long time since such a case had been before the court. People felt that the good name of Penkridge had been spoiled.

Throughout the twenties and the thirties Penkridge gloried in the reputation of its school choir under Mr. Robinson. Hardly a year went past without the choir winning first prize in one of the county's music competitions. In 1923 the judge said that it was unusual to hear a boys' choir sing so well. In 1926 the Chief Inspector of Schools said the success of Penkridge was "a signal victory for the rural schools". In 1932 the choir, in competition with 43 other schools, won five first class certificates in the County Music Festival. The judge said,

"Penkridge had very good marks and in some respects they might have been regarded as the most expert choir in the room. One fault, however, had been detected in pronounciation. It might be local, he did not know. He was not there to dogmatize".

The peak of the choir's fame came in June 1933 when the BBC in the Midlands broadcast the winning choirs at a Festival of Juvenile Song. The Penkridge boys sang a Somerset folk song, "Admiral Benbow".

Despite all these signs of progress there also seems to have been a mood of disquiet and pessimism in Penkridge between the wars. Some people felt that the village was changing and not for the better. Neither could Penkridge escape the effects of national economic depression and social upheaval during these years. The anxiety was expressed by Lord Hatherton at the war memorial in 1921 when he said, "Let each of us live for England, that we may save her from her internal foes." In 1924, when opening the parish fete, Captain Ormsby Gore MP said that they were in anxious times and that people should pull together rather than pull against each other.

Undoubtedly a major cause of this pessimism in Penkridge was the dreadful condition of the coal mining industry in the 1920s. Long before the eruption of the General Strike in 1926 the grossly mismanaged industry was suffering from a dreary catalogue of strikes, threatened strikes, lock outs and wage cuts. A great many Penkridge people felt compassion for the eighty or so mining families in the village while others took a harder line. During the coal strike of 1921 Dr. Nock complained to the District Council that Colonel Whitehead was employing striking miners on the roads while there were genuine unemployed, laid off because of the strike, who needed the work. Whitehead denied that there were many unemployed people thus deprived. He said that the Council were getting good value for their money and the Poor Law Guardians were grateful for the saving on relief payments. He thought it was unlikely that employing the miners was prolonging the strike since many of them were cycling from Penkridge to Bloxwich every day to do their temporary work.

Penkridge miners went through great hardships in the 1921 strike. They suffered similarly in 1925 and 1926. The earning capacity of the miners on Cannock Chase diminished throughout 1925. Trade was slack during the summer months and the autumn and early winter were mild. Many of the pits were idle two or three days a week and thousands of miners had to accept the dole. For Penkridge miners 1925 was "a most anxious and trying year". Almost as worrying for some Penkridge people was the prospect of trade unions organising themselves to protect the living standards of British miners. The guest speaker at the Conservative dinner, held at the George and Fox in April 1926, declared that they,

"Had a far more subtle enemy in Socialism to fight than ever they had in the heyday of the Liberal Party's prosperity."

When the General Strike occurred in May 1926 the Government was well prepared. Part of the smooth organisation that defeated the strike was Colonel Whitehead who was appointed Controller of Transport for the Stafford area by the Minister of Transport. The coal strike outlasted the General Strike but, by August 1926, local miners were drifting back to work. In September 1926 the Poor Law Guardians accelerated the trend by reducing the relief paid to the dependents of striking miners by 25%.

It was to the background of these disturbing events that the Peace Memorial Hall was planned and built. The Parish Council went ahead with the project of building a village hall in the garden of the Littleton Arms as an act of faith since they were not certain that they would be able to raise the £2,250 required. When Lord Hatherton laid the foundation stone in November 1926 the Council were still £550 short of their target. The hall was named to commemorate the end of World War I but there can be little doubt that the social and industrial troubles of the 1920s were also in the minds of those involved in the project. After laying the foundation stone Lord Hatherton said that he

"hoped that the hall would be conducive to the religious and social welfare of the inhabitants of Penkridge and be the means of furthering peace and brotherly will."

When the hall was opened in October 1927 many worries were aired during the ceremony. Lord Hatherton took as his theme, "Give us Peace in our Time, O Lord" and said,

"He had heard some people say, 'Let us forget the war', but that, in his opinion, was a mistake. If they forgot the horrors of the war and the lessons it had taught them, surely they would be more likely to drift into another war before very long".

Mr. James said that the hall was badly needed in Penkridge and then added worries and grievances of his own, saying,

"How long the village would retain its truly rural character was uncertain for there were rumours of industrial development in the dim future. In recent years the character of the village had changed considerably, many of the farm labourers having been displaced by miners. The hall now opened would provide means for innocent recreation and amusement for the tired worker and for his wife after the drudgery of the day's work".

There were many signs that Penkridge was losing its character and independence. In 1930 its strong influence over the welfare of the people in the area was weakened when the Poor Law Union was ended. Also in 1930 the County Council took over the responsibility for the local roads. There were persistent threats to the Rural District Council which faced absorption either by the County Council or by the expansion of the nearby borough councils. The County exerted a growing influence over the local boy's and girl's schools. In 1937 it proposed amalgamating and enlarging them and also building a new senior school in Penkridge for the surrounding area.

Many notable local characters who personified Penkridge's historical roots and sturdy independence died or retired at this time. Joseph Brown, the Wolgarston farmer, died at Reynard Cottage in 1929. Edwin Oakley of Wyre Hall Cottage, the local postman for 35 years, retired in 1924 thus breaking a link with the time when the first delivery round started at 6am and the last finished at 8.30pm and when the postman announced his arrival with a blast on a horn. Frank Dukes, Colonel Whitehead and Joseph Burd, all examples of local public service and self sufficiency, died. James Kempson retired in 1937 after 26½ years as Vicar of Penkridge.

Despite all these changes the greatest threat to and the chief cause of anxiety for Penkridge was the physical destruction of the centre of the village under the County Council road widening scheme in 1931. It was inconceivable that the old parish vestry or Colonel Whitehead at the Rural District Council would have adopted such a scheme. Fred Jones complained to the District Council that 38 buildings, which housed 18 businesses and 31 families, were to be destroyed. He said that there was a strong feeling in the village that the scheme should not go ahead until consideration had been given to people deprived of their homes.

The protests were of no avail. Local business men no longer had the political influence to halt the plans of the County Council. When the County was unable to come to terms with some of the owners it proceeded with the compulsory purchase of the buildings. The main casualties were the chemist's shop belonging to W.F. Fowke, Lloyd's Bank, a shop occupied by Mrs. Mabel Plant at Crown Bridge and two houses occupied by Arthur Morris and Annie Hill. In Clay Street, Barclay's Bank, Arthur Jones' bakehouse, Mr. G. Hodson's garage and a shop occupied by Edward Parker and Maud Crompton were condemned. In May 1931 a public enquiry into the scheme was held at the Peace Memorial Hall. Mr. Fowkes, who owned many of the buildings destined for destruction, took a cynical view of the exercise. "Is it any use opposing the order?", he asked. "So far as we are concerned we look upon it as a matter cut and dried."

The County explained why the scheme, estimated as costing £51,901, was needed. They explained that the road carried some of the heaviest traffic in the county since it was the main road from the Black Country to the North and carried about 3,000 tons a day. The road was very narrow and on a gradient and had been the scene of many accidents. The Council had been considering the problem for 20 years. They had rejected the idea of a by-pass for Penkridge because an eastern route would have required a long viaduct over the unfirm land and a western route would cut through the railway embankment and go too close to the Church and other valuable property.

The main problem with the existing route was the triangle of properties in the middle of the road at its junction with Crown Bridge. The plot contained a house, shop and bakehouse belonging to Arthur Jones and a house belonging to Mrs. Hill. At that point the road was 16½ feet wide and the actual carriage way was only 12 feet wide. It was not unknown that vehicles passing each other at this spot would get jammed and it took a considerable time to move them. The Council proposed to widen 740 feet of road. The new carriage way was to be 40 feet wide with pavements 10 feet wide on the west side of Clay Street and 20 feet wide on the other side. While the road was being excavated the Council would also put in "a comprehensive water supply".

Faced with the inevitability of a road widening scheme one shopkeeper said,

"It is rather late in the day, but I would like to ask if it would not have been possible to have widened the road without practically demolishing the business part of the village?"

The Council explained that the alternative would have been to demolish the Littleton Arms and "the valuable property on the west side". Also, much of the condemned property in Clay Street was dilapidated and overcrowded. Penkridge shopkeepers protested against the bias in favour of residential property and against business. They were being offered no compensation and could not afford to re-start on alternative sites. Mrs. Crompton had taken 15 years to build up her business and Mr. Bridgwater had been a butcher in the same premises for 40 years. Joseph Plant said he could not afford to rebuild even though he had been offered an alternative site at a low figure.

The inquiry heard that several tenants "did not know what they were going to do. They were very concerned as to their position and it was a very anxious time for all of them". A Mr. Parker asked what he was going to do. He had lost a leg during the war and had learned the boot repairing trade with a government grant. Now he was losing his shop. Mr. Kempson, the Vicar, pointed out that there would be a decrease in the rateable value of Penkridge when the businesses disappeared so the people would have to pay for the scheme twice over, through increased rates. The protests had no effect and the demolition soon began, at the New Road junction with Clay Street.

When Mr. Kempson retired in 1937 he reflected upon the changes he had seen during his 26½ years as Vicar of Penkridge. He mentioned the "vast changes brought about by the destruction of the centre of the village." He added that "another change was the fact that for the first time in 500 years a member of the Littleton family was not living in the parish. They could not help feeling that these were not changes for the better." However, at the first Armistice service of his successor, Cyril Jarman, even deeper anxieties emerged. The Church was packed and extra chairs had to be set out. The people of Penkridge listened to a sermon on the meaning of Armistice Days.

"Were they only a vain and empty show, or had they some deeper meaning? What meaning in particular did they have for the younger generation? Surely they were to teach them and continually remind them that the war was not the glorious thing it was so often made out to be in the history books and historical novels, but was fraught with horror, cruelty and sordidness. Had all the sacrifice been in vain? Were they reaping nothing for it? Once at Armistice time they were able to think that the sacrifice had been glorious because it had purchased a new world and conditions, but if they looked around today what did they see? Germany had torn up the peace treaty, persecuted the church, and destroyed democracy; Russia openly declared there was no God."

They were "bound to take precautions to protect the good against the bad. They had been very near to war in the past year, but thanks be to God, they had weathered the crisis".

Penkridge had been making preparations for war since September 1936 when the village received its instructions for air raid precautions from the County Council. On Thursday, May 12th, 1939, sirens wailed over the village as the Staffordshire ARP practiced a complete mobilisation. Some Penkridge people had been afforded a close glimpse of the enemy when, in 1938 a captain in the German airforce gave evidence in a motoring case at Penkridge Police Court. Herr Artur Jacobi, who was also an inspector of road accidents under Goering, had come all the way from Berlin to support a fellow motor cyclist accused of careless driving. The Staffordshire Advertiser reported the case under the startling headline,

"NAZI CHIEF AT PENKRIDGE".

Once the war had started the Peace Memorial Hall was used as a NAAFI canteen. In October 1939 a mobile cinema unit was showing Marx Brothers' films for soldiers.

Penkridge Remembered

Chapter 28

Preparing for Invasion

When the Second World War broke out Cyril Felthouse was ordered to stick poles all over his large fields. It was felt that they were the ideal size and configuration for glider and parachute landings. As Mrs. Felthouse remarked, it was unlikely that they would have stopped the Germans. Technology made rapid advances during the war, however, and a year or so later Cyril Felthouse awoke on several occasions to find his fields covered with strips of silver foil. He didn't know what they were as at the time they constituted one of the deepest secrets of the war. The strips were being dropped from planes to confuse enemy radar.

Quite a few things fell from the sky onto Pillaton farm during the war. Several parachutes came down carrying flares. Cyril was amazed at the beautiful quality of the silk. One parachute was rapidly converted into little flags for the boundary of the cricket pitch. On another occasion a plane had trouble over the farm and made an emergency landing. Cyril remembers being impressed by the way the cool-headed pilot herded all the sheep to the end of the field on one fly past and then came round again and landed, ten yards from the wood. The plane turned over but the pilot stepped out of the wreck. He had been due to go to France the following day and had been making final preparations.

In many ways the start of the war brought a sense of relief. Jack Tweed and Cyril Felthouse had been expecting worse. They were both members of the ARP and had been practising for many months their roles in the event of a gas attack. The ARP had taken over a building at the Top Auction yard by the Railway Inn. They worked by the light of a gas lamp which they had to pump to get started.

Although Penkridge saw no enemy action, ARP duties could be tiring and frustrating. Every time the sirens went Jack Tweed turned out to his post at the Top Auction and his father joined the first aid group stationed at the Haling Dene. Most warnings came at about 11pm. They would spend a couple of hours on duty, the "All Clear" would sound and they would cycle home to bed. Quite often the siren would sound again half an hour later and they would have to turn out again. As well as this, Jack had to take his turn fire-watching some nights at his engineering works at Churchbridge.

Jack often heard the bombers go over. He particularly remembers the night Coventry was bombed as he was returning from visiting his future wife who was living at Gnosall. Cycling along the higher ground there he could see the sky all lit up over the city.

One Sunday morning the authorities organised a big exercise in Penkridge to sharpen up the services in case of attack. Everyone turned out, the siren was sounded, people pretended to be casualties in the street and even planes flew over to lend authenticity. Jack Tweed was allocated the Cannock Road area. He was told to imagine that the old derelict workhouse was on fire and full of poison gas. His role was to report the fire to the fire brigade. Unfortunately, the officer in charge of the brigade was a bit too keen and got the engine there before the siren had sounded. Jack entered the old house wearing his civilian gas mask and searched its three storeys. Eventually, right at the top of the house he found a dummy with a piece of wood lying across it. He pulled the wood off and reported the "casualty".

Cyril Felthouse was stationed down by the Bull Bridge. His main duties were to rescue a young girl named Tonks, who was simulating a sprained ankle by the river bank, and to look for tin canisters labelled "Unexploded Bomb". Cyril is certain that the most enthusiastic participants in the exercise were the mock casualties. When he took the Tonks girl to the casualty post at the Peace Memorial Hall he saw one chap who had taken the trouble of going to the butcher's, buying a sheep's eye and sticking it on his face, as though it had been blown out of its socket. This was so convincing that people were fainting in the Hall and the first aiders were having real cases to practise on.

An inquest was held on the exercise the following week. The Penkridge ARP were castigated for walking casually up the road, and laughing and talking during the "attack". Then an officer complained that someone had removed the "heavy beam" from a casualty in the workhouse which was to have been the main exercise for the Rescue Squad. Jack Tweed decided that he had been in enough trouble for one day and kept his head down.

The busiest place during the war was probably Pillaton aerodrome. A short time after the war started they began night flying there. The planes from the aerodrome used to shoot over the farm at a very low level. They had to take down the electric wires that ran from the road and over the farm.

They used to bring the planes over from Cosford and the trainee pilots came from there by bus. Some of them were real daredevils. They knew that the local bobby, an old constable brought back because of the war, was in the habit of going to their canteen for a cup of tea, so they waited until he was crossing the field and started dive bombing him. He was spread eagled in the middle of the field for ages. They frightened the life out of him.

Another time, one of the pilots decided to have some fun on his way back to Cosford. He flew right through the farm yard, below the level of the trees, over the cricket pitch, tailing his colleagues in the Cosford bus. He intended to "buzz" them at Quarry Heath. Unfortunately he forgot that the land rises there and he hit a bank and turned over in a field of corn. He, too, walked away from the crash.

During the war a Mr. Rosser lived at Francis Dene, which was then the first house in Francis Green Lane. He was in the Home Guard and had an important job at English Electric in Stafford. Because he was always travelling from factory to factory Penkridge people decided he was a Fifth Columnist. Everyone in Penkridge "knew" this, except Mr. Rosser. The local police even went to Stafford to see his firm. When he found out about the rumour he was shocked. His wife asked her neighbour John Thomas Felthouse if he "knew". When he replied, "Yes!" she said, "Why didn't you tell me?"

During the-war, people were given a permit allowing them to kill two pigs a year. A lot of villagers fed up their pigs on scraps and almost lived on greasy bacon. There was a saying in Penkridge that if you ran short of meat you could always go to Wheaton Aston where you could get something "off the ration". The court in Penkridge dealt with rationing offences but one of the top local policemen used to send his chauffeur to Pillaton Farm many times to collect a dozen eggs.

Chapter 29

Penkridge from 1906
Mrs. Harris

Mrs. Harris was born in Penkridge and lived in the village for the first six years of her life before her family moved to Hatherton and Huntington to work in the mines.

"My grandad worked at Otherton farm and we lived on Otherton Lane which is called Boscomoor Lane now. We used to call it Boosmoor Lane. My grandfather's name was Rochell. The old houses are down now and bungalows have been built there.

Walking along Mill Street towards the village there were only four old cottages and a shop on the right. Mrs. Evans used to keep it. She sold all sorts of useful things. A little general store. It was the first house you came to going into the village.

Some of the cottages had a pump but others had to make do with a well. Some of the wells had winders but other people had to throw the bucket down and then pull it up on a long rope. The water was beautiful, cool and clean. The wells were in yards at the back and covered with lids.

There was only one shop in Market Street in those days. It was a grocers, Bellingham's I think. Mrs. Morris used to keep a general store near the Lloyd's Bank. Mr. Bellamy the draper, was a nice man. He had a shop on the corner near to Barclay's Bank.

The Burd's kept the Boat Inn for a very long time. It was a small pub in those days. People didn't have cars so they had to rely on local people going in.

Hills, who sold milk, used to live up Market Street. In the fifties Connie used to come round, door to door, pushing the milk on a trolley but when I was a child we didn't have to bother because grandad used to bring milk back from the farm.

I went to Penkridge school for about a year. It still looks the same from the outside. The teacher seemed very nice. There were not many in the class and the lessons were only reading, writing and arithmetic. At Christmas we had a Christmas tree and a little present each. All the lady teachers wore long dresses and we had to cover our knees with our skirts. The teacher at Huntington was much stricter. She would slap you across the face for nothing at all.

In the houses I remember we had oil lamps. There was nothing else, just candles and oil lamps before the electricity came. No gas.

We always used to keep a pig and kill and cure it ourselves. Granny and Grandad had a pantry with a stone ledge and salted the bacon and hung it up in the house. We always had a flitch of bacon and the hams hanging up. We had fresh milk from the farm, eggs and butter and home made bread. We had a healthy life when we were children and six of us are still alive. It was lovely, quiet and peaceful. The farm workers were happy and peaceful."

(In 1953 Mrs. Harris returned to Penkridge and in 1956 settled in Marsh Lane.

"In 1956 Marsh Lane was a proper country lane. There were no houses. There was a field with two old cottages. Orchard Crescent was just ordinary fields. I don't know why they called it Orchard Crescent - there were no trees there. It was all marshy and in the first place they were going to build the houses where the school is now but when they came to dig the foundations it was too marshy. They took lots of soil up there to build up the hill and built the school there instead. Littleton Crescent was just fields then. Mrs. Bates had a couple of heifers in a field that came up to my garden. There were a couple of old cottages standing on their own.

I worked on the station in 1953. We had a lot of pigeon traffic. They used to come from all the little stations between here and Manchester. I was a porter and had to release them. It was hard work, getting them out of the guards vans and involved a lot of paper work. They came every day of the week. Apart from that the station was not busy. Mr. Grocott, the station master, lived in the station house down below. We used to have a coal fire in the waiting room and if I was ever short I only had to ask the driver of the train and he would throw me some out.

In the fifties there was very little traffic in Penkridge. It was very quiet, even on the main road. They used to drive cattle through the streets to the market, along Mill Street. There was only a cattle market then.")

Chapter 30

Farming at Pillaton
Mr. Cyril Felthouse

Mr. Cyril Felthouse was born on Lower Hanyards Farm, near Stafford in 1901. His father, John Thomas Felthouse, came to Penkridge and farmed Pillaton before retiring to Wyre Hall after the First World War. Wyre Hall belonged to Cyril Felthouse's grandmother, Mrs. Chell. She married at Penkridge in 1868 and her husband Edward Chell farmed Pillaton between 1868 and 1900. She was a skilled lace worker up to the age of 97.

"My father took over the farm at Pillaton in 1905. My uncle Frank Chell had farmed the land for two or three years under Lord Hatherton but had to leave because he was caught shooting hares. Father decided to 'get out' of farming in 1920 but stayed on the farm until I got married in 1928 when he moved to Wyre Hall.

One of my earliest recollections, in 1905 or 1906, is of the Penkridge miners walking past the farm on their way to the Littleton Colliery. They used to come up the road and then cut across the fields. They woke me up at about 5 o'clock in the morning with their clogs going 'clackety-clack'. There were about forty or fifty of them, coming past in two's and three's. Their numbers gradually dwindled as first they got bicycles and then went by bus but they were still going past in the 1920s when I was farming. They were mostly from old Penkridge families and they were ever so good. They would come up and say, 'Gaffer, coming home tonight there was a sheep upside down so I got it on its feet and it's made water so I think it will be all right'. We had a chap called Joe 'Bingy' who had a bad leg and helped out on the farm and rang the bell down at the auction. I think his father was one of the first Penkridge miners.

At first I had a private tutor, Miss Davies, who was the postman's daughter. She taught me at home with another boy, Bill Adderley. He was very naughty and in the end she pushed him in our big boiler and put the lid on. He escaped, rushed down the lane and never came back again. When I was 8 I went to Penkridge School. On my first day I saw a bully hitting a smaller boy. I stepped into the fight to save him and went home with a black eye on my first day. The General Election of 1910 has stuck in my mind all these years. When Mr. George Lloyd the winning Unionist got to Bull Bridge, six lads, including me, were chosen to pull his car into the village for the celebrations.

In 1900 the Heaths were the great farming family with five farms in the area. The Old Man lived opposite us at Pillaton and left in 1919. My father's great friend was Joseph Brown of Wolgarston, the top breeder of Shropshire sheep in the country. People used to come to Wolgarston from all over England for his annual sheep sale. During the First War the Anzac troops stationed on the Chase were particularly interested in the sheep, coming from New Zealand, and visited the farm. As a boy they seemed to me to be huge fellows.

Joseph Brown employed 16 men. He was an excellent farmer and a good boss. When he was marking his sheep I used to help him out. He gave me what looked like, and probably was, a ping pong bat. After the sheep were branded my job was to pat out the flames. Mr. Brown was a grand chap. We used to go trout fishing in his pool with cane rods as thick as your arm. He was a distinguished judge of sheep and used to take me with him to the county show at Leek. Even though he was the best judge in the country he used to say to me, 'Cyril, go and see what the others are talking about'. I sidled up to the other farmers, found out what they thought about the sheep and then told Mr. Brown, to help him make up his mind.

We had a bothy on the farm for the Irish casual labourers who used to work for us at busy times. These people were very friendly and we got on well with them. They were often smallholders back home and knew the farming ways. They needed the extra work to pay their rents. They travelled in small groups and came back to our farm year after year. They wrote to tell us when they were coming and left after we had finished lifting the potatoes. They worked in two's and three's all over the area but came together every Sunday when they went to Mass. During the First War we had a good chap from Galway called O'Connor whose speciality was chasing down rabbits during the harvest and knocking them on the head. He used to put them in the pot, for his dinner. One Sunday he asked me to watch the pot. When he was gone I took the rabbit out, wrapped it in newspaper and put a brick in its place. We had a good laugh when he came back and tested it with a fork to see if it was done! You had to make your own simple fun in those days.

In 1909 I walked across the fields to Teddesley to watch them play cricket there, outside the Hall. One of the Littletons, who was also a racing driver, was playing and the parson from Gailey made a century. I really enjoyed the game and it started off my interest in cricket. While I was there I saw their big, man powered heavy roller with which they rolled the wicket. When they stopped playing cricket at Teddesley they brought the roller into Penkridge and used it to roll the lawn at the Vicarage which is now the Hatherton Country Club. When the Council bought the Haling Dene Centre they decided to put down a grass tennis court and borrowed the roller to settle the soil. They then stopped using it and left it to one side, so one evening in the late 1940s I went down with the tractor and a low loader and, in a terrific thunder storm, took it up to Pillaton for the Cricket Club. We used it for quite a while until we broke one of the shafts. Wolgarston School offered to mend it for us in one of their metalwork classes and it has been there ever since.

When the First War started I went down Market Street and saw a great crowd around the fire engine opposite the post office. The young men were signing up like wildfire to join Kitchener's army, for the King's Shilling. Although I didn't actually see it myself it was well known that girls in Penkridge handed out white feathers to men not in uniform during the war. So many volunteered at once that they could not take them all at first. We had one Penkridge lad on the farm here who was just given an armband. His name was Talbot and he stayed quite a while until he was called up. Another of our workers was a man named Brough. He had been a sergeant in the Royal Marines and was still in the reserves. He was called up straight away.

Pillaton Farm had two Land Army girls during the war. A lot depended upon where they came from. One of them was a city girl from Birmingham and not a lot of use. The other, a good country girl from Durham, was fine. Many of the farms used prisoners of war from the camp on the Chase. If they stayed on the farm they were often housed in the bothies that had been put up for the casual Irish workers. Many of them were Prussian Guards and were excellent workers. (Mrs. Felthouse remembers that at her home at Hatherton they locked up the prisoners in the bothies. They didn't like it and promised not to escape.) Like most farmers we didn't see why the army needed really good horses. When they came down to commandeer horses we took our best one and hid it in the woods.

When the war ended I was working in the fields, cutting turnips. The hooters on all the collieries in Cannock went off. When the vicar left the army and returned to the village he gave a party at the Vicarage. He invited all the young people who had to come in fancy dress, as a country. A.E. Wright's daughter, who lived opposite Haling Dene, went as India. I couldn't find anything so went as England. The party got a bit out of hand with all the farmers' sons and daughters. They were a bit naughty and got into Kempson's bedroom. He was very annoyed and there were no more parties.

I lost three of my best friends because of the depression that set in after the war. They were Colin Robson from the Littleton Arms, Ruffle who was a pupil at Joe Brown's farm at Wolgarston and Jesse Olarenshaw who helped his father at Yew Tree Farm. They were fed up with England and decided to emigrate to Australia. Joe Brown gave them a farewell party at Wolgarston and invited me as well. Jesse was lucky to have got that far. One evening he had been working with his tractor in a Yew Tree field and lit a match to see how much petrol he had left in the tank. He lost all his hair and I heard the explosion at Pillaton. Jesse's father, also called Jesse, retired to Francis Green Lane and lived next door to my father. They had a competition to see who would live the longest. Jesse lasted until the 1960s.

I wasn't yet 21 when I took over the farm and wasn't old enough to sign my own contracts and documents. We didn't have cars in those days so in 1921 I bought a new AJS motor bike so that I could travel to Shrewsbury and Leominster to buy cattle which we would feed up during the winter in the yard with best cake, corn and roots. The 1920s were a difficult time for farmers and sometimes I had to sell the cattle in April for less than I had paid for them in November. But as my father said, 'You had to get muck on the land'. We also had a smallholding at Armitage where we grew fruit. Once, coming back from there with some fruit, I was knocked off my bike by a hit-and-run motorist on the Milford Road. I was concussed, under the bike, and the engine was still going burning my leg. I was rescued by a motorist who turned out to be the Mr. Lloyd who had started the big garage in Stafford in about 1903.

We had a mixed farm of about 208 acres. We had arable crops and about 200 sheep and the 20 cattle we fed in the winter. We employed three men but I did all my own lambing. We had five heavy horses and couldn't afford to exchange them for a tractor until 1930. Then Mr. Tildesley came from the Willenhall garage with a Canadian to demonstrate a new tractor and a Canadian plough. It made a beautiful furrow and eventually we bought one. It cost £120 and had no rubber tyres, just 'splayed luggs' which chewed up all the gravel in the yard. We kept one horse for odd jobs with the cart, and a little horse hoeing.

The men who worked with the horses were called waggoners. We had a first waggoner and a second waggoner. They were responsible for feeding them, fettling them and brushing them down. They used to feed them at 5 o'clock in the morning then go back to their own cottages for breakfast. The waggoners thought the world of their horses. Once, when I was a boy, I was watching the men and horses return from the fields during the harvest. One of the workers picked me up and put me on the back of a horse. The second waggoner got hold of me and threw me right across the lane into a ditch, saying, ' These horses are tired'. Once I was out harrowing when the head waggoner unhooked his horse, ready for feeding, on the other side of the field. My horse saw this and bolted towards them. It got through a half open gate but the harrows and me, trailing behind, demolished the fence.

One of the hardest parts of the job in those days was driving the animals from one place to another. There used to be two auctions in Stafford and when I bought sheep there I had to drive them through the streets of the town before getting into the countryside. When other local farmers realised I was driving them back they put their sheep in with mine and I had a large flock to take down the Brocton Road to Pottal Pool. We didn't use dogs. One man went ahead to stop the traffic while the rest of us drove the sheep from behind. We always used to drive cattle through the streets of Penkridge down to the auction. There were two auctions in Penkridge for a while. The farmers fell out with the private one on Pinfold Lane and ran their own, Farmers' Auction, by the Railway Inn. They formed a committee, which my father was on, and planned to split the profits between them. Unfortunately, more often they split the losses. One of my jobs was to take the butchers into the Inn before the sale and treat them to a drink, to help the bidding along.

Times were hard for everyone in the 1920s so we had to look out for poachers. We were digging up potatoes by hand with forks when one of my piece workers noticed someone in a Morris Cowley taking a 'sample' from a potato clamp and driving away. That night I hid behind a holly bush until I heard the squeaky brakes that all Cowleys had then. I drove into Penkridge to get the police sergeant who I found drinking in the Boat. We drove back to the farm and passed the poachers car. The sergeant didn't want to stop because he thought they were probably a courting couple, so we went up to Mansty and then walked back to the farm behind the hedges. When we saw them we chased them on foot. I picked up some stones to throw but the sergeant shouted, 'Cyril, keep him covered!' and they must have thought I had a gun because one of them surrendered with his arms up in the air. We caught two of them and the police constable, coming up from Penkridge on his bike, caught a third. They had come from Walsall. They had managed to get the potatoes into six bags which the police kept as evidence. On the day of the trial in Cannock the sergeant was quite flustered because one of the bags had disappeared from the police station. Nevertheless he was promoted soon afterwards.

Something that happened quite frequently but always caused great excitement was killing a pig. Farmers' wives had mixed feelings about this because it was usually done in the farm kitchen, since that was where the carcase would be hung. At Pillaton we used to get Ken Lyons' father to come because it was a difficult operation to organise. Four or five people were needed. The butcher hung a little rope with a noose in front of the pig. When it opened its mouth he would slide it in and get a grip on the pig's nose. Someone else would get hold of the pig's tail and between them they would guide it over to a bench. Two other men would brace their knees on this bench, lean over it and pull the pig up onto its back on the bench. Then, while everyone hung on tightly, it would be stuck. After the pig had been hanging for two days and the body had cooled down it was cut up. The butcher came with a big cleaver and cut it from tail to head. Every part of the pig was used. We had scratchings, pork pies, sausages, trotters and bacon. We even used the bladder to store lard in.

In 1920 I joined Penkridge Amateur Football Club. We played friendlies most Saturdays against clubs like Old Edwardians, from Stafford, but our main opponents were Penkridge United who we played in the Charity Cup. Many of their players were miners and they used to come down this road onto our field all black from the pit. They had some very good players. Bradbury was a back and so was Parsons who was the man, I think, who used to play in his cap. Their goalkeeper was Rostance who went on to play for Hednesford Town. We were quite good for an ex-service man's team and United only just used to beat us. Their pitch was just off the Cannock Road where the Cherrybrook estate is now.

(During the Second War I started my own cricket club. I was getting on a bit then, aged 45. We scraped together a few old pads and a cricket ball which I had to take into the village to be re-stitched by the cobbler. Sidney Barnes, the Test cricketer, had rooms at Coppice Farm near Pottal Pool then and he came down and helped the team a lot. He was a grand chap and we liked each other a lot because we both smoked pipes. He wrote us a lovely letter when we made him an honorary member of the club but unfortunately this was stolen from the pavilion.

When the M6 was being built through Penkridge I got to know one of the men who drove the huge earth movers and persuaded him to bring it up to Pillaton. Our cricket field was all in 'butts', uneven, up and down corrugated land. He took off all the top soil and dumped it in the corner of the field. This left the pavilion high and dry above ground level. He then graded it all back and I re-seeded the land. The whole operation cost £700 which was a great bargain. There were big machines on the field again when Shell came to test drill for oil. They hit underground water and it came gushing up just like oil. At first I thought I did have oil on my land!)"

Chapter 31

Penkridge in the 1920s and 1930s
Mr. Jack Tweed

"My family moved from Beacon Hill to Otherton when I was seven. In Lyne Hill Lane by a thatched cottage there was a triangular piece of grass which was our playground. One game was 'Puss, Puss, Come to my Corner'. One person stood in the middle and had to fight his way into one of the corners. Another game was 'Stag, Stagarony'. This involved two children holding each end of a piece of rope and running along the road, catching up other children. This wasn't dangerous in the days before heavy traffic. A good game for the countryside was 'Jack, Shine the Light'. One person had a torch and shone it on and off in a field and the others had to catch him.

More dangerously we used to swim in the canal, there being no swimming baths. Those of us who couldn't swim gathered big bunches of rushes to hold us up. Even then the water wasn't particularly clean with coal barges going backward and forward. Some of the braver lads dived in from the bridges but you had to make sure you were in the middle where the water was deep enough.

We also used to play on the railway line that came into Penkridge from the Littleton Colliery and get into the guards van and have a ride down while they were shunting the trucks. Where the line was built up we used to slide down the bank which we called the 'batters'. Where the brook went under the railway there were two big pipes that you could practically stand up in and in the middle they opened out into a big tunnel, and my friend and I used to push a bath on wheels into the tunnel and pick coal up there. This was down Lyne Hill way, past where the Social Club was built. It was all wide open land in those days. Penkridge railway station was quite a sight then. It was supposed to be the village station with the longest platform in the country. It had a wooden extension for the troops on the Chase during the First War and was probably twice as long as it is now. The extension stretched towards Stafford and the Goods Station, which continued working up until about the 1950s.

Walking out of Penkridge to Otherton, the houses ended at the bottom of Francis Green Lane. Between there and the Cross Keys there were only two buildings, a farmhouse and a house opposite it. The Cross Keys had no water supply and they got it from a spring just down the lane, down a couple of steps. To get to the Cross Keys from Boscomoor Lane you had to cross two fields; Filance Field, over an iron stile and then the field which belonged to the pub. This became difficult when they ploughed the field. Once in a thick fog my father and I lost the path half way across and decided to follow the hedge around. We ended up at the bottom of the field in the opposite corner where we had come in. There were places there called Biddles Bank and Monkey Island.

By the canal there was a place called the Basin which used to ship coal from the colliery onto the coal boats. Mr. Thomas in the village also used to have coal boats and on every Whit Monday the people who belonged to the Chapel used to have a trip to Milford. They scrubbed the coal boat out and were pulled there by the horse. They started out at nine and got to Milford at about twelve. They started back at six and got to Penkridge by nine. It was a great event that people looked forward to in those days. They charged 9d for the trip. Once they had recently tarred the outside of the boat and it was a really warm Whit Monday morning and by the time we got to the first or second lock the tar was all running and the lock- keeper had to plaster all over the side of the boat with newspaper.

Even we could be surprised by some aspects of living in the countryside. One year my father won a goose in a Christmas whist drive and sent my cousin and me to pick it up from Mr. Powell, the saddler. When we got there we found it was still alive. We tied a piece of string round its neck and led it to Boscomoor Lane. When we got it home it walked around the house, quite tamely. Then my father had to kill it.

Old Mr. Flynn who farmed out at Whiston and Bickford used to deliver milk in the old fashioned way. He brought it in a bucket and tipped it into your jug. He was a good man and worked hard for people. I can just remember the 1926 Coal and General Strike. Among the many things that he did to help the miners, he organised a tea in the field by the Top Auction. There was some sympathy for the miners, in Penkridge.

I left school in 1933 and the village really changed just prior to that when the road was widened. The left hand side of the road up Clay Street going towards Wolverhampton was all knocked down. The piece next to where the chapel is now was a sandy area which they used to call The Rabbit Holes, opposite the Railway Tavern. They knocked it all down. The old chapel stood more or less where you go through the gate to the Sunday School now, on the corner of New Road. It was built in 1828 and the old school building stood at the back of that, where the new chapel stands today. In front of the old chapel there were houses. In fact there was only a narrow alley that went down the side of the old chapel to the school building at the back. They knocked the old school building down and then they built the new chapel. When they built the new chapel they wanted it to be made of Penkridge Stone, just like the Church, so they built the Chapel and a piece leading to the old chapel which was the vestry and the kitchen, and the idea was that they would knock the old chapel down and build a new school room of stone, just like the rest when they had the money. Unfortunately, with the increase in costs, that never came to pass.

The new chapel was opened in 1934. I went to the stone laying. It absolutely poured down all day long. At the time I had just left school, and had had a month out of work. The chap who lived next door to me was the treasurer of the Methodists and the architect wanted all the steel window frames painted because they were standing there in the rain. He asked me to paint the windows and I gave them two coats with paint that I got from Fred Rostance's. I was told that in the past the Methodists had a chapel opposite the Fox where the furniture store is now. In the thirties there was still quite a split between the Chapel and the 'Big Church' as we called it. Penkridge children used to call the vicar, Mr. Kempson, 'Black Jim' because he had jet black hair parted down the middle. His vicarage is now the Hatherton Country Club. They held the village fetes there and they were very special events with dancing on the lawns till late at night.

The road was very narrow before 1933. The bar door of the Littleton Arms opened straight out onto the Wolverhampton Road. There was no footpath at all. Opposite there, on the other side of the road, was Plant's paper shop. The pavement on that side was about two feet wide. A lad who lived in one of the little houses further up the street was standing looking in the paper shop window one day and a lorry mounted the pavement and killed him. That accident really started off the scheme to widen the road. Even though lorries were much smaller then, two of the bigger ones could hardly pass each other there. If they did they brushed the lintel of the Littleton Arms bar door and you could see the marks there for many years.

The other side of the road, from St. Michael's Square leading to Stafford, was also knocked down. Bridgewater's butchers shop would be somewhere in the middle of the road now. Their slaughterhouse stood where the motor repair shop is today, where it backs onto the bowling green. After the widening, the Bridgewaters built their shop across the road, where the Staffordshire Building Society is now.

The road widening meant that there was a lot of new building. This led to some controversy. I worked for Billy Rostance, the builder. He used to live and have his yard in Bridge House, which is a hotel now. We were building the new paper shop for the Plants, and Joe Brooks, another Penkridge builder, was building the new Bridgewater's butchers shop. When we put the spouting on the paper and bicycle repair shop it overlapped the boundary, so he made us take it down and if you look up there now you can see a little retaining wall and no spouting.

They knocked the old George and Fox down and built a new one behind it.

The Crown pub used to stand on the other side of Pinfold Lane where the tool hire shop is now, though much nearer the White Hart as the road was so narrow.

In the middle of Penkridge, not exactly where the traffic island is now, but a bit further out into the main road, was a little island made up of Jones's bakery and fancy cake shop. It formed a triangle in the centre of the village.

On Crown Bridge, past the telephone box and near the modern bakery shop, was where the fire station was located. When I was a boy there were two fire engines there, one motor and one horse drawn, although I never saw the old horse drawn one taken out. The old building carried on round to where the paper shop is but all the rest were knocked down in the road widening.

The blacksmith's shop used to be behind Cheadle's garage and he used to be a fireman. Cheadle and Hodson used to be together before they split up and Hodson's set up on their own. A cousin of mine used to work in the blacksmith's shop and I went down there often to see him shoeing horses and mending the tackle and doing a bit of welding. Bill Burgess was the blacksmith and people now don't realise how skilful the blacksmith's trade was. He had his own lathe and even his hammers, which he made himself, were precision instruments. I worked in the edged tool trade at Churchbridge and made engineer's hammers which I sometimes gave to him. It wasn't good enough to offer him a 2½ or 3lb hammer. It had to be precisely 2¾ lb to knock out the toe pieces on the shoes of heavy horses.

Bill Burgess used to go to the Littleton Arms for a 'fourpenny'. I suppose, being a blacksmith, he couldn't afford beer at the usual 5d a pint. At that time the passage leading from the car park into the Littleton went all the way through to the front door. I had my first drink by the Wolverhampton Road door which was about halfway up the stone passage. There was a little room called the Coffee Room one side of the passage and three bars on the other. The main clubroom is now the restaurant. In those days two halves of beer were enough to make you 'wobbly'. The landlord was old Billy Robson. We thought him a bit of a character because he always used to wear old fashioned knickerbocker trousers.

The Boat used to be a tiny pub run by the Burd family. There wasn't much room in there except for the club room. Winnie Burd was a very prim and proper landlady and you had to mind your 'ps and qs' when you went in the Boat. The house in Market Street called 'Two Steps' was the Blacksmith's Arms pub. It was always known as 'Two Steps', even then, because you went up two steps to get in. The Star pub in my time was the Co-op and I used to deliver my mother's order there when I went to school.

The car park in front of the Star Inn was my school playground, although in those days it was rough stones, not tarmac. The boys' school was where the two doors are. The infants' school was down Bellbrook. There were only two rooms in the boys' school. Standard 1, where you started, had a part of a room, separated from standards 2 and 3 by a curtain. Two teachers worked in this room. Standards 4,5,6 and 7 were all together in another room being taught more or less the same things except when old Mr. Robinson, the Headmaster, taught maths to standards 6 and 7. There was a stove at one end of the room and a fire at the other.

The boys were divided into four teams or houses, England, Ireland, Scotland and Wales, with a prefect for each house. If you met Mr. Robinson in the street you were expected to salute although he explained that you were saluting the School, not him personally. Mr. Robinson was a bit deaf but it did not stop him keeping discipline. You knew you were in trouble when he walked from the front to his desk in the corner, because he kept his big stick there.

I was a prefect and considered top boy in the school but it did not stop me getting into trouble. On rare occasions 'Black Jim' came to take us, it being a Church School. The teachers wanted to put on a good show but unfortunately we pupils didn't always co-operate. He asked questions and we didn't answer. He was taking a science lesson and asked us who discovered the laws of gravity. I said to the boy next to me,'William Tell'. He burst out laughing and Old Robinson, who was sitting at his desk said, 'What are the silly asses up to now?' The Rev. Kempson told him what I had said and I was called out to the front. Robinson gave me a chance by asking if I really believed what I had said. Not wishing to look a fool, I said, "No" and got the stick.

Mr. Robinson's main interests were painting and singing. We did practical work every afternoon. A teacher came from Stafford to teach us woodwork on Tuesdays and we painted on the other days. We brought something in to copy every Monday and put it in a jar at the back of the class for the rest of the week. If you brought something like gooseberries and didn't get them painted by Monday you sometimes found they had disappeared by Wednesday. Mr. Robinson marked the work out of six and made the sixes stand at the front, the fives at the side, and the fours at the back. At the end of the week the two boys with the best marks were rewarded by being allowed to sit at a special desk, with a much better paint box, for the following week. My friend and I were not very good at painting but won once when we copied some blackberry leaves which were just turning colour, and really splashed on the paint. When we sat at the top desk my friend hadn't a clue what to do or which paint to use. He told me that he was colour blind and up till then had memorized the position of the paints in the much smaller boxes.

Mr. Robinson, himself, was a very good painter and one of his pieces of work hangs in the church just where you go behind the organ. He used to paint the scenery for the Young Conservatives' annual pantomime in the 'back lobby' of the school. The school used to put on excellent productions. I particularly remember 'A Midsummer Night's Dream'. The lad who played Bottom wasn't a brilliant scholar but he took the part really well. The school choir won prizes all the time in Stafford Music Festivals. Early in the 1930s everyone was very excited when they sang on the wireless - a great honour in those days. Mr. Robinson used to send me across the road to the shop, with 1 shilling to buy him 20 Players. They used to cost 11½d but he never gave me the halfpenny for going.

I had to walk to school. When we lived at Beacon Hill the journey was about 2 miles if I cut across the fields or 3 if I used the roads. Because it was so far the people living in Mill Street used to look after me sometimes during the day, as they knew my granny and sister. It was an area of little cottages stretching from the post office and part of it was called ' The Tanyard'. It had the reputation of being the roughest part of Penkridge. All I know is that people living there would do anything they could to help you. You could depend on them.

It is quite difficult to remember the position of the old shops in Penkridge as they have changed such a lot. The flower shop at the top of Market Street used to be a saddlers. The chemists was once a fish and chip shop. The insurance office in Market Street used to be Paynes the butchers. We used to call Mr. Bellamy, who had a draper's shop near to the modern hairdressers, ' The Calico Farmer' because he also had a smallholding. Mrs. Plant had a clothes shop and sold children's games. We used to call her ' Mother Duck'. The shop where I used to buy Mr. Robinson's cigarettes also sold ice cream. In those days it was like buying thick slabs of custard. On the corner of New Road Miss Bastone had a shop in the old house. She was an old lady then and sold liquorice sweets. They were kept unwrapped in the shop window and you could see the blow flies walking all over them. You paid by putting your money through a slot in her really old fashioned counter. Little boys took advantage of her by saying, 'I've put the money in the slot, Miss Bastone', when her back was turned getting the sweets.

The village doctor was Dr. Nock who lived at Ivy House. He delivered me. You couldn't say he was well liked but in those days doctors were like gods to us. He was respected as a good doctor though, and he worked hard. He took his surgery in the morning, mixed his own medicine and then did his rounds. He was at the beck and call of people for the rest of the day. Once, I cut open my lip at work and they brought me back to Penkridge for my doctor to put the stitches in. Dr. Nock's sister made me a cup of tea afterwards. When I went back a few days later Dr. Nock was talking to the new doctor in the village, Dr. McCollum, and he took the stitches out. Just after the war I fell off my motor bike and cut my elbow. I particularly remember this accident as it was the first time Dr. Nock was able to prescribe the new drug, Penicillin, for me.

Penkridge didn't have its own dentist in those days. Mr. Rudge used to come from Cannock on two mornings a week and rented a room in an old house on the corner of the Square. He was an asthmatic and acted as starter on the school sports' day. When you went to see him you sat down in a normal sitting room armchair. He gave pain-killing injections and kept his forceps hidden in his pocket as he approached the chair, so as not to alarm his patients.

By the 1940s, old Mr. Smith had a dental surgery over where the furniture store is now. Once he took one of my teeth out and charged me 3/6d. I had never paid more than 2/- before and complained. He said, 'Well isn't it worth it?' It had been very painful so I replied, ' No'! Years later he took the place in Pinfold Lane where Mr. Emms is now. His surgery was upstairs and the waiting room was downstairs. If you made an appointment to have all your teeth out he used to say things like ' You're going gummy tomorrow.' Once he asked for £2 to repair some false teeth I had broken in a football match. When I replied that this was too much he said, 'Go bloody gummy, then'! After Mr. Smith had a stroke Mr. Guthrie from Cheslyn Hay took over, until Brian Smith came out of the forces.

When I left school the main jobs available were farming, working for one of the three Penkridge builders - Brookes and Fred and Bill Rostance (who were not related), engineering in Stafford at a place like Bagnalls and working at the coal mine. No jobs were easy in those days but it is true that miners used to say that their sons would never go down the pit. My father was a miner and he used to wear moleskin trousers. These got so wet that when he came home on cold nights they used to stand up on their own, frozen solid. I used to see the Penkridge miners standing outside The Boat in the mornings, waiting for the bus that took them to the Littleton Colliery. They returned at the end of the shift, still black, and had to wash at home. Many of the miners used to play for Penkridge United. Sometimes, when they had a Saturday morning shift, they didn't have time to wash and played with black faces. Charlie Bradbury played in his mining cap. If it fell off during the match he would stop to pick it up no matter what the state of the game was. The team used to get changed at The Boat and then walk to their pitch which was where the Cherrybrook estate is now. The team folded in about 1933. When football started again in the 1950s they had to be careful about using the name Penkridge United because the old team had left a few debts behind them. The miners gradually disappeared. Charlie Bramwell was the last miner I remember coming back to Penkridge with a black face."

Chapter 32

The Leading Inhabitants of Penkridge
1793 - 1892

Compiled from trade directories

Elizabeth Adams	1818	gentlewoman, Clay Street
Eliza Adams	1872	straw bonnet maker
Richard Adams	1818	coal and lime merchant, Market Street
William Adams	1851	coal dealer, Crown Bridge
Orlando Adcock	1818	victualler, White Hart
Ann Adcock	1834	White Hart
Thomas Adcock	1851	joiner, Cannock Road
Joseph Adcock	1892	private resident
Isaac Akers	1793	taylor
Thomas Akers	1793	carrier, Husbandman Street
William Akers	1818	tailor, Market Street
Miss Allen	1891	schoolmistress
George Allen	1892	farmer, Yew Tree Farm
Thomas Allen	1892	insurance agent, Clay Street
John Alston	1851	tinner, brazier, Market Street
Henry Anderson	1851	maltster, Horse and Jockey
William Anslow	1818	tin plate worker, brazier, victualler Blacksmith's Arms
William Aston	1818	maltster, Pinfold Lane
Robert Bagnall	1834	clock maker, Market Street
William Bagnall	1872	solicitor, Whiston Lodge
Richard Bailey	1834	draper, plumber, painter, Market Street
Edward Baker	1841	tailor, High Street
Emma Baker	1851	milliner, dressmaker, Clay Street
Mrs. Baker	1872	private resident
Miss Baker	1891	infant schoolmistress
Mary Baldeley	1841	provision dealer
Richard Bannister	1818	grocer, flour dealer, Crown Bridge
Richard Bannister	1834	maltster, Mill Street
Sarah Barber	1851	

Frederick Barber	1892	collector of poor rate, school attendance officer
George Barnacle	1884	stonemason, Quarry Heath
Joseph Barnfield	1793	butcher
Edward Bartlam	1818	gentleman, Mill Street
Caroline Bastone	1892	shopkeeper, poulterer
Francis Bate	1834	fellmonger, New Road
Mary Bate	1851	fellmonger, New Road
Samuel Batte	1884	White Hart
Miss Beaumont	1884	schoolmistress
George Bennett	1818	solicitor
John Bennett	1851	solicitor, Clay Street
Edward Biddle	1818	shoemaker, Stone Cross
Thomas Blakeman	1851	wheelwright, Swan Lane
Mrs. J.W. Blakemore	1851	boarding school, Crown Bridge
Jonathon Blakemore	1851	saddler, Crown Bridge
George Blaylock	1872	inland revenue officer
Frederick Boldero	1872	surgeon, medical officer, public vaccinator, Ivy House
Richard Boothby	1834	beer house, Market Place
George Botton	1793	saddler
George Boulton	1818	mercer, grocer, corn miller, Market Street
Miss Boulton	1851	Clay Street
Samuel Bowdler	1834	beer house, Wire Hall Street
Thomas Boyd	1851	wharfinger
Catherine Bradbury	1818	gentlewoman, Crown Bridge Street
Astley Bridgewater	1892	butcher, Crown Bridge Street
George Bridgewood	1851	beer house, butcher, Cannock Road
William Broadhurst	1851	relieving officer, assistant overseer, Market Street
Clement Bromley	1872	painter, plumber
William Bromley	1892	painter, sign writer, paper hanger and grainer, Mill Street
William Brooks	1892	builder, Reynard's Cottage
John Brown	1818	locksmith, Market Street
George Brown	1892	farmer, Wolgarston
James Burn	1834	Blacksmith's Arms
Thomas Burns	1884	shoemaker
Mary Burns	1892	boot and shoe dealer
William Burns	1892	tailor, outfitter
Joseph Burrows	1841	beer retailer
Samuel Campion	1818	fellmonger, Stone Cross
Rupert Capewell	1834	saddler, Clay Street
Michael Causer	1818	grocer, flour dealer, Stone Cross
Joseph Chamley	1793	carrier
Arnold Chapman	1834	chapman
Thomas Chapman	1834	shoemaker, High Street
Henry Cheadle	1793	smith

John Cheadle	1818	blacksmith, Market Place
Thomas Cheadle	1818	blacksmith, Market Place
William Cheadle	1834	blacksmith, Market Street
William Cheadle jnr	1851	blacksmith, parish clerk, agricultural implement maker
John Cheadle	1892	blacksmith
Elizabeth Cheadle	1834	beer house
Joseph Cheadle	1851	shoemaker
Edward Chell	1884	farmer, Pillaton
Thomas Chidlow	1851	White Hart
Thomas Clark	1818	joiner, Market Street
Charles Cliff	1834	baker, Market Street
George Cliff	1834	wharfinger, coal dealer, Wire Hall Street
Phoebe Cliffe	1851	baker, High Street
George Cliffe	1884	baker
James Cluett	1851	hairdresser, High Street
Francis Collins	1834	academy
John Collis	1851	solicitor, magistrates clerk, Wyre Hall
George Cooke	1884	station master
Charles Cooper	1834	tailor, Market Street
John Cooper	1851	tailor, Cannock Road
George Cooper	1892	wheelwright, blacksmith
William Cope	1793	victualler, Horse and Jockey
William Cope	1818	plumber, glazier, house painter, Market Place
Edward Cope	1834	draper, hatter, High Street
William Cope	1851	grocer, draper, Clay Street
E. Cope	1851	agent to Crown Life Office
Thomas Cope	1834	plumber, painter, Smallbrook Street
Thomas Cope jnr	1851	plumber, builder, Crown Bridge
C. Cotterill	1879	parochial committee guardian
Mrs. Cotterill	1884	farmer
Mrs. Cotton	1793	farmer
John Cotton	1818	farmer, Market Street
Thomas Cotton	1818	shopkeeper, rag dealer, Clay Street
William Cotton	1818	victualler, Littleton Arms
William Cotton	1851	gentleman, Penkridge Villa
Charles Cox	1834	grocer, druggist, High Street
Cornelius Cox	1851	grocer, druggist, High Street, (1872 Cuttlestone House)
Thomas Cox	1872	cowkeeper
William Cox	1884	draper, grocer, Wyre Hall
Joseph Cox	1892	beer retailer
Joseph Cresswell	1872	carrier, farmer, grocer, Market Street
John Critchley	1841	esquire, The Villa
Richard Croydon	1818	esquire, Rock House
Mrs. Margaret Croydon	1851	private resident, Rock House
Richard T. Croydon	1892	Rockhouse
John Croyden	1834	corn miller, Mill End, (1872 Compton House)

Edward Croyden	1872	corn miller, Penkridge Mill
Miss Croyden	1872	private resident, The Villas
Thomas Croyden	1892	Market Street
David Dagley	1885	White Hart
Sarah Dale	1884	milliner
John Davis	1872	cowkeeper, Woodbank
Thomas Davis	1892	farmer, Lyne Hill
Charles Day	1872	private resident
Mrs. Jane Day	1892	private resident
James Deakin	1851	grocer, High Street
Humphrey Devie	1818	tanner, farmer, Mill Street
Joseph Devie	1793	tanner
Mrs. Ellen Devie	1834	gentlewoman, Clay Street
Mrs. Jane Devie	1851	gentlewoman, Clay Street
Peter Devey	1872	cowkeeper, Woodbank
John Doughty	1841	The Star
Edward Doughty	1872	boot maker
Richard Doughty	1872	carpenter, sexton
Miss Louie Doughty	1892	dressmaker
Joseph Dugmore	1834	The Boat
Jonathon Dugmore	1851	grocer, Clay Street
Thomas Dukes	1872	painter, plumber, sub-postmaster, Superintendent Fire Brigade
Abraham Duncalf	1793	grocer, mercer
Abraham Duncalf	1793	hatter
William Dyke	1872	George and Fox
Joseph Dyke	1892	shopkeeper
Thomas Eaton	1793	gardener
Joseph Eccles	1818	grocer, chandler, Stone Cross
Mary Eccles	1818	widow, Clay Street
Joseph Edwards	1884	Boscomoor
Robert Edwards	1841	beer retailer
Robert Edwards	1872	carrier, Brookhouse
Mary Ann Emery	1834	shopkeeper, Clay Street
Charles Evans	1892	beer retailer
William Evans	1884	beer retailer
Thomas Evans	1891	The Star
Walter Faulkner	1872	builder, bricklayer
Rev. James Fell	1872	vicar, rural dean, Vicarage
Henry Fiddler	1892	Horse and Jockey
John Finey	1793	carpenter, joiner
John Fleetwood	1834	attorney, Wire Hall Street
William Ford	1892	grocer, ironmonger, seedsman
Mary Ford	1834	boarding school, Ivy House
George Frape	1872	corn, flour dealer, Market Street

Edward Gilbert	1851	builder, insurance agent
Edmund Gilbert	1872	architect, surveyor, Deanery House
Mrs. E. Gilbert	1891	Mill Street
Robert Gilbert	1851	builder, brick, tile, pipe maker, Clay Street
Alfred Gilbert	1892	builder, stone merchant
Mary Glover	1818	town baker, Market Street
H.B. Gray	1884	curate
Charles Green	1892	White Hart Inn
Edward Green	1892	grocer
Henry Greensill	1851	farmer
John Gretton	1872	glass and china dealer, fish monger
Hannah Gretton	1892	china and glass dealer
Frank Griffin	1892	commercial traveller
George Griffiths	1872	painter, plumber, glazier
William Griffiths	1884	The Boat
Joseph Groves	1793	baker
William Groves	1872	shopkeeper
Charles Hales	1818	butcher, Crown Bridge
William Hales	1851	butcher, Crown Bridge
John Hall	1818	seedsman, boot and shoe maker, Market Street
Rev. Edward Hall	1851	incumbent
Edward Hall	1851	grocer, draper, insurance agent
Mrs. Rachael Hall	1851	Clay Street
Thomas Hammersley	1834	The Swan, Swan Lane
Richard Handy	1851	
Nancy Hanslowe	1793	victualler (Anslow)
Philip Harrison	1793	cooper
Harry Harvey	1892	drapery and drug store
Thomas Haycocks	1892	tailor, newsagent
John Hazeldine	1818	grocer, chandler, Clay Street
John Hazeldine	1851	gentleman, Rose Villa
Thomas Henshaw	1851	The Lord Nelson
Leonard Heywood	1841	The Swan
Eli. Higgins	1851	The Boat
John Hill	1851	beer house, wheelwright, Railway Tavern
Henry Hill	1872	wheelwright, farmer, smith
Mary Hill	1884	beer retailer, Railway Tavern
William Hill	1872	draper, grocer
H. Hobson	1879	parochial committee, ratepayer
Thomas Hodgetts	1851	tailor, grocer, Mill Street
John Hodson	1793	gentleman
John Hodson	1818	esquire, land agent, Husbandman Street
Joseph Holt	1892	carrier
Sarah Hordern	1793	draper, mercer, Clay Street
Elizabeth Hordern	1841	
Martha Horton	1893	The Star
Edward Huntley	1892	private resident, Town End

Edward Ingram	1892	farmer
Frederick Ingram	1892	stone merchant, Woodbank
Rev. Owen Jackson	1892	curate
Jane Jacks	1892	cowkeeper
Philip James	1818	governor of House of Industry, acting overseer, Husbandman Street
John James	1892	Horsebrook Hall
Mary Jackson	1793	grocer
Ann Jackson	1851	shoemaker, Mill Street
H. Jeavons	1884	Cuttlestone House
Sarah Jeavons	1885	Cuttlestone House
Henry Jenk	1884	inland revenue officer
George Jones	1818	butcher, Crown Bridge Street
Rees Jones	1841	grocer, draper, sub-distributer of stamps
Richard Jones	1872	baker, grocer
William Jones	1872	farmer
Edward Jones	1892	farmer
Miss Keeling	1872	Congreve Cottage
Miss Keeling	1892	The Square
Miss Keeling	1892	Sunnyside
Walter Keeling	1891	Sunnyside
George Keeling	1872	Deanery Farm
Charles Keeling	1872	Yew Tree Farm, (1892 The Cedars)
Mrs. R. Keeling	1884	Pinfold Lane
Richard Keller	1793	ropemaker
William Kirk	1793	peruke maker
William Kittridge	1818	victualler, maltster, George and Fox, Stone Cross
Betty Kittridge	1834	shopkeeper, Market Street
Benjamin Lawrence	1872	chemist
Elizabeth Lawrence	1891	chemist
Miss Lawrence	1891	music teacher
Charles Lea	1851	manager, Mill End
Thomas Lea	1851	Bridge Cottage
Mary Lees	1818	victualler, The Boat, Husbandman Street
Ann Lees	1834	shopkeeper, Wire Hall Street
Margaret Lees	1841	straw hat maker
Augustus Lewis	1793	surgeon
John Lewis	1793	carpenter, joiner, builder, timber merchant, Bellbrook
John M. Lister	1851	surgeon, Clay Street, (1872 Ivy House, 1884 St. Michael's Lodge)
Mrs. Lister	1892	St. Michael's Lodge
Rev. Cecil Littleton	1892	Vicarage
Rev. Henry Lovatt	1872	boarding school, Mill Street
John Lymer	1818	joiner, Husbandman Street
Alfred Lyons	1892	monumental mason

Elizabeth Lyons	1892	shopkeeper
John MacKnight	1872	insurance agent
Joseph Maden	1818	breeches maker, Pinfold Lane
Joseph Maiden	1793	glover
Samual Mapp	1818	joiner, Mill Street
Isaac Marshall	1884	The Deanery
Edward Masefield	1834	Horse and Jockey
Mrs. Masfen	1892	The Grange
Francis Mason	1834	draper, druggist, Market Street, (1851 Deanery Hall)
Robert May	1793	taylor, Clay Street
Ann Molinuex	1793	White Hart Inn
John Morrall	1872	tailor
William Morris	1872	The Boat, shopkeeper
George Nagington	1892	farmer, miller, Penkridge Mill
William North	1818	joiner, builder, Market Place
Edward North	1851	joiner, beer house, Market Place
William Nickson	1834	beer house, Clay Street
William Nickson	1834	shoemaker
James Nixon	1834	overseer, governor of workhouse, Wire Hall Street
Jonathon Noday	1841	hairdresser
John Oakley	1834	tinman, Market Place
Edward Oakley	1851	gentleman, Clay Street
Charles Oakley	1892	carter
George Onslow	1793	butcher
William Onslow	1793	tinman, brazier
Edward Oxenboulds	1834	National School, Market Place
John Page	1892	Cuttlestone House
William Parker	1818	hairdresser, Clay Street
James Partridge	1834	supervisor, Clay Street
Rev. J. Payton	1893	curate
William Pearson	1872	saddler, harness maker, assistant overseer, Crown Bridge Street
Annie Pearson	1892	haberdasher, milliner
Samuel Pearson	1892	bricklayer, carrier
Joseph Peel	1818	corn miller and dealer, Husbandman Street
William Perrin	1793	surgeon
Mary Perrin	1818	Post Office, seminary for young ladies
Ann Perrin	1851	school mistress, Crown Bridge Street
James Phillips	1872	saddler, harness maker, Clay Street
Samuel Pickering	1884	farmer, Park Gate
Thomas Pike	1851	farmer, high constable Cuttlestone Hundred, Parkgate Farm
Henry Pike	1892	butcher
Henry Plant	1872	Wire Hall
Henry Platts	1818	solicitor, Stone Cross

George Poole	1872	Blacksmith's Arms
Hannah Poole	1884	Blacksmith's Arms
Elizabeth Potts	1818	gentlewoman, Mill Street
Henry Powell	1818	cooper, turner, Market Place
Samuel Powell	1872	cooper
John Powell	1834	shoemaker
Francis Powell	1851	shoemaker, Mill Street
William Powell	1851	locksmith, Clay Street
William Preston	1793	turner
George Price	1851	grocer, Cannock Road
Joseph Ransford	1885	beer seller
Arthur Raybould	1893	Crown Inn
Mrs. Reynolds	1834	High Street
William Richards	1884	grocer, farmer, George and Fox
Rev. R. Ridge	1884	curate
Thomas Riley	1834	joiner, Market Place
Rev. Albert Roberts	1851	curate, Clay Street
Thomas Robins	1818	farmer, Market Street
Henry Robson	1851	Littleton Arms
Thomas Robson	1879	assistant overseer, manager gasworks
Mrs. T. Robson	1891	Littleton Arms
Catherine Robson	1892	Littleton Arms
Charles Rodwell	1872	chimney sweep
Francis Rodwell	1892	chimney sweep
George Rogers	1818	cooper, turner, Market Street
Henry Rogers	1872	farmer, Wolgarston
George Rogers	1884	farmer, Wolgarston
William Rogers	1872	cooper
Samuel Rogers	1892	Clay Street
John Rostance	1834	shoemaker
William Rostance	1851	shoemaker, town crier
John Rostance	1884	carpenter, Market Street
Maria Rostance	1892	newsagent
Thomas Rostance	1892	boot and shoe maker, town crier
James Rushton	1851	butcher, farmer, High Street
Charles Russell	1884	beer seller
John Rutter	1872	farmer, Lyne Hill
John Salt	1834	maltster, High Street
Thomas Sanders	1818	surgeon, Market Street
William Scarlet	1818	surgeon, Clay Street
James Scholey	1793	victualler, the Fox
Mrs. Serjeant	1892	Upland Villa
John Seaville	1851	maltster, Market Place
Ann Seaville	1872	beer retailer
Jesse Sebridge	1818	bricklayer, Market Place
Lady Shakerley	1892	Haling Grove

Eli Shaw	1841	registrar, relieving officer, National School
John Shutt	1872	Penkridge Villa
Ann Shutt	1884	Upland Villa
Matthews Shutt	1872	machinist, wheelwright
Rev. Richard Slaney	1793	perpetual curate
Edward Slater	1851	tailor, High Street
Robert Sloman	1851	organist, Crown Bridge Street
Thomas Smith	1834	cider dealer, Wire Hall Street
Joseph Smith	1851	coal dealer, George and Fox
Joseph Smith	1892	butcher, farmer
John Southern	1793	bricklayer
William Southern	1818	builder, maltster, Market Street
Jonathon Southern	1834	beer house, bricklayer, Mill End
James Stafford	1793	vicar
John Starkey	1818	boarding school, insurance agent, sec. of Savings Bank
Frederick Steele	1892	tailor
Thomas Stringer	1872	wharfinger, shopkeeper
Miss Stubbs	1872	The Villas
Jeremiah Taylor	1818	baker, grocer, High Street
Jonathon Taylor	1851	maltster, Crown Bridge Street
Samuel Thursfield	1818	sawyer, Market Place
William Thurstance	1818	tailor, Market Street
James Tildesley	1892	J.P., The Firs
Thomas Timbs	1818	saddler, Clay Street
John Toft	1818	butcher, High Street
Thomas Toft	1818	joiner, builder, Crown Bridge
Joseph Tomlinson	1793	baker
James Turner	1793	farmer, gentleman, Husbandman Street
Edward Turner	1872	baker
Isaac Turner	1872	cowkeeper
William Turner	1892	Boat Inn
Thomas Vickers	1851	gentleman, Ivy House
Mrs. Wade	1872	Bridge Cottage
Thomas Walford	1892	tobacconist, Crown Bridge
George Walker	1793	maltster
John Wall	1892	market gardener, The Marsh
John Wallace	1892	scrap iron dealer
Thomas Warburton	1818	tailor, Mill Street
James Warburton	1851	tailor, Clay Street
William Watkins	1834	nail, spade and edge tool maker, Smalbrook Street
Ann Webb	1818	dressmaker, Clay Street
Thomas Webb	1793	tanner

Thomas Webb	1818	gentleman, Clay Street
William Webb	1818	butcher, Stone Cross
William Webb	1851	beer house, High Street
William Webb	1851	butcher
Michael Webb	1851	Crown, High Street
Humphrey Webb	1834	carrier
Charles Webb	1872	chimney sweep
Richard Wedge	1851	surveyor, land agent, Clay Street
Richard Wedge jnr	1851	railway inspector, Clay Street
Richard Wedge	1892	collector of poor rates, sanitary inspector, The Villas
Joseph Wells	1851	station master
Thomas Westwood	1851	shoemaker, Mill Street
William Whilton	1818	butcher, Market Place
Mary Whilton	1851	butcher, Market Place
Misses Whilton Fanny and Isabella	1872	butchers
Mrs. White	1793	huckster
William Wild	1818	blacksmith, Clay Street
John Wilkinson	1892	physician, surgeon, Mill Street
Richard Williams	1818	saddler, Stone Cross
Joseph Willington	1834	wine and spirit merchant, Market Street
William Wise	1793	smith
George Wise	1834	blacksmith, Clay Street
Owen Withams	1793	taylor
Mrs. Ann Wood	1851	Haling Grove
Miss Maria Wood	1884	Haling Grove
Thomas Wood	1851	Robin Hood Inn, Market Street
Thomas Wood	1851	joiner, High Street
Charles Wootton	1851	farm bailiff, Cannock Road
Elizabeth Worsey	1818	victualler, Horse and Jockey
William Worsey	1834	George and Fox
John Worsey	1793	victualler
John Wright	1851	Deanery
Nancy Wright	1793	Littleton Arms
James Wyatt	1818	shopkeeper, shoe dealer, Clay Street
John Yerl	1834	coal dealer, Mill Street
Mrs. Youard	1892	Crown Bridge
Thomas Youard	1892	Railway inn

Bibliography

Published Sources

John Clare.	Autobiographical Writings OUP. 1986
John Clare.	The Parish. Penguin Classics. 1986
Celia Fiennes.	The Journeys of Celia Fiennes. MacDonald. 1983
Daniel Defoe.	A Tour Through the Whole Island of Great Britain. Penguin. 1971
F.W. Hackwood.	Inns, Ales and Drinking Customs of Old England. W.S.L.
J.L. Hammond.	The Village Labourer. Longmans, Green. 1932
L.F. Hobley.	The Fire Service. Allman. 1968
Pamela Horn.	Labouring Life in the Victorian Countryside. Alan Sutton. 1987
David Horovitz.	Brewood
Penkridge Parish Council	Penkridge Parish 1976
W. Pitt.	A Topographical History of Staffordshire. 1817 W.S.L.
W.E. Tate.	The Parish Chest. Phillimore. 1983
J.C. Tildesley.	History of Penkridge. 1886
Robert Charles Wilkes.	The Story of Penkridge. Penkridge Parish Council. 1985

Main Documents

Churchwarden Accounts	1779 - 1881 D1354/4
The Committee at Stafford	1643 - 1645 S.H.C. 1956
Court Rolls Edward III and Richard II	1327 - 1383 S.H.C. 1893
Thomas Croyden, Memoirs,	1876 D260/M/F/5/99
Cuttlestone Hundred Court	D1798/22
Deanery Farm Labour Bills	1861-1866 D1158/20
Deanery Manor Court	D1798/20
Enclosure Award	1827 D1354/5
George Inn	1811 464M/26a - 11
John Hinckley, will	1793 464M/27a-h
Hearth Tax Returns	1666 S.H.C. 1927
Littleton Estate Map	1754 D260/M/353a
Sir Edward Littleton's Fox Hunting Diary	S.H.C. 1960
Littleton v. Wyatt. Staffordshire Tracts	P.N. 4246 (W.S.L.)
William de la More	S.H.C. 1885
Medical Club	D260/M/F/5/122
Manorial Court Books 18th C.	W.S.L. D1798/4/'Bs 328 - 330

Main Documents *contd.*

Muster Roll	1539	S.H.C. New Series Vol. V
National Schools	D260/M/F/5/117 - 122	
Parish Magazines	1883 - 1899	1354/2/2
Penkridge Gas Company	D1179/1	
Penkridge Parish Register	W.S.L.	
Pewing mid 19th C.	D1354/5	
Poll Tax	1379-81	S.H.C. 1896
Preston Vale Farm	1864-1865	D1108/5
Quarter Session Rolls	1594-1609	S.H.C. 1929, 1930, 1932, 1935, 1940, 1948.
Reading Room	1888	D1121/P/8/10
Savings Bank	1818	Salt Pamphlets, volume VIII
Staffordshire Advertiser	1795-1939	W.S.L
Staffordshire Muster	1640	S.H.C. 1894
Subsidy Roll	1327	S.H.C. 1886
Vestry Minute Book	1853	D1354/3/1
Vestry Minute Book	1887-1921	D1354/3/2
Workhouse Minute Book	1836-1843	D36/A/G/3

Abbreviations:

W.S.L	William Salt Library
S.H.C.	Collections for a History of Staffordshire
D	numbers refer to County Record Office catalogue

Author's note:

Family and location names in old documents often differ in spelling from modern usage. In some places I have 'modernised' spellings for the sake of clarity and/or continuity and trust that the reader will suffer this liberty.

R.M.